CULTURAL IMPERIALISM
A CRITICAL INTRODUCTION

John Tomlinson

Pinter Publishers
London

© John Tomlinson 1991

First published in Great Britain in 1991 by
Pinter Publishers Limited
25 Floral Street, London WC2E 9DS

Reprinted 1994

British Library Cataloguing in Publication Data

A CIP catalogue record for this book is available from the
British Library
ISBN 0-86187-746-2   Hardback
   0-86187-751-9   Paperback

Typeset by Florencetype Ltd, Kewstoke, Avon
Printed and bound in Great Britain by SRP Ltd, Exeter.

For anny and the boys

You were the first to teach us something absolutely fundamental:
the indignity of speaking for others.

Gilles Deleuze to Michel Foucault

Contents

Acknowledgements

I should like to thank the following people who have helped me in various ways in the writing of this book: Martin Barker, Conrad Lodziak, Philip Schlesinger and Dave Woods. Many of the ideas were tried out with groups of students on the B.A. Communication Studies degree at Nottingham Polytechnic and I am grateful for their stimulating responses. I am also grateful to Nick Lockett for permission to reproduce the excellent photograph from his collection *Beaming the Dreamtime – a story of Aboriginal Television*. Above all, thanks to Anny Jones for everything, not least the peripatetic discussions during which the book was effectively written.

1

The Discourse of Cultural Imperialism

Consider this picture. It's really a very ordinary domestic scene, a family watching television – something millions of us do every evening.

Yet there is clearly something extraordinary about the image, something that immediately strikes an exotic note. The family is watching in the open air; instead of armchairs, they are seated on blankets and oil-drums or on the desert sand. These people are obviously not Westerners, and the starkness of the setting seems to concentrate our attention on the Western technology that is absorbing them. The presence of the television is made strange in this context by the lack of the usual trappings of Western affluence. This is an extraordinary image of transported ordinariness.

There is a text accompanying the photograph which tells us the family is part of an aboriginal community, watching television in a remote part of Australia on the edge of the Tanami desert. It also suggests that their culture is under threat from what these people are doing, and notes that the community have set up their own broadcasting organisation – the Walpiri Media Association – 'to try to defend its unique culture from western culture'. Knowing this, we will probably read the picture in a certain way, inferring a domination from the image. The picture can thus quickly be grasped as representing cultural imperialism.

What follows is an attempt to understand what *kind* of domination is registered in images like these.

In fact, the picture invites us to see the television itself as the focus of domination. Its baleful light dominates the scene; all (or most) attention is fixed on it. The accompanying text speaks of '*Dallas* and *Sale of the Century* . . . beamed to the Australian deserts by satellite'. But is it what the people are seeing that threatens their culture? Does imperialism lie in the contents of foreign programmes? If so, how does this influence work? The screen appears to be blank; we can't see what the people are watching. But doesn't this blankness also signify our incapacity to know how alien texts are read, and the cultural effects they may have? What are these people thinking as we view them, as we might ourselves so easily be viewed, gazing at the shining monster?

Or perhaps it is a question of what they are actually *doing* – sitting and

1

watching television, a practice linked to a technology which is in a sense 'alien' to their culture? And if this is where the domination lies, perhaps the television is merely emblematic of a wider cultural imperialism – the spread of a certain Western-modern lifestyle? Why, then, shouldn't we see the ice-box on which it is standing as equally indicative of cultural threat? And doesn't the obvious poverty of the family have some connection with the idea of cultural imperialism? Is this poverty itself a cultural question, or is there another distinct form of imperialism at work? If there is, what is the relation between these – economic and cultural – kinds of domination? And finally, what could it mean to speak of a practice people seem to *choose* to engage in – like watching television – as a form of domination?

These are some of the questions we will examine. But let us first stand back from the image and try to see it in a certain context. When I first saw this photograph, it had below it the caption: SEASON'S GREETINGS. It was on a Christmas card sent out by a British television company.[1] The company actually supports the Walpiri Media Association as part of its corporate charity funding. Now this context complicates the signification of the image in a variety of ways, which I shall not try to spell out here. But it is worth taking up the point that, in this context, the picture is for Western consumption. The juxtaposition of an image of cultural domination with such a strong marker of Western culture as a Christmas greeting has a certain irony. But it also illustrates a more general point – that the discourse we're concerned with is inescapably lodged in the culture of the developed West. At issue is a discourse about other cultures and their right to flourish, but one that circulates primarily in the heart of the 'imperialist' West. 'Cultural imperialism' is a critical discourse which operates by representing the cultures whose autonomy it defends in its own (dominant) Western cultural terms. It is a discourse caught up in ironies that flow from its position of discursive power. This is, of course, as true for this book as for any other text it will discuss.

The concept of cultural imperialism

The term 'cultural imperialism' does not have a particularly long history. It seems to have emerged, along with many other terms of radical criticism, in the 1960s and has endured to become part of the general intellectual currency of the second half of the twentieth century. There is no shortage of attempted definitions of the term and yet, as one well-known writer on the subject has admitted:

> It is always with a certain apprehension that the problem of imperialism is approached and especially what is known as cultural imperialism. This generic concept has too often been used with ill-defined meaning[2]

Part of the problem, as Mattelart implies, is that 'cultural imperialism' is a generic concept, it refers to a range of broadly similar phenomena. Because of this it is unlikely that any single definition could grasp every sense in which the term is used. My approach will avoid initial definition: I will argue that the concept of cultural imperialism is one *which must be assembled out of its discourse.*

To appreciate why I take this approach we can consider the hybrid nature of the term. It brings together two words which are themselves extremely complex and problematic, in an attempt to provide a covering concept for a very broad range of issues. This complexity is masked somewhat by the term's superficial appeal. For example, the following definition may seem quite appropriate to describe what is going on in the picture of the aboriginal family:

> [T]he use of political and economic power to exalt and spread the values and habits of a foreign culture at the expense of a native culture.[3]

However a moment's reflection will show that the practice of watching television cannot be deemed to be straightforwardly *imposed*, that the *intention* of the broadcasters may not be directly to 'exalt and spread' values and habits, and that the notion of the process being at the 'expense of a native culture' is extremely ambiguous. The problem with this sort of working definition is not simply that it is partial, but that it can impose its own directions and limits on analysis from the outset. So working from this sort of perspective we may be inclined to think of cultural imperialism as *essentially* about the exalting and spreading of values and habits – a practice in which *economic* power plays an instrumental role. But as the dictionary entry from which this definition is taken goes on to acknowledge, much of the writing on cultural imperialism assigns a more central role to economic practices. Often the implication is that *these* are what are really at stake, and that cultural factors are instrumental in maintaining political-economic dominance. Thus, for example, Martin Barker:

> There are hardly any precise definitions of 'cultural imperialism'. It seems to mean that the process of imperialist control is aided and abetted by importing supportive forms of culture.[4]

This definitional contrast – economic power in the service of cultural domination and vice-versa – signals much deeper intellectual and political divisions, as we shall see. The point for the moment, however, is that either definition sets an analytical agenda which is controversial.

To produce a non-controversial definition – one that could accommodate at least this difference in perspective – would be extremely difficult. This is because the divisions here derive from differing understandings of the constituent parts of the term. So, briefly, setting out to define 'cultural imperialism' non-controversially would require a broadly accepted view of both 'culture' and 'imperialism'. But to attempt this would be to produce a sort of *Tristram Shandy* of a discussion, in which the hero is not born until half-way through the book or, perhaps, in our case never! To appreciate the difficulties involved here, we may turn to Raymond Williams's short essays on these constituent terms in his book *Keywords*.

Williams notes in particular two strands in the development of the term *imperialism*: one in which the term refers primarily to a *political* system and one to an *economic* system. He suggests that it is this difference in emphasis – the first growing out of nineteenth-century English usage in reference to colonial rule, the second having its roots in early twentieth-century Marxist analysis of the stages of development of modern capitalism – which accounts for an abiding ambiguity in the use of the term. For, he argues, imperialism is used today to describe and denounce the practices of both America and the Soviet Union. 'American imperialism', however, refers to a primarily economic denomination associated with the global reach of capitalism but not having the political form of 'colonialism', whereas 'Soviet imperialism' has been used by critics of Soviet Marxism to describe a primarily political denomination of its Eastern bloc 'satellites' by the Soviet Union. Thus, he notes that the same word is used negatively to describe the two most conspicuously opposed politico-economic systems in the world at that time. Imperialism, he concludes:

> . . . like any word which refers to fundamental social and political conflicts, cannot be reduced, semantically, to a single proper meaning. Its important historical and contemporary variations of meaning point to real processes which have to be studied in their own terms.[5]

We shall return to some of the ambiguities of the term imperialism in the fourth section of this chapter; the important point for the present is the procedural one that Williams makes here and indeed throughout *Keywords* – that these politically and intellectually problematic terms – what W.B. Gallie once called 'essentially contested concepts' – cannot be taken in isolation from their discursive context and the 'real processes' to which this relates.

This is even more evident in the case of 'culture' which, Williams warns, is 'one of the two or three most complicated words in the English language'.[6] The complexity involved is evidenced in the huge variety of attempted definitions that exist. In a famous study from the 1950s, two anthropologists, A.L. Kroeber and Clyde Kluckhohn, collected over 150 definitions from English and American sources alone.[7] This would suggest that either there is a considerable amount of confusion here, or that 'culture' is so large and all-embracing a concept that it can accommodate all these definitions: they all grasp some aspect of a complex whole. In fact the latter position has probably been the most popular: it is implied by an often-quoted definition by the nineteenth-century British anthropologist, E.B. Tylor:

> Culture is . . . that complex whole which includes knowledge, belief, art, law, custom and any other capabilities and habits acquired by man as a member of society.[8]

This sense of culture as a 'complex whole' is obviously attractive in that it reflects a perception that human life is experienced as a 'totality': there ought, therefore, to be some way of describing this totality of lived experience. 'Culture' thus provides an organising concept for descriptions of 'the way of life' of a collectivity. This sense clearly emerges in the attempts of the delegates to a UNESCO conference on cultural policy to come to grips with their subject. After recording various stabs at a definition the report states, or rather *admits*: 'In the view of other delegates culture permeated the whole social fabric and its role was so pre-eminent and determining that it might indeed be confused with life itself.'[9]

Now one has to sympathise with this view to the extent that 'life itself' is the complex whole that ultimately counts for people. But the difficulty in what Clifford Geertz has described as this '*pot-au-feu* theorising about culture'[10] is precisely its impossible ambitions. To make sense of 'life itself', people inevitably analyse the complex whole into areas and elements which seem to be somehow distinct. 'Culture' is almost always marked off against other areas of social life (as it is on the very same page of the UNESCO report that stresses its all-pervasive character). In the case of the concept of cultural imperialism, culture is used in distinction from the *political* and *economic* spheres of life which are the concern of 'imperialism' in its more general sense.

Trying to tie down culture to some broadly acceptable definition is thus likely to lead to a level of generality which makes the definition theoretically useless. In an article on the sociology of culture, Roland Robinson resists defining the concept, suggesting that 'we ought to entertain Nietzsche's dictum that that which has a history cannot usefully be defined'.[11] The force of this comment is that the very complexity of the term, as it has developed historically, is what is important. What we need to understand is not what culture is, but how people *use the term* in contemporary discourses.

This is precisely the approach Raymond Williams takes when he identifies three 'broad active categories of [modern] usage': (1) as a description of 'a general process of intellectual, spiritual and aesthetic development'; (2) as indicative of 'a particular way of life, whether of a people, a period, a group, or humanity in general'; or (3) as a reference to 'the works and practices of intellectual and especially artistic activity'.[12] In the discourse of cultural imperialism it is the second and third of these usages which are dominant.

The sense of a 'particular way of life' is clearly the Tylorian one of the complex whole; but here the important word is 'particular'. What is at stake is the idea that we can speak of distinct and particular *cultures*. As Williams points out, this pluralising of the concept of culture – which can be traced to the ideas of the eighteenth-century German Romantic, Johann Herder – was a decisive development in the career of the concept. To speak of 'cultures' in the plural is to dispute the idea that there is one 'correct' pattern of human development – as is implicit, say, in the Eurocentric notion of 'civilisation'. The pluralism introduced by the sense of 'a culture' as a distinct way of life of a collectivity is of major importance in modern

(Western) thought. It can be seen, for example, as a founding concept in anthropology, the academic discipline which more than any other claims 'culture' as its object. But it has much wider implications. It implies a sense of the *sovereignty* of particular cultures: the idea that 'how life is lived' is a judgement to be made by the particular collectivity that possesses this culture, *and by no one else*. This idea is a very strong one in modern liberal thought generally, and it is fundamental to the notion of cultural imperialism. Much of the opposition to cultural imperialism is implicitly founded in the liberal values of respect for the plurality of 'ways of living'. The fact that these very values have a particular historical and cultural provenance (*Western* liberalism) is a complication which is rarely probed.

Williams's third 'active usage' also helps us to grasp an important aspect of the discourse of cultural imperialism. As he says, the sense of the 'works and practices of intellectual and especially artistic activity' is probably the most widespread everyday understanding: for most people, culture means, 'music, literature, painting and sculpture, theatre and film'.[13]

This usage cuts down the 'complex whole' to more manageable proportions. It is possible to think of these aspects of 'how life is lived' in distinction from others: reading a novel is different from washing the dishes; watching a film is different from driving to work. Now when people speak of cultural imperialism they often employ a *form* of this third usage. But it is a form which expands the sense from the slightly 'high-cultural' tone of 'intellectual and artistic practices' to include 'popular culture' and entertainment and, importantly, the mass media. As Williams recognises elsewhere, this wider sense – which actually represents a certain confluence between usages (2) and (3) – is common in contemporary cultural studies, where culture is seen as the 'signifying practices' of a society, 'from language through the arts and philosophy to journalism, fashion and advertising'.[14]

This sense of culture as essentially a *signifying system* has inclined much of the discourse of cultural imperialism towards a focus on the mass media, which are generally seen as the most important set of signifying practices in modern societies. Indeed, as we shall see, cultural imperialism for some theorists translates into 'media imperialism'. But to restrict the sense of culture to just these practices would be misleading. To fully grasp the implications of the arguments about cultural imperialism, we need to see other mundane practices as 'cultural' ones. For example, we will see in Chapter 4 that a lot hangs on the sense in which global capitalism can be seen to have a distinctly cultural dimension, threatening other 'ways of life'. In order to grasp these arguments, we must recognise culture as involving, for instance, the practices of *consumption* within an intensive market setting. These practices will involve some 'signifying practices' (for example, advertising) but also other practices (for example, shopping, as both routine necessity and as 'leisure pursuit') which are 'cultural' without being directly 'signifying'.

For our purposes, a sense between the all-embracing 'complex whole' and the more restricted 'semiotic' sense of 'signifying practices' is required. What we are after is a general sense of culture as the *context* within which people give *meanings* to their actions and experiences, and make sense of their lives. This aspect of 'how life is lived' is (in certain ways) distinguishable from those practices by which people manage to satisfy their material needs – which we might call, broadly, economic practices. It is also separable from those aspects of life which involve the distribution of power within and between collectivities – which we might call political practices. In fact this level of distinction, crude and problematic as it is, is all we need to grasp the most general thrust of arguments about cultural imperialism. For what is claimed is that a form of domination exists in the modern world, not just in the political and economic spheres but also over those practices by which collectivities make sense of their lives.

This level of specificity is as far as it is sensible to go. Having described the three active usages, Williams goes on to advise against the search for one 'true' meaning of the term:

> It is clear that, within a discipline, conceptual usage has to be clarified. But in general it is the range and overlap of meanings that is significant. The complex of senses indicates a complex argument about the relations between general human development and a particular way of life, and between both and the works and practices of art and intelligence.[15]

Now it is just this complex of senses, and the arguments it signals, which is at issue in the 'cultural' component of the hybrid term 'cultural imperialism'. For we are dealing here with a term that is not restricted to the technical vocabulary of an academic discipline, but that appears across a range of discourses – academic, polemical, literary, bureaucratic, and so on. Within these discourses the degree of overlap between usages is considerable and our purpose will be to try to grasp the deeper arguments underlying the various nuances in usage. Indeed, if we accept Williams's point that the term 'culture' is still developing, then we must accept that meanings generated in the use of the term 'cultural imperialism' may *add* to the range of nuances of the component terms. It is quite possible that specific senses of 'culture' and 'imperialism' may be generated out of the use of the term 'cultural imperialism' itself. The sensible procedure would seem to be to begin with the active usages of the term 'cultural imperialism'. This is what I mean by the need to assemble the concept of cultural imperialism out of its discourse.

It is worth summarising the argument of this section, for it has important implications for all that follows. I have suggested that it is of little value to attempt to *define* cultural imperialism at the outset, even in terms of a rough and ready 'working definition'. This is because the concept has such complex ramifications at an abstract level, largely owing to the complexities and controversies surrounding its constituent terms. Added to this, the active use of the concept produces special nuances of meaning which not only could not be derived from analysis of its constituent terms, but also, in a reflexive manner, may actually *contribute* to the range of meanings of these constituents. It is necessary, then, to look at the way the term has been used in a variety of discursive contexts: to proceed via conceptual synthesis rather than analysis. This is liable to be less neat and tidy, but it has more chance of grasping the significant ongoing intellectual and political *arguments* which, as Williams rightly argues, are the real substance of cultural studies.

The cultural imperialism thesis: the blind men without the elephant

The thirteenth-century Sufi teacher, Rumi, told the tale of a group of blind men trying to describe an elephant by touch alone. One felt the trunk and described it as a rope; another felt the leg and described it as a tree while a third felt the ear and described it as a fan. The point of the story was to show how the unenlightened may miss the truth of the whole: the elephant as coherent reality.

In this section I want to suggest that something like the *reverse* of this may arise in academic references to cultural imperialism: the impression may be given that a unified coherent set of ideas exists, where it doesn't. This is most likely to happen when terms like 'the cultural imperialism thesis' are used, as for example by Tunstall:

> *The cultural imperialism thesis* claims that authentic, traditional and local culture in many parts of the world is being battered out of existence by the indiscriminate dumping of large quantities of slick commercial and media products, mainly from the United States.[16]

Notice that here we have something like a *definition*, quite a reasonable one in fact, though still in some ways controversial if we wanted to probe it. But what is interesting is that there exists here an *implied speaker*. To state a 'thesis' is to imply that someone, somewhere has formulated and articulated it. It is different from simply defining a phenomenon. To talk of a 'thesis' entails the idea of an explicit or implicit speaker. The literature on cultural imperialism is full of this sort of reference. Laing, for example, in an article on the music industry, writes, 'the cultural imperialism thesis is clearly an idea of the left'. Sinclair, in a discussion of advertising, gestures towards 'theorists closer to a cultural imperialism approach'.[17]

Obviously this sort of writing is using the formula of 'the cultural imperialism thesis' as a sort of academic shorthand, and this is quite understandable. Indeed in what follows we will often use this sort of shorthand. But it is worth considering what is implied in speaking of *the* cultural imperialism thesis. The major implication is to give what is said about cultural imperialism a sort of artificial *coherence*. It is to imply that it is a coherent body of ideas shared by a group of theoretically specifiable speakers.

Well, what is wrong with this? Precisely that this coherence does not exist in the various writings and sayings about cultural imperialism. When

Marxist critics use the term they are speaking in a very different way from when a liberal critic uses the term, or a national representative in UNESCO. And this disagreement is actually *fundamental* – it is not as though there were some basic thesis which could be given a certain Marxist or liberal or nationalist slant or inflection. To speak about 'the cultural imperialism thesis' is thus to be tempted to think of some original reference point in relation to which we might judge the various 'versions' of it. The 'cultural imperialism thesis' does not exist anywhere in this original form: there are *only versions*.

A better way of thinking about cultural imperialism is to think of it as a variety of different articulations which may have certain features in common, but may also be in tension with each other, or even mutually contradictory. One way of putting this is to speak of the *discourse of cultural imperialism*. To speak of a discourse rather than a thesis is to recognise the multiplicity of voices in this area and the inherently 'unruly' nature of these articulations.

Indeed the 'thesis' formula may be seen as a way of 'taming' this unruly discourse. To understand this we can turn, briefly, to one of the most acute analyses of the operation of discourse in societies, that of Michel Foucault. In his paper, 'The Order of Discourse', Foucault writes:

> in every society, the production of discourse is at once controlled, selected, organised and redistributed by a certain number of procedures whose role is to ward off its powers and dangers, to gain mastery over its chance events, to evade its ponderous, formidable materiality.[18]

One of the points that Foucault wants to make is that discourse is in principle boundless – it 'proliferates to infinity'. Anything can be said, but societies regulate this anarchic proliferation with various practices of containment. One of the most obvious practices is that of 'prohibition'. As the term implies, this involves direct restriction of discourse – placing a taboo on certain subjects, elaborating a ritual around the circumstances of speech (as, for example the formalities involved in Parliamentary debates) or restricting the right to speak in certain contexts to 'qualified' people (judges in court-rooms, priests in religious rituals, 'experts' asked to comment in the media coverage of news items). All such practices have the effect of containing discourse by limiting what is said and who is allowed to say it. But perhaps the more interesting of the practices Foucault describes are those which regulate discourses, as it were, *from within* – not prohibiting discourse, but keeping it in check by tying it to certain regulative principles. Foucault calls these practices 'procedures of rarefaction'. 'Rarefaction' is a complex term but it has the general meaning of 'becoming less dense' thus of 'refinement' or 'purification', but also of a 'thinning out' of the dense mass of what is said about a subject.[19] So here Foucault is trying to describe the various ways in which the unruly density of possible discourse is managed in the formal discursive practices of societies.

Two of these procedures seem particularly relevant to the way of speaking that involves the concept of 'the cultural imperialism thesis'. First the principle of the academic *discipline*. Roughly, Foucault wants to argue that the disciplines enforce control of discourse by establishing their own rules of what counts as legitimate knowledge within their boundaries: the notion of a 'discipline' is taken fairly literally here, as something which enforces order and control. Now in using the term 'thesis' we implicitly recognise this academic discourse (which is built within the institutional structures of Western academic practices) as the *appropriate* one for discussion of cultural imperialism. But we must also recognise that discourse extends beyond the tidy realm of the academic. Foucault claims that each discipline, in staking out the limits of its own legitimate knowledge domain, 'pushes back a whole teratology of knowledge beyond its margins'.[20] A 'teratology' is a tale of the marvellous or the monstrous. Foucault reminds us that anything can be said: mundane, rational, marvellous or monstrous. What academic practices do, in one sense, is to 'police the boundaries' of this saying, keeping the marvellous and the monstrous at bay. So, since we will deal mostly with the discourse of the academic, we need to remember that this is not the only way to speak about cultural imperialism. This is perhaps especially important where we speak in the language of Western rationalism of the cultural practices of other cultures. We should remember that the 'monstrous' is only a way of describing what lies beyond our own intellectual boundaries, in the same way as the medieval cartographers imagined monsters to inhabit the lands beyond the known world.

Secondly there is the principle of *the author*. Foucault means by the author-principle not simply the real individual who wrote a particular text, but 'a principle of grouping of discourses, *conceived as a unity and origin of their meanings, as the focus of their coherence*'.[21] To speak in terms of authors is, in a way, to suggest coherence, because we think of the *authorial self* as coherent. What Foucault wants to draw our attention to is the author-principle as a *limiting function* of discourse, something that organises what is said by implicitly referring it to 'an identity which has the form of individuality and the self' (p. 59). Thus, if we consider the various books and articles which directly address 'cultural imperialism' (this one included) we probably understand each one by thinking of it in relation to its author who is, as it were, at the centre of its meaning. Foucault wants to get us to see discourse as existing in a much more problematic relationship to authorial intentions. But this (contentious) point is of less direct consequence for us than the idea that authorship provides a sense of *coherence*. Now the idea of 'a thesis' is interesting here since, as we saw earlier, it simply *implies an author*. Thus to speak of 'the cultural imperialism thesis' refers all sorts of discourse about the matter to the principle of unity and coherence of an (assumed but unnamed) author. This includes all actual authored texts (which may be contradictory), but also all those other masses of sayings which, as Foucault says, 'circulate without deriving their meaning or their efficacy from an author to whom they could be attributed: everyday remarks which are effaced immediately', and so on.[22] The rhetoric of the 'thesis' thus works to gather all the possible discourse of cultural imperialism into the manageable bounds of an implied set of authored statements. In this book we will, of course, mostly discuss the ideas of authors and, in a sense, 'call them to account' for their words. But we must not imagine that, by this process, we can grasp all that is said about cultural imperialism as coherent and unified. Rather, as Foucault argues:

> Discourses must be treated as discontinuous practices, which cross over each other, are sometimes juxtaposed with one another, but can just as well exclude or be unaware of each other . . . we must not imagine that the world turns towards us a legible face which we would have only to decipher . . .[23]

This, I believe, is precisely how the various discourses of cultural imperialism need to be approached. We must not take what is said to 'totalise' into a single coherent whole. The blind men, we should recognise, may have been wise not to assume the existence of the elephant.

Who speaks?

Once we admit to the existence of these discontinuous and proliferating discourses of course, we open a Pandora's box. Part of the aim of the academic rhetoric of 'theses' and so on is the purely *practical* one of limiting and containing this massive and ultimately *unknowable* realm of discourse – for how can we know everything that has been said or written on a subject? – within manageable bounds. The thesis formula is thus also shorthand for 'those books and articles to which I have had access, and which I can predict are circulating in the academic community I am addressing'. But this is likely to be only a very small fragment of the sum of statements about cultural imperialism. What get excluded are probably writings in difficult or obscure foreign languages, ephemeral writings like newspaper articles, slogans on walls and leaflets distributed at demonstrations, and almost everything people say but do not write down.

This is true of all academic writings and there is, of course, a sense in which it has to be taken for granted that the formalised discourse of academic and intellectual debate is just one form of talk amongst others, and that in criticising it we are simply engaging in one delimited 'language game'. However the issue of 'who speaks?' is of peculiar sensitivity in the context of cultural imperialism. This is because there is a danger of the *practice* of cultural imperialism being reproduced in the discussion of it.

One fairly obvious fact to consider here is that the vast majority of published texts on the subject will be in a European language. Indeed the majority of *all* published texts are in European languages. According to UNESCO estimates, 'more than two thirds of printed materials are produced in English, Russian, Spanish, German and French'.[24] When we consider that some 3500 verbal languages and some 500 written ones are estimated to exist in the world, this fact might strike us as at least emblematic of some sort of cultural imperialism. The paradox might then be that the mere fact of writing in one of these dominant languages reproduces this imperialism. This may be so, not just in the rather loose sense that writing in English somehow adds to the total amount of English texts filling up the global bookshelves. The more significant point is that the thoughts I have on the subject of cultural imperialism will be fed by texts either originating in English or translated from a (probably) European language. There may be discussions of cultural imperialism written in Quechua or Guarani, but I don't know of any. My ignorance here is the central issue for, however well intentioned, I will produce a text which excludes these possible influences and so in a real sense 'silences' certain voices.

Once we start down this road, the possibility of writing *anything* that does not reproduce 'cultural imperialism' looks threatened. I write in English because it is the only language I *can* write in adequately; because I assume any likely readership to be English speaking; and so on. Similarly I rely for the main part on translations for my sources. And even if I were to any extent polyglot, this would probably be limited to a relatively few major European languages. It would be unlikely to extend to the 1250-odd languages spoken on the continent of Africa.[25] These are all *practical* and unavoidable determinants of my discourse. Yet it is also true that these practical determinants exist within – it could be argued are determined by – an historical context which is the context of a European imperialist and colonialist past and present. The reasons for the effective absence of Quechua or Guarani discussions of cultural imperialism are no doubt complex and involve both the suppression of these languages by the original Spanish colonists of Peru and Paraguay, and the present institutional mechanisms ordering academic publication and communication. When I write within this context of the 'silencing' of these voices – however remote the mechanisms producing this are from my own relationship with my text – I produce a discourse *implicated* in the processes of dominance which I wish to describe.

There is obviously no simple way out of this difficulty. There is no practical alternative for me but to write as if this problem did not exist. But this need not mean that we are trapped within the same unwitting reproduction of dominance as every other English text. To recognise the problems involved does at least disturb complacency. I should have an uneasiness about speaking in the place of others, because of the privilege my language enjoys, just as you should have a suspicion of this text on the same grounds. There is more that can be said about this: there is an attitude we can adopt in our mutual construction of this text which may distinguish it from a text which actually failed to recognise the problem. But since this touches on several other issues, I shall postpone the discussion until the final part of this chapter.

Apart from this problem of the 'dominance' of languages themselves, the question of 'who speaks?' can be posed in terms of the access of nations and cultures to a 'voice in the world'. What is at stake here is how nations and cultures become included in, or excluded from, the argument over cultural imperialism.

First we can ask what it means to be included in the argument in a 'world' sense. An initial trap awaiting us is that of talking as though nations or cultures actually 'speak'. There is, of course, a straightforward metaphorical sense to this, as for example in the biblical resonance of the motto of the BBC – Nation shall speak peace unto nation. But this sort of expression is familiar from many other contexts: international diplomacy, newspaper headlines, political speeches and so on, and what is really intended here is that certain *representatives* of nations or cultures speak. This may sound obvious, but there is a danger that using the shorthand may conceal issues about just *how* representative representatives are. This is a problem we will shortly return to. But let us for the moment continue to use the shorthand, bearing in mind its implications, and identify two major ways in which nations or cultures may be said to 'speak' about cultural imperialism.

The first is the idea of an ongoing 'argument' or 'debate' amongst scholars, academics, intellectuals through the pages of scholarly journals, books, conference papers and so on. This is what academics often mean when they refer to that other popular formulation, 'cultural imperialism *debate*'. The notion involved here is that there exists a sort of global community of scholars united by common intellectual interests and ideals. This is to some extent true: there *are* international conferences and international journals – some even publishing articles in more than one language. Books *do* get translated, academics *do* go on lecture tours and on academic exchanges. In these senses it is quite possible to think of something like a global community of scholars.

But it would be illusory to think of this community of scholars in any more than a loose sense. There can be no real organised structure of global intellectual communication outside of global institutions. When we ask what global institutions are we are faced with another puzzle. There are of course bodies like the United Nations, the World Health Organisation, the International Monetary Fund and so on. But all of these exist as collections of member states: this is to say that they exist within an *international* rather than a global or 'world' order. In so far as member states choose to fund and participate in these international organisations, they exist. But there is no overarching 'global' order that guarantees their existence. The United Nations Peacekeeping Force is sometimes loosely referred to as a 'world police force', yet it is commonly recognised that it is a police force without any powers of arrest. This is because the world has no real integrating system of political institutions in the way that its constituent states have. It is this institutional context of the state which makes a police force with real powers meaningful. Since there is no 'world state' there can be no real world police force. So though we can speak meaningfully about international institutions, *global* ones are rather more problematic. The significance of this for the discourse of academics and intellectuals is that, outside of specialist international organisations like those of the United Nations, whatever is said, discussed and recorded will be determined by conditions relating to the reality of global existence. This reality is one of *internationalism* – in a system of nation states – and, it must quickly be added, *multinationalism* – in a system of capitalist production.

To see what is at stake here, we may briefly consider the question of academic publishing. The context of this, in the West at least, is that of a set of private capitalist enterprises – publishing houses – whose major determinants are those of the market in academic books, journals, and so on. Decisions on what gets published – that is 'who speaks' – will therefore be made primarily in commercial terms, in terms of market demand. The way this works is that certain books and journals come to circulate in the most powerful and affluent nations. This circulation will generally be taken to represent the material existence of the 'global debate' on any particular issue. Yet it is clear that this circulation of texts is determined, at one level, by the interests of the (relatively) affluent academic institutions of the capitalist West which provide the market for the (often multinational) academic publishing houses. It is by no means clear that this situation can be seen as a 'global argument' in the fullest sense of the term. Added to this is the question of translation. The decision to translate a text either from or into one of the dominant languages will not usually be made in the light of some ideal of global understanding, but in pragmatic terms of market demand. Thus, whether or not this book is ever translated into another language will depend on its perceived quality as the intellectual commodity it becomes on publication, on the nature of the market in this sort of book and so on. However, it will almost certainly never be translated into Guarani or Quechua. This is because there is simply never going to be a viable market for such a translation. So the effective exclusion of certain cultures – here those of South American Indians – from the 'global conversation' of intellectuals and scholars indicates how loosely we speak in speaking of a global community of scholars. The point is not that academics aim to practise as an exclusive club, however true this may be in some cases. It is, rather, that the underlying material context of intellectual debate is that of *all* 'global communication'. This is the context of national institutions connected largely through an international and multinational capitalist market.

My sources of ideas and information are predominantly those produced under the constraints of this intellectual market context: this is what it means to write an academic text, whether about cultural imperialism or quantum physics or W.B. Yeats. The mistake we must avoid is that of taking this context-bound discursive practice for anything so grand as 'the global debate about cultural imperialism'. It is better to see academic discussions as a privileged voice within a *potential* global conversation, which never actually takes place.

But there is a second sense in which a global conversation is imaginable. This is through those international organisations I have mentioned: for our purposes, mainly the United Nations and particularly its specialised subsidiary body concerned with cultural issues, UNESCO. Such bodies notionally exist to promote 'global conversation'. The constitution of UNESCO, for example, contains this statement:

Parties to this Constitution believing in full and equal opportunities for education for all, in the unrestricted pursuit of objective truth, and in the free exchange of ideas and knowledge, are agreed and determined to develop and to increase the means of communications between their peoples and to employ these means for the purposes of mutual understanding and a truer and more perfect knowledge of each other's lives.[26]

UNESCO may seem to offer a more genuine global forum. It is at least distanced from the immediate commercial constraints of the communications market. As Thomas McPhail suggests, it represents an attempt 'to move the debate beyond the cash register to the social, cultural and human dimensions of international exchanges'.[27] But we must remember that United Nations bodies are not global, but international organisations, in the sense described above. The overriding implication of this is that their very existence is subject to the continuing will to conversation of national constituent members. This fact is the major qualifier of any claim made about the access to discourse that UNESCO provides.

At the time of the drafting of the original constitution of UNESCO (1945), there were twenty signatory nations. Among these, the old European colonial powers and the United States had the dominant voice.[28] Between the 1940s and the 1980s, however, the number of participant members of UNESCO grew to some 160. An interesting history attaches to this growth, since it reflects the entry into the 'global conversation' of what were euphemistically known as the 'emergent nations' – that is the countries which, one after another since the end of World War II, had gained political independence from their European colonisers. Political independence did not, of course, mean *economic* independence or anything like global political power. These countries, which we now know variously as 'Third World', 'less developed' or 'developing' countries, remained economically dependent on the 'developed nations', in many cases their own former colonising power.[29] One of the central arguments of theorists of neo-imperialism has thus been that the series of flag lowering and raising ceremonies that marked 'independence' for Third World countries were in a sense cynical or, at best, empty gestures. What they *did* produce, however, was some formal acknowledgement of 'nationhood' within bodies like UNESCO. This acknowledgement translated into a 'voice' – and equal voting rights.

It was hardly surprising that Third World nations should begin to use their voices and votes in these bodies to raise the many issues of their obvious disadvantage: their economic dependence and the consequent continued poverty and immiseration of their people, their global marginalisation in political, cultural and communications terms. Third World voices became increasingly organised during the 1960s and 1970s until, by the mid-1970s, they had become a considerable voting bloc in both the United Nations and UNESCO.[30] Their influence on debates came to be symbolised in two initiatives: in the United Nations, the call for a 'New International Economic Order' made in a declaration of the General Assembly in 1974 and, following on from this, the call in UNESCO for a 'New World Information and Communications Order'.

The resolution calling for a New International Economic Order (NIEO), 'which shall correct inequalities and redress existing injustice [and] make it possible to eliminate the widening gap between developed and developing countries'[31] was, in effect, a recognition within the UN of the exploitation of the Third World by the First. This recognition was made possible by the changing composition of UN members, but also by external factors, notably the newly found economic clout of one sector of the 'Third World', the OPEC countries.[32] The resulting shift in the terms of debate was, if anything, amplified in UNESCO, where, from the mid-1970s, the idea of a New World Information and Communications Order (NWICO) became the dominant discursive theme. The significance of this newly found voice for the Third World should not be underestimated. The famous 'MacBride Report', *Many Voices, One World*, was just one of a number of important documents issuing from UNESCO conferences and commissions which in various ways took the developed world to task over its cultural and communications hegemony. It has to be said that without these the notion of a global coversation would look particularly threadbare.

The point to notice is that the voice afforded the Third World in UNESCO is a *provisional* one. Both the NIEO and the NWICO are unpopular topics of conversation with the developed countries. This is because, behind the guarded diplomatic language, 'UN-ese', of the reports there lies a direct challenge to the global 'order', that is, to the economic and political dominance of the developed nations. So what keeps the developed countries at the discussion table? The short answer is, ultimately, nothing. As the diplomatic ambiguities gave way to more direct challenges, as, through the late 1970s and early 1980s, UNESCO became more and more forthright in condemning neocolonialism, so two of its most important founding members simply left. The United States withdrew from UNESCO in January 1985 and the United Kingdom followed in January 1986. Behind the official justifications for these withdrawals can be glimpsed the entirely provisional nature of the UNESCO conversation.[33] Quite simply, economically dominant nations, particularly those with a right-wing administration, will tolerate only a certain degree of radicalisation of the debate. The voice of the Third World in UNESCO, though in one sense powerful, is nevertheless only a tolerated voice, and this toleration has a significant material aspect. When the US and the UK went, they took their financial contributions with them. In the case of the US this was considerable – approximately 25 per cent of UNESCO's income.[34] Further withdrawals of funding by the developed countries would obviously threaten its very existence. So it must be concluded that the global conversation UNESCO provides is highly circumscribed and ultimately limited by the existing distribution of global economic power. This conclusion invokes a more general truth: that access to discourse is *always* linked to material – meaning, in a capitalist global order, economic – power.

Notice how we have slipped easily into the shorthand of 'nations speaking'. I want now to take up the warning issued earlier about this shorthand: that the question 'who speaks?' includes a question of *representation*. When nations are said to speak in bodies like UNESCO, it is really individuals, or groups of individuals, who *speak for* them. For our purposes, this raises two major problems: who is represented, and how are they represented?

To have a voice in the world as represented at UNESCO means to be a nation. This excludes ethnic and cultural minorities which may have separate cultural identities and interests *within* nations. So neither the Quechua nor the Guarani have UNESCO representatives. Nor, indeed, do the Basques or the Catalans in Spain, the Catholic minority in Northern Ireland, the Tamils in Sri Lanka, the Lithuanians in the USSR. There is a *discourse about* minority cultures in UNESCO,[35] but there is no *discourse of* minority cultures. This is a major issue in relation to cultural imperialism for, explicitly or implicitly, much of the discourse here refers to the dominance of national cultures. We have to ask: what is a national culture, and how does it exist in relation to minority cultures within it? We shall ask these questions, and return to the discourse of UNESCO, in Chapter 3.

But even if we ignore these problems there remains the problem of how the representative represents. Even if we assume UNESCO delegates speak for their nations – that is the majority culture, the 'national culture' – they may not adequately represent it. Michelle Mattelart describes a good instance of this situation. She refers to the speech by the French representative at the UNESCO World Conference on Cultural Policies in Mexico in 1982. This speech contained a forthright critique of US cultural imperialism, in the sense of their domination of the production and distribution of cultural goods (TV programmes such as *Dallas*) and a call for the protection and strengthening of national cultures. Mattelart describes the public reaction within France to this speech:

> The speech inspired a noisy polemic in the French press: cries of indignation against chauvinistic isolationism and jingoism, protesting the suicidal folly of this rebellion against a hegemony seen as natural, hence both fated and justified. The T.V. page of *Le Monde* took this opportunity to speak against the pusillanimity of 'French television and the boredom it exudes'. The masses were called upon to exercise their plebiscite, to voice their will regarding the only culture deemed to be theirs in this advanced industrial age.[36]

Some quite complex issues of representation are involved here. To begin with, the UNESCO delegate 'speaks for France': his legitimate representation cannot be challenged within UNESCO, since this would be to undermine the entire basis of the institution's discursive order. However, his representation *is* challenged in the French press, which in effect claims to 'speak for France' in contradictory terms. Neither, of course, has any real claim to represent 'France': both simply represent notions of French cultural opinion, each having some real constituency no doubt, but certainly not that of the entire nation. What we have are two privileged voices 'wrapping themselves in the tricolour'. When the French press rhetorically urges 'the masses . . . to voice their will', it is curiously inviting 'France' to speak for herself the words that have already been spoken for her.

But France cannot speak. All that can happen is that certain *versions* of 'French national culture' get represented: the leftish national intellectual establishment version of the UNESCO representative; the implied 'vox pop' version of the press. There is a sense in which both of these versions have a real existence in the values and beliefs of the people who may agree with them. To this extent it is clear that there will not be a single, monolithic entity called 'French national culture'. Just as in the case of the 'cultural imperialism thesis' there will only be competing versions. But notice also that the implied supporters of each version never actually speak: they are always spoken for. This happens continually in the discourse of cultural imperialism: we are always working with texts which 'represent' cultural affairs in a dual sense. They represent in the sense of describing or depicting a state of affairs ('French culture under threat'/'French culture struggling against the isolationism of its political leaders') and they represent in the sense of (often implicitly) speaking for a culture.

As with the problems of language mentioned earlier, the problems of representation have considerable theoretical depth.[37] In order to maintain our present discussion at our chosen level of generality, it is inevitable that we simply 'bracket' most of these philosophical issues. But as with the vexed question of language, we do need to be aware of the existence of these problems. For example, the layers of representation involved in the quotation I have just given are far more complex than we have so far allowed. In her text, Mattelart represents the issues, but she also speaks from a position (as a Marxist cultural critic) which implies a 'speaking for' – for the left, for radical cultural critics, for the reader even, in so far as s/he is invited, via the rhetorical style, to 'collude' with the text. Add to this *my* representation of Mattelart (and your collusion in this) and we have a situation in which the notion of the simple 'issue' seems constantly to retreat. Obviously we cannot (I cannot!) maintain a discourse for long at this explicit level of awareness of meta-levels of representation. What we can do is maintain the same *attitude* in the construction of this text as I mentioned in the discussion of language. We shall return to this at the end of the chapter.

The point of these various considerations of the question 'who speaks?' is to help us to organise the way in which *we* speak in this text of cultural imperialism. It should at least be clear that we cannot without risking misrepresentation (in both senses) say 'National cultures under threat speak' or 'the Third World speaks' or 'the left speaks' or even 'intellectuals speak'. As the implied coherence of the 'cultural imperialism thesis' is misleading, so is that of bodies of voices or of their legitimate representatives engaged in an ordered global conversation. The discourse of cultural imperialism is far more unruly than this: some speak but are never heard; some speak, though with questionable mandate, for others, and so on. How should we, to minimise further misrepresentation (which we can never entirely avoid), speak about this unruly and fragmented discourse? The answer, as I will argue in the following section, is by organising our discourse around a number of ways in which it is *possible* to speak about cultural imperialism: that is to speak of not one, but a number of possible discourses.

Four ways to talk about cultural imperialism

Actually, five, but we can dispose of the first one quite briefly. Sometimes critics of cultural imperialism refer to it as cultural domination.[38] Is there a substantive issue at stake in this distinction? I don't think so. Both the terms 'imperialism' and 'domination' have a fairly high level of generality, but any possible preference turns on one being the more precise. Thus it may be argued that 'imperialism' grasps a specific form of domination, that associated with 'empire'. So, in the case of cultural imperialism in the Third World, this term might point towards the links between present domination and a colonial past. We will recall from the citation of Raymond Williams on imperialism (p. 4) that the term is ambiguous between a set of economic and a set of political meanings; this ambiguity has significant implications for the way we think about the Third World today. To maintain the sort of specificity we might desire in choosing the term 'imperialism', we would have to engage with these ambiguities to the point of choosing one particular inflection of the term 'cultural imperialism': as a pattern of inherited colonial attitudes and practices say, or as the practices and effects of an ongoing system of economic relations within global capitalism. Going for precision in this context means closing off available meanings.

'Domination' might then be favoured precisely because of its generality. It might also be more appropriate because claims about cultural domination are frequently made in relation to nations which have historically been colonisers rather than colonised: for example France dominated by the United States. Ultimately, I don't think the choice of terms much matters: both have sufficient conceptual latitude and ambiguity to accommodate most uses to which they are put. There may be some interesting nuances to be teased out, but we must exercise some restraint here. Chasing these nuances may make us lose sight of the more important issues: we might fall into what Ian Craib has nicely termed, the 'brain-teaser trap'.

This refers to one of several possible traps which attend the discussion of social theory generally. The 'brain-teaser trap' is that of being drawn into intriguing 'second-order problems' of a logical or philosophical kind which have little direct bearing on the issue at stake. As Craib says, there is a certain intellectual satisfaction to be had from playing with these puzzles, 'the same sort of pleasure that can be derived from the "brain-teasers" sometimes to be found in the "quality" Sunday papers'.[39] But this sort of fascination can easily make us lose sight of our proper concerns. And since many of these intriguing abstract problems are, as Craib says, in a certain sense 'insoluble', we might finish up producing elegant arguments on *either* side of the case without advancing the 'concrete' issue at all. This would probably be true of the potential argument over 'imperialism' or 'domination' if we pushed it far enough. Consequently, we must continually exercise judgement as to when a 'real' theoretical issue is likely to turn into a 'brain-teaser'.

At their most usefully general, both 'imperialism' and 'domination' contain the negatively marked notions of power, dominion, or control. The real problem for us is that there are various *orders* of power, dominion or control involved in claims about cultural imperialism: those exercised by nations for example, or by capitalism, or some global process of development or context of modernity. So we come to the problem of representing this diversity without referring our discussion to some implicit 'master narrative' of cultural imperialism: without, that is, blindly assuming the existence of the elephant.

The best approach I can devise for this is to think in terms of different ways in which it is *possible* to speak of cultural imperialism. What I mean by this is simply reasonably coherent ways of speaking intelligibly about the subject. I shall suggest and briefly describe four here, and these will form the basis of the following four chapters. In discussing these I shall, of course, refer to specific texts and authors. But it would be a mistake to identify particular texts too closely with each general way of speaking: sometimes two or more possible ways exist within the same text, occasionally, though not always, in tension.

One of the virtues of this approach is to keep our discourse reasonably open to other possibilities: there are *other* ways of speaking, voices not heard in this text, nor indeed in the 'global conversation'.

Cultural imperialism as 'media imperialism'

The great majority of published discussions of cultural imperialism place the media – television, film, radio, print journalism, advertising – at the centre of things. There is, however, an argument about the actual use of the terms 'cultural imperialism'/'media imperialism' which we ought to acknowledge at the outset. We can do this by referring briefly to the way this distinction is handled in Chin-Chuan Lee's account of media imperialism.

Lee argues that 'neo-Marxists' prefer the broader term 'cultural imperialism' because they 'adopt a more holistic view of the role of the media', seeing them as necessarily implicated in a larger totality of domination. 'Non-Marxists' on the other hand are said to 'prefer to deal with media imperialism rather than the all encompassing "cultural imperialism"', since they do not accept, a priori, the implied broader context of domination, nor media imperialism's situation within it. The non-Marxist preference is for a term which grasps 'a more specific range of phenomenon [*sic*] that lends itself more easily to a rigorous examination'.[40]

This is a fair general assessment, and the point which emerges from it is that the term 'media imperialism' is often used in a deliberately restrictive sense by 'non-Marxists' or as we might call them, 'pluralist' theorists.[41] Pluralist views of 'media imperialism' thus tend to be theoretically unassuming, and to locate themselves fairly close to what are seen as the empirical grounds of the debate. They tend to keep the focus on the media so as to try to establish the 'facts' without making more general theoretical assumptions about cultural imperialism. In this perspective, Lee suggests, whatever links exist between the media and other aspects of culture, or indeed the connections between 'economics, politics and culture' generally, are not assumed in terms of a grand theory at the outset. They remain to be seen – that is, empirically demonstrated. Though Lee attempts to find some sort of balance between Marxist and pluralist approaches, the general drift of his book seems at least to accept the pluralist view that 'media imperialism' is a viable term on its own (deliberately restrictive) grounds.

This approach seems to me to be mistaken for two reasons. First, though the media may be analytically separable from other aspects of culture, it is clear that they are intimately connected with these other aspects in terms of people's 'lived experience'. People's experience of television, for example, is very often within the cultural context of the family and this context has a significant mediating effect. The general principle, then, of abstraction from a cultural totality is highly problematic. Secondly, there is a danger with the pluralist, anti-theoreticist approach that any *critical* sense of the term 'media imperialism' will be lost. I suggested earlier that the notion of 'domination' is essential to the notion of imperialism: thus to speak of 'media imperialism' is to understand a priori a context of domination. This is a theoretical assumption underpinning the term. Now it is clear from the general context of Lee's book that he would accept at least this level of theoretical assumption; yet to minimise theoretical assumptions is to risk losing any critical edge. As Fejes has suggested, within the literature of 'media imperialism' there do, in fact, exist *non-critical* accounts:

> Most importantly, without theory, there is lacking the critical standpoint and set of standards and concepts by which one can judge and evaluate the research efforts which deal with the issues raised by this approach. A good example of this last point is William Read's study *America's Mass Media Merchants* (1976). As an empirical work the subject of this study – the expansion of American media overseas – falls within the concerns of the media imperialism approach. But the study's overall purpose and conclusion – to demonstrate that 'through the market place system by which America's mass media merchants communicate with foreign consumers, both parties enjoy different, but useful benefits (Read, 1976:181) – is diametrically opposed to the central thrust of the previous work done in this area.[42]

That is, Read speaks of media imperialism without the notion of domination. I would argue that the pluralist argument for theoretical modesty – which lies behind preference for 'media imperialism' rather than 'cultural imperialism' – could ultimately license studies like Read's.

This discussion has necessarily moved towards more general theoretical issues, so let's bring it back in summary to the central question of media imperialism as a way of talking about cultural imperialism. I have argued that it is necessary to see arguments about the media as aspects of cultural imperialism and not to try to separate out a discrete range of phenomena called 'media imperialism' having no imputed connection with a broader cultural totality. Media imperialism then, as I understand it, is a particular way of discussing cultural imperialism. It is not simply a name for the study of the media in developing countries or of the international market in communications. It involves all the complex political issues – and indeed, the political *commitments* – entailed in the notion of cultural domination.

Having established our view of media imperialism as a way of talking about cultural imperialism, we can now mention some of the more interesting questions that arise from this way of talking. I shall simply 'trail' these issues here and we will return to them in detail in Chapter 2.

The main cluster of issues arising out of the discourse of media imperialism has to do with the way in which domination is said to occur. Critics of media imperialism often concern themselves with the structural and institutional aspects of the global media. By focusing on such issues as the 'dumping' of cheap television programmes in the Third World or the market dominance of Western news agencies, they produce critiques of what are basically political-economic forms of domination. The assumption seems to be, in this sort of discourse, that this is all that 'cultural imperialism' actually is. In contrast with these approaches are those which recognise a specifically 'cultural' level of domination, but which merely *assume* that imported cultural goods like television programmes, adverts, comics and so on have a self-evident cultural effect. Both of these assumptions are problematic and represent general difficulties in the discourse of cultural imperialism. The discourse of media imperialism provides us with a first context in which to consider the general problem of what cultural dominance actually means.

But talking about cultural imperialism as media imperialism also generates another important issue: the question of the centrality of the media in claims about cultural imperialism. Sometimes writers use the two terms as synonyms[43] and this might imply that the media have an overwhelming importance in the processes referred to as 'cultural imperialism'. We must consider quite carefully what is at stake in attributing this massive central significance to the media. On the one hand, it is clear that the mass media are constantly and rapidly expanding in terms of technical power and penetration, coverage and representation of both public and private life in the West. To this extent it is tempting to see the media as the central cultural reference point of modern Western capitalism. And if this is so, then cultural imperialism might be seen to centre on the media in two ways: either as the dominance of one culture's media (texts, practices) over another; or as the global spread of 'mass-mediated culture' as such. These two understandings have quite different dimensions of implication, the second being much the wider. But both involve the idea that the media are at the crux of modern culture.

However, as Conrad Lodziak has pointed out in a very useful corrective to the general drift of writings on media sociology, media theorists often have a tendency to exaggerate the broader social significance of their subject of study.[44] People in modern societies may watch a lot of television, but they do many other things besides, and to overemphasise the representational aspects of cultural action and experience is, perhaps, to end up with a rather narrow view of culture. Indeed, as we shall see, the more radical theorists of media-as-culture seem to believe that this narrowness is the reality of the lived experience of people in modern capitalism. Though it has a certain iconoclastic attraction this idea is, I think, ultimately implausible. To understand claims about cultural imperialism we need to examine the relationship of the media to other aspects of culture without assuming its 'centrality' from the outset.

Cultural imperialism as a discourse of nationality

If the media are the most common *focus* for discussions of cultural imperialism, the idea of the invasion of an indigenous culture by a foreign one is the commonest way of articulating the *process* involved. Nearly everyone who talks about cultural imperialism talks in this way at some point. We have already met a typical example in Tunstall's definition, where he speaks of the threat to 'local cultures' posed by cultural exports from the United States.

The reason why this discourse has such common currency is that it is a highly ambiguous way of speaking and thus very accommodating. We shall spend a fair amount of time in Chapter 3 sifting these ambiguities. Here is one to be going on with: 'indigenous culture'. This trips pretty easily off the sociological tongue, but what does it mean? 'Indigenous' may be taken uncontroversially as a synonym for 'native', meaning 'belonging to a geographical area'. But *how* does a culture 'belong' to an area? A subsidiary sense of 'indigenous' is that of 'belonging *naturally*',[45] and though this may offer a sort of answer to how a culture belongs, it is one fraught with theoretical problems. For if we can take anything for granted about culture, it is that it is *not* a natural phenomenon. Culture is entirely – even definitively – the work of human beings. So it is not merely implausible that a culture may belong to a region in the sense that flora and fauna are 'natural' to it; it is theoretically incoherent to juxtapose culture and nature in this way. Yet this does not prevent a lot of discourse proceeding as though 'authentic' cultures were somehow 'natural'.[46]

So we need another sense of 'belonging'. How about something like 'being accepted or established practices in an area'? This moves, rightly, from a 'natural' to an *historical* way of speaking. But how is a cultural practice 'established' through time? How long does the process take? Is it merely length of time that produces 'authenticity'? Is the process of cultural establishment ever finished? The answers we give to these questions will be heavy with implications for judgements of cultural imperialism.

Let us try substituting 'local' for 'indigenous'. This displaces (but does not conjure away) the problems of 'belonging': yet it creates its own difficulties. How local is local? Do we mean the culture of a village, a region, a nation or a supra-national region (for example, Latin America)? In fact, as we shall see, the talk is mostly of nations. Talk in UNESCO is indeed in a certain sense restricted to nations (see p. 17). This being so, the arguments we shall have to examine cluster around the idea of a *national cultural identity* and the threats posed to this by cultural imperialism. In dealing with this (dominant) discourse of national cultures we shall inevitably confront the other levels of 'locality' at which cultural imperialism may be said to operate.

The other main area of ambiguity in this discourse has already been mentioned: the question of how specifically *cultural* domination is said to occur. Whereas in Chapter 2 we will be interested in distinguishing cultural from political and economic domination, and in considering how the cultural 'effects' of, for example, TV programmes are felt, in Chapter 3 we engage with a more general issue of value. This is the question of the grounds for attributing domination (expressed in the peculiarly martial language of 'invasion', 'attack', 'assault' and so on) rather than the neutral or even positively valued notion of 'influence'. To put this another way, we will begin to examine the critical basis of the concept of cultural imperialism.

One attractive candidate for such a ground is the principle of *cultural autonomy*. We shall have to decide, first, what this could mean and, second, whether indeed it provides any stable basis for a critique of cultural imperialism. This problem of critical grounds is a major one for all discourses of cultural imperialism. It will not be settled here but will recur throughout the book, providing a paradoxical unifying thread to the various discourses; a common unresolved question of cultural value. We will only bring this issue to an uneasy rest in Chapter 5, where I will suggest that what is at stake is not any particular cultural values but, rather, the capacity of a collectivity to generate *any* satisfying narratives of cultural meaning in the conditions of social modernity. But this is to anticipate another way of speaking about cultural imperialism, and to move from a mode of thinking which is governed by the geographical (local and foreign cultures) to one governed by the historical (tradition and modernity). A major subtext of Chapter 3 will be an argument for the benefits of such a move: to see cultural imperialism in the broader terms of the global, historical, advance of capitalist modernity.

Cultural imperialism as the critique of global capitalism

This way of speaking is typical of neo-Marxists. In a sense it follows from the Leninist tradition of inflecting the term 'imperialism' towards the economic rather than the political.[47] It usually involves seeing the world as a political-economic *system* of global capitalism, rather than the more common view of it as a collection of political entities called nation-states. This has the consequence of casting capitalism itself, rather than particular nation-states, as the real imperialist power. So it is a way of speaking which should be quite distinct from the previous one. But critics who set out to speak in this way soon find themselves in theoretical difficulties and begin to speak of the activities either of nation-states (and particularly the United States) or of 'multinational corporations'. In both cases they implicitly recognise the common view of the world as a set of nation-states. The reasons for this compromise have to do with the difficulty of thinking through the *existence* of capitalism in global terms. Neo-Marxists rightly wish to emphasise the enormous and globally integrated and integrative power of capitalism, but they face problems in 'mapping' this system on to the 'political existence' of the world as nation-states. Such problems are major ones for general, political-economic theories of neo-imperialism, and as such stretch beyond our chosen level of specificity. Yet it is important to acknowledge them, and we can do this conveniently by referring to the way they arise in the theoretical assumptions of certain neo-Marxist writers on cultural imperialism.

'Cultural imperialism' is a rather uncomfortable discourse for Marxists. Apart from the tensions that arise in the attempt to map capitalist domination on to the relations of domination between nation-states, Marxism has difficulties with the notion of 'culture' itself. This problem usually presents itself at a surface level in what is often called the 'economic reductionism' of Marxist analysis. Crudely, this refers to the tendency for (some) Marxists to represent everything (in this context, specifically cultural processes) in terms of a supposed underlying and, in some sense, *causal*, political-economic process. We shall meet this for the first time in Chapter 2, where we discuss the tendency of the moment of culture to recede in neo-Marxist accounts of media imperialism: that is, for the specific element of cultural domination to be reduced to questions of ownership, control and transfer of cultural goods within the global capitalist market. But there is another sense in which specifically cultural issues may become subordinated in neo-Marxist accounts. This is where the processes of cultural imperialism are seen as having a functional role to play in the spread of capitalism as an economic system and a set of class relations. In this case the arguments become shaped by the presumption that the cultural goods on offer from the capitalist West are almost a set of trinkets offered the Third World in exchange for their labour power. As we shall see, there is a marked tendency, particularly among some of the Latin-American accounts of cultural imperialism, to see 'culture' in this servicing relation to class domination. This misrepresents not only the nature of cultural processes, but also, perhaps, the nature of the reproduction of capitalism itself.

Lurking behind these specific difficulties is the big general problem of how we are to think about capitalism as culture. Capitalism, as Marx certainly saw,[48] is more than a 'mode of production'. It implies a cultural totality of technical-economic, political, social-relational, experiential and symbolic moments. There ought, therefore, to be a way of speaking of cultural imperialism as the global dominance of capitalist culture. The best of the Marxist accounts strive to articulate this sense. But this is a considerable task, made the more difficult by our cultural immersion in the 'totality' of capitalist culture. We will consider two main approaches.

The first is the claim, common to many critical discourses of cultural imperialism, that capitalism is an *homogenising* cultural force. The perception here is that everywhere in the world is beginning to look and to feel the same. Cities in any part of the world display uniform features determined, for example, by the demands of automobiles; architectural styles become similar; shops display a uniform range of goods; airports – the potential gateway to cultural diversity – have an almost identical 'international' style; Western popular music issues from radios and cassette players from New York to New Delhi. In the discourse of neo-Marxists, it is the economic imperatives of multinational capitalism that are behind this cultural convergence. There are disputes about the scale and pace of this process and about the potential for cultural resistance to the Juggernaut of multinational capitalism. But I think the evidence of a general drift towards cultural convergence at certain levels is undeniable. What we shall be mainly concerned with is how this process may be seen as a form of domination. This involves another quite separate judgement about the culture of capitalism: that it is in some way inherently incapable of providing meaningful and satisfying cultural experience.

This is the second approach, focusing on the claim that the spread of capitalism is the spread of a culture of consumerism: a culture which involves the commodification of all experience. This is, again, a very common claim, both in the discourse of cultural imperialism and in the wider neo-Marxist critique of capitalist societies. But there are difficulties both with the view that a consumer culture is *imposed* on developing societies, and with the criteria used to judge 'consumerism' as a cultural ill in the wider sense. The issues here are complex and will occupy the larger part of this chapter. But the general conclusion here will be that the difficulties of conceiving of 'capitalist culture' derive from the way it is abstracted, in much neo-Marxist discourse, from the broader social-cultural context of *modernity*. The discourse of cultural imperialism which takes capitalism as its target needs to be connected with that which addresses the discontents of modernity itself.

Cultural imperialism as the critique of modernity

The final way of speaking is that which stresses the effects of cultural imperialism not on individual cultures but, as it were, on the world itself. It is what we may call the critical discourse of *modernity*. This discourse is not the domain of theorists who claim to speak directly about something called cultural imperialism; rather it is a way of speaking about global historical developments which encompasses, and in certain ways reformulates, the claims of the theorists of cultural imperialism.

'Modernity' as we shall understand it, refers to the main cultural direction of global development. Thus the drift towards a sort of global cultural homogeneity that is recognised (with certain qualifications) in Chapter 4 is seen in this discourse to derive from the dominance of a particular – 'modern' – way of life which has multiple determinants. These include capitalism (seen as a set of productive and consumerist practices) but also urbanism, mass communications, a technical-scientific-rationalist dominant ideology, a system of (mainly secular) nation-states, a particular way of organising social space and experience and a certain subjective-existential mode of individual self-awareness. Cultural imperialism as a critique of modernity implies a critique of the dominance of these global cultural determinants.

This critique can have more or less theoretical depth. At its most superficial it can appear as the simple complaint against homogenisation and the championing of cultural diversity which I shall criticise in Chapter 4. Another simplification it always risks is the reduction of the idea of modernity to that of 'capitalist society'. Though we must recognise the major significance of capitalism in the making of modern societies, it is important to maintain that capitalism is a certain *inflection* of modernity and not vice versa; and not least because there are senses in which Marxism, the major critical perspective on capitalism, can itself be situated within the cultural context of modernity.

But on another theoretical level the critique of modernity becomes an argument against the dominant trends of global development. Indeed, it involves an argument about the meaning of 'development' itself. This is because the goal of development for what is considered the 'underdeveloped world' is generally conceived of as 'modernity'. 'Modernity' and 'development', though by no means necessarily linked as concepts, have become closely identified. The most interesting arguments about the dominance of modernity, then, are those which question its claims to be, in some way, the destination of all cultural development.

What is centrally at stake in this critical discourse is a way of responding to the ambiguous cultural condition of modernity. Critics of modernity within the West have tended to harp on its cultural and existential discontents, whilst taking its material benefits for granted. But this sort of anxiety will probably seem less pressing for those Third World societies which do not share the general level of material provision of the West. To put it crudely, they may think the prospect of 'modern' clean water worth the cultural risk. And if clean water, why not motorways, fast food, personal computers, hypermarkets? The problem for the critique of modernity is how to criticise its discontents whilst recognising its comforts, thus to avoid the self-indulgence involved in romanticising 'tradition'.

This problem will occupy us most in Chapter 5; in addressing it we will have to problematise not just those cultural practices characterised as 'modern', but the underlying cultural 'narrative' that sustains them: a narrative rooted in the culture of the (capitalist) West, in which the abstract notions of development or 'progress' are instituted as global cultural goals. Reformulating the discourse of cultural imperialism in this way may allow us to see the claims of its critics as part of a broader refusal to accept this narrative as the 'one true story' of how human beings should organise their collective affairs.

These then are the four discourses within which our discussion will be organised. This, of course, imposes our own 'discipline' on what is said. The processes of classification adopted in this text represent my attempt, in Foucault's terms, to 'gain mastery over the chance events' of the unruly discourse of cultural imperialism. This element of domination in represent-ation is unavoidable: it is a function of academic discourse. But it is useful to bear in mind, in a text which purports to speak of domination, Foucault's claim that all discourse is 'a violence we do to things'. In the following brief section I suggest an attitude which may disturb the complacency induced by the familiar academic voice.

Some advice on reading from Blaise Pascal

In this chapter we have come across a number of what we might call 'meta-problems' that arise in trying to write about cultural imperialism. They attach to *our discourse*, to the practices – and crucially, the *power* – involved in the writing and reading of this text.

First there is the question of language. As I said earlier, we should share a certain uneasiness over the fact that our text is written in one of the 'arch-imperialist' languages in the world today. There is a sense in which writing in English, and drawing primarily on English-language sources, may be reproducing the practices of cultural imperialism in the very act of discussing them. My writing and your reading in English helps to maintain this whole debate as the cultural property of the English-speaking world. And this is not merely accidental: a whole history of global dominance – of imperialism and colonialism – stands behind our present privileged discursive position.

This connects with the broader problem of representation, of 'who speaks' in the discourse of cultural imperialism. We shall keep returning to the question of 'who speaks' throughout this text, since speaking about cultural imperialism nearly always involves a politically problematic 'speaking for' others. But what we will not be able to sustain is an *explicit* sense of the complex problems of representation involved. For example, we will soon inevitably take for granted the fact that I 'speak for' the whole debate. But this is a source of severe limitations on the discourse. For not only will I, through ignorance, 'silence' voices in the discussion, I will also organise and 'discipline' the discourse via my discursive categories: the chapters and sub-sections I choose; the way I frame the arguments. Now, of course, my intention here is to clarify issues, but if we follow Foucault we must recognise the 'violence' this does to ideas and events. To write within the broad conventions of the academic text is to 're-present' a discourse in a very particular way. We have to remember that the (Western) academic voice is simply in a privileged cultural position vis-à-vis other voices: it assumes for itself a critical position 'raised above' other forms of discourse. But the nature of our subject does not allow us to indulge this complacency. If we are to speak of the rights of cultures to define the terms of their own experience we cannot assume that they have any obligation to conform to our critical categories. In a text like this, violence is done by advancing a style of thought which is culturally specific (Western rationality, a certain form of liberalism, and so on) as the 'master discourse'.

There is little we can do *within the text itself* to avoid these difficulties. As I write, I forget the power of the language I write in, I forget the voices I silence and the 'culturally relative' nature of the critical categories I employ. You, the reader, will probably do the same – for it is simply not practicable to maintain an explicit awareness of these meta-problems. To do this would be to load the text at every turn with qualifications – and there will be plenty of these in any event – so as to make it impenetrable.

But there is something we can do. We can adopt a certain *attitude* in the writing and reading of this text. And in this we can take advice from a rather unlikely source, the seventeenth-century French philosopher, Blaise Pascal. In his *Discourses on the Condition of the Great*, Pascal offers advice to a young nobleman on the way he should regard his privileged social position. He begins by telling a parable of a man cast by shipwreck on an unknown island. The inhabitants of the island mistake the man for their lost king and treat him accordingly. The man, after some misgivings, 'gives himself' up to his good fortune' and allows them to treat him as their king;

> But as he could not forget his real condition, he was conscious, at the same time that he was receiving this homage, that he was not the king whom this people had sought, and that this kingdom did not belong to him. Thus he had a double thought: the one by which he acted as king, the other by which he recognised his true state, and that it was accident alone that had placed him in his present condition.[49]

Pascal tells the young nobleman that if he is to lead a moral and Christian life in the condition in which God has placed him, he should think of his rank and fortune as similarly the result of 'an infinity of chances' and not as deriving from any personal merit or natural worth:

> What follows from this? that you should have a double thought, like the man of whom we have spoken, and that, if you act externally with men in conformity of your rank, you should recognize, *by a more secret but truer thought*, that you have nothing naturally superior to them.[50]

Now the attitude we can adopt in the construction of this text is that of Pascal's 'more secret but truer thought', what he goes on to call 'the thought in the back of the mind'. Our situation is similar to that of the mistaken king and the young nobleman to the extent that our actual practices (the text itself) will not *explicitly* recognise all the 'accidents of fortune' that place us in a privileged discursive position. It is possible to read this text as the straightforward academic discourse (produced for cultural consumption in the West) that, at one level, it is. But if we keep the 'thought in the back of the mind', we may construct the text differently. This thought should be the awareness of the conditions of power out of which texts like this are born: the power of Western capitalist modernity. What this amounts to is an attitude of constant *problematising* of the values and concepts we employ when we speak, from the heart of the capitalist West, about other cultures.

Of course, this attitude changes nothing in the real world. As Louis Marin observes of Pascal's thought at the back of the mind, 'it is a thought, a form and not an action. It is a judgement that leaves action and in particular political action intact . . .'.[51] The pretend king continues to act as a king, the nobleman as a (perhaps slightly more benign) ruler, our text remains embedded in the assumptions and styles of thought of its cultural location. In the same way, merely being conscious of our cultural privilege does not alter the political-economic reality of domination from which it derives. All it can do is to give us justifiable misgivings about the cultural practice we are engaged in here.

Notes

1. The photograph and text are from a Christmas card published by Central Television, Birmingham, 1989.
2. A. Mattelart (1979) in A. Mattelart et al. (eds), *Communication and Class Struggle, Volume One*, New York, International General, p.57.
3. A. Bullock and O. Stallybrass (eds) (1977) *The Fontana Dictionary of Modern Thought*, London, Fontana Books, p.303.
4. M. Barker (1989) *Comics: Ideology, Power and the Critics*, Manchester, Manchester University Press, p.292.
5. R. Williams (1983), *Keywords*, London, Fontana, p.160.
6. Ibid., p.87.
7. A.L. Kroeber and C. Kluckhohn (1952) 'Culture: a Critical Review of Concepts and Definitions', *Papers of the Peabody Museum of American Archaeology and Ethnology*, Harvard, Vol. 47.
8. E.B. Tylor (1871) *Primitive Culture*, quoted in J. Goudsblom (1980) *Nihilism and Culture*, Oxford, Basil Blackwell, p.56.
9. UNESCO (1982) *Final Report of World Conference on Cultural Policies: Mexico City*, Paris, UNESCO, p.8.
10. C. Geertz (1973) *The Interpretation of Cultures*, New York, Basic Books, p.4. Geertz comes as close as any anthropologist to the sense of culture we are after, in his view of it as a *context of meaning* within which practices can be intelligibly described (p.14).

11. R. Robinson (1988) 'The Sociological Significance of Culture: Some General Considerations', *Theory, Culture and Society*, Vol. 5, pp.3–23, (p.4).
12. Williams, op. cit., p.90.
13. Ibid.
14. R. Williams (1981) *Culture*, London, Fontana, p.11. The term 'signifying practices' is indicative of the influence of semiotic analysis – in particular the work of Barthes – on contemporary cultural studies. A *narrowly* semiotic approach might try to analyse every sort of social action as a form of signification (as, for example, was the ambition of one pioneer of semiotics, Charles Peirce). But, in fact, 'signifying practice' is frequently used in much looser ways, and in discussions of cultural imperialism the strict semiotic sense is much attenuated.
15. Williams (1983), op. cit., p.91.
16. J. Tunstall (1977) *The Media are American*, London, Constable, p.57.
17. D. Laing (1986) 'The Music Industry and the "Cultural Imperialism" Thesis', *Media, Culture and Society*, Vol. 8, pp.331–41, (p.331); J. Sinclair (1987) *Images Incorporated: Advertising as Industry and Ideology*, London, Croom Helm, p.157.
18. M. Foucault (1981) 'The Order of Discourse', in R. Young (ed.) *Untying the Text*, London, Routledge and Kegan Paul, p.52. It is also worth mentioning at this point Edward Said's application of Foucauldian thought in his analysis of the Western discourse of 'orientalism' – see E. Said (1979) *Orientalism*, London, Routledge and Kegan Paul. Said's work is of major importance in understanding the cultural and power relations between the 'West' and the 'East'. I do not discuss his work in any detail, since it has more bearing on the representation of other cultures *within* the West than with the direct arguments about cultural imperialism.
19. See Young's discussion, op. cit., p.49.
20. Foucault, op. cit., p.62.
21. Ibid., p.58 (emphasis added).
22. Ibid.
23. Ibid., p.67.
24. S. MacBride (1980), *Many Voices, One World*: Report by the International Commission for the Study of Communication Problems, Kogan Page/UNESCO, p.49. Anthony Smith notes that 'Asia alone has more than 140 English-language daily newspapers'. Part of the explanation for this is, as he points out, an economic one: 'it takes far less newsprint to reproduce the same information in English as in most Asian writing systems.' – A. Smith (1980) *The Geopolitics of Information*, London, Faber and Faber, pp.48–9.
25. MacBride, op. cit., p.49.
26. Quoted in H. Eek (1979) 'Principles Governing the Use of the Mass Media as Defined by the United Nations and UNESCO', in K. Nordenstreng and H.E. Schiller, *National Sovereignty and International Communication*, New Jersey, Ablex, p.176.
27. T.L. McPhail (1987) *Electronic Colonialism: The Future of International Broadcasting and Communication* (revised 2nd edn), Beverley Hills, Sage, p.89.
28. See ibid., pp.67–8.
29. For a discussion of these issues see the excellent collection: H. Alavi and T. Shannin (eds) (1982) *Introduction to the Sociology of 'Developing Societies'*, London, Macmillan, and in particular the introduction, pp.1–8.

30. Anthony Smith even suggests that 'UNESCO has in fact been the object of a kind of Third World takeover' (Smith, op. cit., p.61).

31. United Nations (1974) *Declaration on the Establishment of a New International Economic Order*, quoted in McPhail, op. cit., p.79.

32. See ibid., p.81.

33. As McPhail says, the US State Department officially based its decision to withdraw from UNESCO on three criticisms of its conduct: 'the politicization of issues', 'the promulgation of statist concepts' (that is, a hostility towards the free market economy), and 'budget and management issues' (the claim that the organisation was extravagant and wasteful of resources). British withdrawal, predictably, followed the same lines of argument, the decision being taken personally, and against the advice of the House of Commons Foreign Affairs Committee, by Margaret Thatcher. See ibid., pp.258–63, and 277–80.

34. See ibid, p.267.

35. See, for example, MacBride, op. cit., pp.168–9. The issue of qualification to engage in discourse in United Nations bodies is exemplified by the case of the Palestinian people. The Palestinian Liberation Organisation is recognised by the UN to the extent of granting it *observer* status in its organisations, including UNESCO, but no rights to speak. See E. Said and C. Hitchen (1988) *Blaming the Victims*, London, Verso, p.249.

36. M. Mattelart (1988), 'Can Industrial Culture be a Culture of Difference: A Reflection on France's Confrontation with the US Model of Serialized Cultural Production', in C. Nelson and L. Grossberg (eds) *Marxism and the Interpretation of Culture*, London, Macmillan, p.430.

37. Again, Foucault provides one of the most subtle approaches to these issues. See particularly M. Foucault (1970) *The Order of Things: an Archaeology of the Human Sciences*, London, Tavistock.

38. For example, H.E. Schiller (1976) *Communication and Cultural Domination*, New York, M.E. Sharpe.

39. I. Craib (1984) *Modern Social Theory*, Brighton, Wheatsheaf Books, p.12.

40. C-C. Lee (1979) *Media Imperialism Reconsidered*, Beverly Hills, Sage, pp.41–2.

41. Lee cites, for example, the work of Jeremy Tunstall (op. cit.) and Oliver Boyd-Barrett (see Chapter 2, notes 9 and 67).

42. F. Fejes (1981) 'Media Imperialism: an Assessment', *Media, Culture and Society*, Vol. 3(3) pp.281–9 (p.282), citing W. Read (1976) *America's Mass Media Merchants*, Baltimore, Johns Hopkins University Press.

43. For example, Laing, op. cit., p.331.

44. See C. Lodziak (1986) *The Power of Television: a Critical Appraisal*, London, Frances Pinter.

45. I take this and all definitions, unless otherwise stated, from *The Concise Oxford Dictionary*.

46. On this, see Barthes's claim that one purpose of cultural criticism is 'to establish Nature itself as historical' – R. Barthes (1973) *Mythologies*, London, Paladin, p.101. Some of the most precise analysis of the confusion of nature and culture comes, of course, from the literature of feminism. See, for example, C. Delphy (1984) *Close to Home: A Materialist Analysis of Women's Oppression*, London, Hutchinson.

47. See V.I. Lenin (1966) *Imperialism: The Highest Stage of Capitalism*, Moscow, Progress Publishers. Also, Williams's discussion (1983) op. cit., p.159.

48. See, for example, the discussion of the cultural experience of capitalism in the

'Manifesto of the Communist Party', in L.S. Feuer (ed.) (1969) *Marx and Engels: Basic Writings on Politics and Philosophy*, London, Fontana.

49. B. Pascal (1910) 'Discourse on the Condition of the Great', in C.W. Eliot (ed.) *Blaise Pascal: Thoughts, Letters, Minor Works*, New York, Collier, p.378.

50. Ibid., p.379 (emphasis added).

51. L. Marin (1979) 'On the Interpretation of Ordinary Language: A Parable of Pascal', in J.V. Harari (ed.) *Textual Strategies: Perspectives in Post-Structuralist Criticism*, London, Methuen, p.253.

2

Media Imperialism

In Chapter 1 I trailed the discussion of media imperialism by arguing against the view that it can be conveniently separated out into a tidy discourse of media practices and institutions – the professional province of media theorists. This is a significant argument for what follows. Media theorists have their own axes to grind, but in grinding them they produce a substantial element of the discourse of cultural imperialism. Though their discussions of media imperialism often remain tied to the particularities of media institutions and forms they are always, if sometimes unwittingly, in the thick of the conceptual and normative problems of cultural imperialism. Our aim is to explore these problems *through* the discourse of media imperialism and this should, and will, severely limit our scope.

We shall be concerned with three main issues. The first is the problem of specifying 'the cultural' within a wider context of political/economic domination. The discourse of media imperialism often tugs back to one of economic domination, in which the specific moment of the cultural seems forever to recede. Looking at claims about media imperialism, then, will help us form a first view of what should and should not count as cultural domination.

The second issue is related to the first. Because of the constant tendency to revert to an economic account, where cultural 'effects' of media imperialism *are* posited, they are invariably problematic. Either they are simply assumed and allowed to function in the discourse as a self-evident concomitant of the sheer presence of alien cultural goods, or else they are inferred using fairly crude interpretative assumptions. The second issue is the *hermeneutic naivety* of much of the discourse of cultural imperialism. Not only do the claims of some media analysts provide nice examples of this, there is an existing debate within media theory generally about the problems of inferring 'media effects' to which we can conveniently refer.

The third issue has to do with the way in which the media figure in contemporary Western culture, thus in cultural imperialism seen as the 'imposition' of this. The media are generally located at the centre of the culture of the capitalist West and there are several reasons for this, ranging from the pragmatic to the more theoretically principled. To understand the notion of cultural imperialism, we therefore need to think about the 'mediated' nature of contemporary Western culture and to ask what it is that is 'imposed' on other cultures. Is it simply a set of 'media images' or a more complex 'mediation' of cultural experience?

In pursuing these three issues we shall be parasitic on the discourse of media imperialism. This chapter will be neither a survey of the 'media imperialism debate', nor will it involve itself directly in many of the specific and detailed arguments of media analysts. So, for example, arguments about the particular implications of direct broadcast satellites or the relative importance of TV and radio in Third World countries, or about the market structure of Western multinational news agencies will not be our direct concern. These are issues which media analysts typically focus on and they have generated a substantial literature, largely of an empirical nature, in the process.[1]

There is a strategic reason for us to avoid the fine grain of the media analysts' discourse, apart from the obvious question of space. This is the need to maintain the critical distance of our discourse from the various ways in which cultural imperialism has been discussed. Each particular discourse will tend to draw us in to its particularities. We can think of them, changing the metaphor from Chapter 1, as 'settled areas' in the terrain of cultural imperialism. What we must do is to resist becoming settlers as we visit each area. We must keep our distance. Ours must be a *nomadic* discourse.

Media imperialism theory and the retreat of culture

In 1981 Fred Fejes wrote an assessment of the state of play of research into media imperialism. His main conclusion was that the area was heavy on 'empirical description of concrete examples of media imperialism', but light on unifying theory. What was mostly going on, Fejes argued, was a mass of detailed descriptions of the global operations of the media industries, focusing on the control exercised by the Western transnational corporations over the flow of information and the dissemination of media products worldwide. If there was to be any progress, he argued, this empirical description needed a coherent theoretical framework. Fejes spent much of his time arguing that the documentation of ownership and control of the global media be integrated into a broader political-economic analysis of relations between developing and developed societies.

Towards the end of his discussion – and the priority afforded the issue is significant – Fejes turned to media imperialism as cultural imperialism:

A third concern that the media imperialism approach must address if it is to progress is the issue of culture. While a great deal of the concern over media imperialism is motivated by the fear of the cultural consequences of the transnational media – of the threat that such media poses to the integrity and the development of viable national cultures in Third World societies – it is the one area where, aside from anecdotal accounts, little progress has been achieved in understanding *specifically the cultural impact of transnational media on Third World societies*. All too often the institutional aspects of transnational media receive the major attention while the cultural impact, *which one assumes to occur*, goes unaddressed in any detailed manner.[2]

The key phrase here is 'specifically the cultural impact of transnational media on Third World societies'. This implies that there is a form of domination involved in the practices studied as media imperialism which can be recognised as 'specifically cultural' as distinct from – what? Well, presumably a media domination which is, in some sense, describable as *other* than cultural. Immediately we are confronted with the problem of specifying 'the cultural'. If we use too broad an approach it will be difficult to exclude *any* human practices and certainly no activity associated with the media. So, what understanding of 'the cultural' is implied here by Fejes? We can see that he means to distinguish between 'the institutional aspects of transnational media' and the effects of media products on their consumers.

On the one hand there is that cluster of issues which has to do with the ownership and control of the media worldwide: with the manner in which media products – TV programmes, advertisements, news – are produced and distributed, and particularly with the market dominance of the powerful multinational corporations. On the other hand, there is the question of the *implications* of this market dominance for the people on the receiving end of these cultural goods. How does the consumption of foreign TV programmes and so forth affect the patterns of culture within a society? Does it significantly alter cultural values, for example spreading Western 'consumerism'? Does it destroy, swamp or crowd out authentic, local, traditional culture?

The first cluster of issues would normally be considered as one of political economy, or of the 'macro-sociology' of institutions. The domination involved here could be described largely in economic terms: it is part of the neo-imperialism which structures the overall relations between the First and the Third World. This is the domination which the 'dependency theory' of developing societies advocated by Fejes describes. The second cluster of issues is 'specifically cultural' in Fejes's formulation, as distinct from this economic imperialism. The idea implicit here is that there is a distinct level of analysis involved, having to do with the content of media texts, the reception of this content, and the impact of the reception, 'on the lives and human relationships of Third World populations'. This is 'the cultural dimension of the media' which, according to Fejes and others,[3] theorists of media imperialism have generally failed to confront. This failure, Fejes suggests, derives from the inherent difficulties of 'the cultural dimension': 'There is very little consensus on the basic formulation of the questions to be asked, much less agreement on methods and criteria.'[4]

We can agree with Fejes in a lot of this. Certainly much of the output of the media analysts *does* have to do with matters of political economy or media institutions. Equally, at the time that Fejes was writing, there was very little attempt to confront the issue of media effects in relation to media imperialism. Since then some attempts have been made and we will consider these in the next section. But we need to hold as *provisional* the view of 'the cultural' that Fejes presents. If it were simply and indisputably the case that the cultural is the domain of texts and their reception, matters would be much more straightforward. The inherent ambiguity of the concept of culture with which we are saddled makes things rather more complicated.

In order to understand this complexity, let us look now at a representative discussion of media imperialism of the kind that Fejes criticises for stopping short, in his terms, of the specific moment of 'the cultural'.

The text we shall consider is a short paper by Herbert Schiller, 'Transnational Media and National Development', which appeared in a much-cited collection edited by Nordenstreng and Schiller, *National Sovereignty and International Communication*, in 1979. Schiller is one of the best known and most prolific writers on media imperialism and has maintained a consistent line on these issues over a long period. There are some ways in which his work is idiosyncratic and we shall refer to these later. He is, however, quite typical in his focus on institutional issues rather than on media texts.

Schiller begins by presenting a picture of how the world works economically. Following Wallerstein,[5] he describes a 'modern world system' consisting of a global capitalist market economy in which the 'core' countries of the developed industrial West (his analysis excludes the state-planned societies of the Eastern bloc) dominate the allocation of human and natural resources. The nations of the Third World are located, according to this model on the 'periphery', at a distance in terms of economic, technological, strategic and political power, from the centres of control. Thus, Schiller argues, Third World countries do not have the control of their economic (and even, arguably, of their political) development in the way that the term 'national development' implies. Forces outside of nominally 'independent' sovereign nations actually determine how development proceeds.

The ideas of a 'world system' and a 'core–periphery' model of global political-economic power are typical of the broadly neo-Marxist paradigm in development studies known as 'dependency theory'.[6] Dependency theory obviously stresses the way in which formerly colonial countries remain dependent on the West, but perhaps the key to the thinking here – at least in the version Schiller adopts – is the integrated and *systematic* nature of modern global capitalism. The multinational corporation (MNC) – sometimes transnational corporation (TNC) – is of central importance in this approach, since it is generally held to represent the most significant unit in the 'system' of global capitalism. The enormous economic power of the MNCs (in many cases far greater than that of individual nation-states)[7] and their interests in exploiting markets, natural resources and labour forces worldwide has, for many critics, come to represent the high point of capitalist development and the major determinant of the economies of the Third World. Dependency theory has much to recommend it, especially considering the paradigm in development studies – 'modernisation theory'[8] – which it displaced. However, it must be said that Schiller tends to present a fairly simple version which glosses over some of the tricky conceptual problems involved and in which the notion of 'the system' becomes reified and operates in a rather crude and rigid 'functionalist' manner. This is one of the areas in which he has attracted the most criticism,[9] but is not our major concern at present.

Schiller is out to show how the media fit into the world system of capitalism and his focus is on their provision of 'the ideologically supportive informational infrastructure of the modern world system's core – the multinational corporations'.[10] Multinational media corporations thus act as agents for 'the promotion, protection and extension of the modern world system and its leading component, the MNC in particular'.[11]

At the centre of Schiller's argument is the notion that media imperialism is an extension of the sort of commercial role the media have in developed societies – particularly in the United States – in relation to the 'developing' societies. This role is described very briefly, in just under half a page, in the familiar terms of critical media theory. That is to say, the media are seen primarily as vehicles for corporate marketing, manipulating audiences to deliver them as 'good consumers' of capitalist production:

> The apparent saturation through every medium of the advertising message has been to create audiences whose loyalties are tied to brand named products and whose understanding of social reality is mediated through a scale of commodity satisfaction.[12]

The point to note is that there is simply an *assertion* of the manipulative and ideological power of the media here. Critical media theory has long grappled with the problems of assessing 'media effects' and there are, as we shall later see, major difficulties involved. Schiller is not interested in these problems; what he wants to do is to chart the way in which 'the system' spreads its tentacles. So, dwelling only long enough to register the manipulative role of the media within his analysis, he moves quickly on to the needs of the system to gain more and more markets and areas of exploitation, and to the strategies employed towards this end. The picture he draws is of the incorporation of successive media practices (print and broadcast media production, advertising, market research, public relations) and successive technologies (computing and data analysis, information technology, satellite broadcasting) into the integrated and integrative world system of capitalist domination. This description, with an accompanying suggestion of the clandestine role of US agencies like the CIA in 'stabilising' the system's spread throughout the world,[13] occupies the rest of the paper.

Schiller's conclusion is most revealing. His summary describes the trans-national media as, 'inseparable elements in a worldwide system of resource allocation generally regarded as capitalistic', which 'create and reinforce their audiences' attachment to the way things are in the system overall'.[14]

But he goes on from this specifically to *deny* the point of attempts to measure media effects at a detailed empirical level. Individual media texts are mutually reinforcing in their demonstration of the attractions of consumerism and the 'American way'. Their effects, though not directly quantifiable, are cumulative and 'totalising' and 'are observable as typifying a way of life'. Thus the 'effect' of the transnational media in Third World countries is, for Schiller, the institution of a developmental path:

> It is what has come to be recognised, with apologies to the Chinese, as the capitalist road to development. In this process, the media, now many times more powerful and penetrative than in an earlier time, are the means that entice and instruct their audiences along this path, while at the same time concealing the deeper reality and the long term consequences that the course produces.[15]

Schiller employs a broad notion of culture as a 'way of life' – the culture of capitalism – and what is really significant about this way of life is the centrality of 'the system' within it. He has a strong view, recalling some of the themes of the 'critical theory' of the Frankfurt School,[16] of the incorporative power of the capitalist system. This is seen as shaping the way things are at all levels of Western societies, from the military-industrial complex to the personal-existential experience of citizen-consumers. Because this 'totalising' view is so strong, Schiller sees neither point nor possibility in attempting to isolate and investigate, for example, the consumerist attitudes or the political values that exposure to particular media texts are said to promote. The evidence, as he sees it, is in the inexorable and undeniable spread of capitalism. Schiller sees his task as the monitoring and charting of this spread, and the ever new strategies it employs. It is this project which consistently shapes his analysis along political-economic lines. Six years on from this paper, his argument is essentially the same only more so. A paper from 1985, 'Electronic Information Flows: New Basis for Global Domination?' simply picks up the story: 'The latest developments foretell the creation of a still more thorough-going and all-embracing information control.'[17] Subheadings like, 'The Transnational Corporate Business Structure' and 'Information for Sale' structure a discourse which remains doggedly at the 'macro level'.

Schiller is not idiosyncratic in this. Much of the output of an equally prolific writer on media imperialism, Armand Mattelart (some of whose work we will examine in the following section) has a similar focus on media institutions and multinational corporate strategies.[18] Nor is this general approach without its intellectual-strategic justification. Golding and Murdock, for instance, state that: 'Cultural dependency is itself, however, an aspect of a more fundamental system of economic domination, and only *comprehensible* as such.'[19] There is a strong sense in many of the media critics of the *priority* of a political-economic analysis in both analytical and political terms. A good example of this strategic sense is found in an article by Rohan Samarajiwa documenting the control exercised by the Western transnational news agencies over the global news market. Samarajiwa's paper is not theoretically 'totalising' in the manner of Schiller. It is a careful and informative discussion, which demonstrates how the sheer economics of the global news market acts as a barrier against the entry of agencies from the Third World. This sort of analysis is clearly most important in understanding the structural underpinnings of the silencing of Third World voices. But what is significant for us is the justification Samarajiwa offers for his analysis:

> This approach does not imply that news is nothing more than a commodity or that it should always be treated as a commodity. *The Third World interest in news derives precisely from its political and cultural significance.* . . . However the political and cultural objectives can be achieved, and the present order challenged, only by the adoption of realistic strategies that take into account the strengths and weaknesses of the present structure. A politico-economic analysis of the world market in news is an indispensable step in the formulation of such strategies.[20]

There are clear differences between a careful empirical analysis like Samarajiwa's and the more polemical heaping up of instances of domination in Schiller's work. But they share a sense of the priority of what they are doing. Reading the mass of research generated by the media analysts, there is a definite sense of the conceptual problems of the 'moment of the cultural' being forever deferred. As Michael Tracey has put it:

> Those who favour the idea of cultural dominance through television have tended to study company reports, rather than the realities of individual lives; to describe the flow of communication in the abstract, rather than the cultural meaning of those flows.[21]

There are good reasons – particularly for Marxists – to try to clarify the material context of domination. But the question remains whether this sort of analysis will ever grasp the specificity of cultural domination.

Fejes clearly thinks it won't. For him there are questions of 'cultural impact' to be addressed at the level of individual consumers. Part of his criticism of theorists like Schiller is that their broad sweep involves the unexamined *assumption* of the manipulative effects of media products:

> Generally, a perception of the cultural consequences of the control of various media products is based on a view of the mass media as primarily manipulative agents capable of having direct, unmediated effects on the audience's behaviour and world view.[22]

Schiller's totalising approach tends to assume that capitalism *is* culture; that the 'effects' of the spread of the system are evident in the immersion of individuals within it. For Fejes, there is another stage in the analysis to be undertaken. This concerns the difficult question of *how* people experience the culture of capitalism. Perhaps it is not so powerfully manipulative – or its effects are experienced differently by different individuals? Perhaps the export of consumerist values and the ethics of the market-place are mediated by other factors as they cross cultural boundaries? Religion might be an obvious example of such a mediating influence. Such considerations suggest that Schiller's approach is too broad, too shallow, and perhaps too pessimistic.

The question remains, then, of how to get closer to the cultural implications of the political-economic analysis of media imperialism. Fejes suggests that we pursue media products into the realm of their reception by audiences. We need to examine the way in which media texts are *interpreted* and how these interpretations may be mediated in different cultural contexts. Is this a fruitful area of investigation and will it give us an adequate sense of 'the cultural'?

Reading Donald Duck: the ideology-critique of the 'imperialist text'

Contrasting with the broad sweep of Schiller's work are analyses that focus on particular media texts and aim to disclose their imperialist nature. These analyses are not nearly so numerous as the institutional analyses but they have a celebrated exemplar in a study by Ariel Dorfman and Armand Mattelart: *How To Read Donald Duck: Imperialist Ideology in the Disney Comic.*[23]

As the title suggests, Dorfman and Mattelart aim to demonstrate the imperialist nature of the values 'concealed' behind the innocent, wholesome facade of the world of Walt Disney. The Disney comic is taken to be a powerful ideological tool of American imperialism, precisely because it presents itself as harmless fun for consumption by children. What Dorfman and Mattelart offer is an 'oppositional reading' of Disney, which penetrates this veneer of innocence to reveal the ideological assumptions that inform the stories and that can, arguably, naturalise and normalise the social relations of Western capitalism. As Martin Baker summarises Dorfman and Mattelart's argument: 'American capitalism has to persuade the people it dominates that the 'American way of life' is what they want. American superiority is natural and in everyone's best interest.'[24]

How To Read Donald Duck was written in Chile in 1971 during the brief flowering of revolutionary socialism of Salvadore Allende's Popular Unity government and is closely identified with the revolutionary politics of this period. After the military coup of 1973 which, with the connivance of the United States, brought the junta led by General Pinochet to power, the book was publicly burned and its authors forced into exile. It was subsequently widely translated – the English translation being, for a time, banned in the United States – and has become somewhat of a classic of recent anti-imperialist cultural critique. John Berger, reviewing the English translation for *New Society* wrote: 'It has become a handbook of de-colonization. It examines the meaning of Walt Disney comics: in doing this one thing precisely and profoundly, it illuminates a global situation.'[25]

The Disney comics, which have been widely distributed in the Third World since the 1940s, could certainly be seen as potential 'carriers' of American capitalist cultural values. In this sense, Berger is right to say that Dorfman and Mattelart's analysis 'illuminates a global situation' in which media texts of Western origin are massively present in other cultures. But the key question is, does this presence represent cultural imperialism? Clearly the sheer presence *alone* does not. A text does not become culturally significant until it is read. Until it is read it has the same status as imported blank paper: a material and economic significance, but not a directly *cultural* significance. At this level of analysis, then, reading the imperialist text becomes the crucial issue in judging cultural imperialism. Thus, following Fejes's call for attention to the 'cultural impact' of media texts, we need to ask how textual analyses – readings – like Dorfman and Mattelart's stand as evidence of cultural imperialism.

How to Read Donald Duck is a rather difficult book to assess. It is not a careful academic study, but an openly polemical work with a self-consciously political aim. Its analysis is not crude, but it is, as David Kunzle has said, 'enraged, satirical and politically impassioned'.[26] It is as much a *refusal* of American consumer-capitalist values as it is an analysis of them and their ideological effects on Chilean society. It also tends to conflate 'America' with capitalism itself as 'the class enemy'. Because of these features, which arise from the particular historical context of the book's production, it is rather unfair to treat it as a coherent argument about the workings of cultural imperialism. But what it does contain is an implicit model of these workings which relies on the central notion of the *power of ideology* in the 'imperialist text'. There are two basic theoretical moves in the book: the identification of imperialist ideology, and the theorisation of its effect.

The first move receives by far the most attention. Dorfman and Mattelart reveal a catalogue of ideological themes in the comics: an obsession with money and a 'compulsive consumerism'; the constant reference to 'exotic' (that is, Third World) lands as the source of wealth 'there for the taking' by adventurers from the West; the depiction of Third World nations in terms of racial and cultural stereotypes (and in particular the 'infantilisation' of the peoples of these countries); the presentation of capitalist class relations as natural, unchangeable and morally justified; direct anti-communist and anti-revolutionary propaganda; the representation of women in stereotypically subordinate terms, and so on.

In many cases their interpretations are plausible and, to the 'politicised' reader, often compelling. But in the very nature of interpretation there is always room for disagreement. The book is, of course, conceived as a disagreement with the self-representation of the Disney comics. But Dorfman and Mattelart's readings would also, no doubt, diverge from the 'naive' readings of most children and, probably, a majority of adult readers. There is certainly evidence that other critics of the Disney comics see things differently. Martin Barker's most interesting recent discussion points out how one central theme of Dorfman and Mattelart's critique – the obsession with money, as personified in the character of Donald's 'Uncle Scrooge' – has been interpreted dramatically differently by different critics.

Dorfman and Mattelart read Uncle Scrooge as a device for concealing the organised power of the capitalist class behind the 'pathetic sentimental solitude' of a comic millionaire-miser.

> [Uncle Scrooge] is set up so as to leave intact the true mechanisms of domination. Attacking Scrooge is like knocking down the gatekeeper, a manifest but secondary symptom, so as to avoid confronting the remaining denizens of Disney's castle. Could this garishly dramatized Mammon figure be designed to distract the reader's attention, so that they will distrust Scrooge and no one else?[27]

Their reading here is along fairly typical Marxist lines, wherein ideology acts to conceal and 'mystify' the true nature of social – that is, class-structural – relations in capitalism. Wealth is made to appear 'naturally' in the hands of certain individuals, and its power is hidden by casting the individual 'millionaire' as a harmless eccentric. But, as Barker shows, three other critics have given this theme three quite different interpretations. One reads the Scrooge character as a deliberate mockery of the absurdity of 'money-fetishism', another extends this to see a 'closet critique of capitalism' in the stories, with Scrooge as 'a biting parody of the bourgeois entrepreneur in the competitive stage of capitalism', while a third sees the whole discourse of money as subservient to the larger theme in the stories of 'the ways in which human beings deceive and destroy themselves'. As Barker neatly puts it, 'The same information, interpretable four different ways'.[28]

This is, of course, the besetting problem of this sort of textual ideology-critique: it implies that the critic has penetrated the 'superficial' meaning of the text to arrive at the 'true' ideological meaning. The Disney comics aren't *really* about small furry and feathery animals sent off by a comic uncle to have adventures searching for gold in fantasy lands called Inca-Blinca, Aztecland or Unsteadystan: they are about the capitalist-imperialist world-view implicit in the narrative. But who is finally to say? Disney represents its comics as 'innocent', Dorfman and Mattelart as 'guilty'. Barker suggests that 'they are too diverse and complicated to be either': they must be seen as establishing 'a complicated "contract". . . . with their readers, including those in Latin America'.[29] This is surely right. What is finally at stake is not the literary-critical merits of Dorfman and Mattelart's interpretations, nor indeed the correctness of their socioeconomic analysis, but the crucial question of how ordinary readers read the comics: that is, the questions of if and how the text has its ideological effects.

Unless they can establish a convincing account of the influence the ideology they detect has on ordinary readers in Chile, Dorfman and Mattelart's work remains at the level of a politicised reading of the 'imperialist text', not an argument about cultural imperialism. They do offer a sort of argument about influence, but it is scarcely a developed one. The most concentrated discussion comes in their final chapter, 'Power to Donald Duck?':

> But how can the cultural superstructure of the dominant classes, which represents the interests of the metropolis and is so much the product of contradictions in the development of its productive forces, exert such influence and acquire such popularity in the underdeveloped countries? Just why is Disney such a threat?[30]

How, in fact, does the American Dream travel? The first response Dorfman and Mattelart give to their own question is to stress the location of cultural imports like Disney within the wider economic context of dependency: 'Our countries are exporters of raw materials and importers of super-structural and cultural goods.'[31]

This explains the presence of alien cultural texts, but not yet their effects. They go on:

> To service our 'monoproduct' economies and provide urban paraphernalia, we send copper, and they send the machines to extract copper and, of course, Coca Cola. Behind the Coca Cola stands a whole superstructure of expectations and models of behaviour, and with it, a particular kind of present and future society and an interpretation of the past.[32]

So, imported cultural goods – Coke, Disney – somehow 'contain' the values of American consumer capitalism and offer an implicit interpretation of the good life. Still, we have yet to see how these cultural goods are supposed to transmit the values they contain and the social vision they 'offer'. When the explanation comes, it is frankly disappointing:

> The housewife in the slums is incited to buy the latest refrigerator or washing machine; the impoverished industrial worker lives bombarded with the images of the Fiat 125. [in the same way]. . . . Underdeveloped peoples take the comics at second hand, as instruction in the way they are supposed to live and relate to the foreign power centre.[33]

When it comes to the crucial question of ideological effects, Dorfman and Mattelart can only offer an unproblematised notion of the manipulative power of the media text. They simply *assume* that reading American comics, seeing adverts, watching pictures of the affluent *yanqui* lifestyle has a direct pedagogic effect. Their model of effects is thus precisely the one that, as we saw in the previous section, Schiller employs and Fejes criticises. For all that they focus on texts rather than institutions, Dorfman and Mattelart do not significantly advance the argument about cultural imperialism beyond Schiller. Any advance in this approach to cultural imperialism is dependent on an analysis of *the relationship between text and audience*. This is something that, as Boyd-Barrett points out, few critiques of cultural imperialism have addressed:

The orthodox view of audiences in the West is now one that stresses the social context in which communications are received, and which stresses the individual's capacity for active selection and selective retention. This view does not seem to have carried over sufficiently to Third World contexts. . . . Individual capacity for psychological compartmentalization and rationalization is underestimated to an extraordinary degree. Much more attention needs to be given to the processes by which individuals and groups interpret, translate and transform their experiences of foreign culture to relate to more familiar experiences.[34]

Since Boyd-Barrett wrote this, some work has been done on these problems. In turning to this we shift our focus from Disney to another, more recent, *bête noire* of the critics of cultural imperialism, *Dallas*.

'Watching *Dallas*': the imperialist text and audience research

For many critics, the American TV series *Dallas* had become the byword for cultural imperialism in the 1980s. Ien Ang's study, *Watching Dallas* takes as its central question the tension between the massive international popularity of the Texan soap opera:

> . . . in over ninety countries, ranging from Turkey to Australia, from Hong Kong to Great Britain . . . with the proverbial empty streets and dramatic drop in water consumption when an episode of the series is going out . . .

and the reaction of cultural commentators to this 'success':

> *Dallas* was regarded as yet more evidence of the threat posed by American-style commercial culture against authentic national identities. In February 1983 for instance, Jack Lang, the French Minister for Culture . . . had even proclaimed *Dallas* as the 'symbol of American cultural imperialism'.[35]

Ang detects amongst European cultural critics an 'ideology of mass culture' by which she means a generalised hostility towards the imported products of the American mass culture industry, which has fixed on *Dallas* as the focus of its contempt. She quotes Michelle Mattelart:

> It is not for nothing that *Dallas* casts its ubiquitous shadow wherever the future of culture is discussed: it has become the perfect hate symbol, the cultural poverty . . . against which one struggles.[36]

The evident popularity of *Dallas* juxtaposed with its hostile critical reception amongst 'professional intellectuals' and the linked charges of cultural imperialism poses for us nicely the problem of the audience in the discourse of media imperialism. For the cultural critics tend to condemn *Dallas*, like Donald, with scant regard to the way in which the audience may read the text. Cultural imperialism is once more seen as an ideological property of the text itself. It is seen as inhering in the images of dazzling skyscrapers, expensive clothes and automobiles, lavish settings, the celebration in the narrative of power and wealth and so on. All this is seen to have an obvious ideological manipulative effect on the viewer. As Lealand has put it:

> There is an assumption that American T.V. imports do have an impact whenever and wherever they are shown, but actual investigation of this seldom occurs. Much of the evidence that is offered is merely anecdotal or circumstantial. Observations of . . . Algerian nomads watching *Dallas* in the heat of the desert are offered as sufficient proof.[37]

However, encouraged by developments in British critical media theory,[38] some writers have attempted to probe the audience reception of 'imperialist texts' like *Dallas*. Ien Ang's study, although it is not primarily concerned with the issue of media imperialism, is one such.

Ang approaches the *Dallas* audience with the intention of investigating an hypothesis generated from her own experience of watching *Dallas*. She found that her own enjoyment of the show chafed against the awareness she had of its ideological content. Her critical penetration as 'an intellectual and a feminist' of this ideology suggested to her that the pleasure she derived from the programme had little connection with, and certainly did not entail, an ideological effect. In reacting to the ideology in the text, she argues, the cultural critics overlook the crucial question in relation to the audience: 'For we must accept one thing: *Dallas* is popular because a lot of people somehow *enjoy* watching it.'[39]

Ang saw the popularity of the show, which might be read as a sign of its imperialist ideological power, as a complex phenomenon without a single cause, but owing a good deal to the intrinsic pleasure to be derived from its melodramatic narrative structure. The show's ability to connect with 'the melodramatic imagination' and the pleasure this provides were, Ang thought, the key to its success, and these had no necessary connection with the power of American culture or the values of consumer capitalism. What the cultural critics overlooked was the capacity of the audience to negotiate the possible contradictions between alien cultural values and the 'pleasure of the text'.

Ang's study was based on a fairly informal empirical procedure. She placed an advertisement in a Dutch women's magazine asking people to write to her describing what they liked or disliked about *Dallas*. Her correspondents revealed a complex set of reactions, including evidence that some did indeed, like Ang herself, manage to resolve a conflict between their distaste for the ideology of the show and a pleasure in watching it. For example:

> *Dallas*. . . . God, don't talk to me about it. I'm hooked on it! But you wouldn't believe the number of people who say to me, 'Oh, I thought you were against Capitalism?' I am, but *Dallas* is just so tremendously exaggerated, it has nothing to do with capitalists any more, it's just sheer artistry to make up such nonsense.[40]

Ang found such a high level of disapproval for the cultural values of *Dallas*

Can I use arguments ie active?

in some of her correspondents that she speaks of their views being informed by the 'ideology of mass culture' of the cultural critics. These viewers, she argues, have internalised what they perceive as the 'correct' attitude towards mass-cultural imports – that of the disapproving professional intellectuals. They thus feel the need to justify their enjoyment of the show by, for example, adopting an ironic stance towards it. Alternatively, she suggests, an opposing 'anti-intellectual' ideological discourse of 'populism' may allow the *Dallas* fan to refuse the ideology of mass culture as elitist and paternalist, and to insist (in such popular maxims as 'there's no accounting for taste') on their right to their pleasure without cultural 'guilt'.[41]

Ang's analysis of the ideological positioning and struggle around the text of *Dallas* is not without its problems.[42] But her empirical work does at the very least suggest how naive and improbable is the simple notion of an immediate ideological effect arising from exposure to the imperialist text. The complex, reflective and self-conscious reactions of her correspondents suggest that cultural critics who assume this sort of effect massively underestimate the audience's active engagement with the text and the critical sophistication of the ordinary viewer/reader.

The same message comes from most recent studies of audience response. Katz and Liebes, for instance, also looked at reactions to *Dallas*, but in a rather more formal empirical study than Ang's. Their work involved a large-scale cross-cultural study of the impact of *Dallas*, comparing different ethnic groups in Israel with a group of American viewers. Katz and Liebes situate themselves within the growing perspective in media research which sees the audience as active and the process of meaning construction as one of 'negotiation' with the text in a particular cultural context. They argue that this perspective:

consider passive media

> raises a question about the apparent ease with which American television programmes cross cultural and linguistic frontiers. Indeed, the phenomenon is so taken for granted that hardly any systematic research has been done to explain the reasons why these programmes are so successful. One wonders how such quintessentially American products are understood at all. The often-heard assertion that this phenomenon is part of the process of cultural imperialism presumes, first, that there is an American message in the content and form; second, that this message is somehow perceived by viewers; and, third, that it is perceived in the same way by viewers in different cultures.[43]

Katz and Liebes, like Ang, are generally dubious about the way in which the media imperialism argument has been presented by its adherents:

> Since the effects attributed to a T.V. programme are often inferred from content analysis alone, it is of particular interest to examine the extent to which members of the audience absorb, explicitly or implicitly, the messages which critics and scholars allege they are receiving.[44]

Their study of *Dallas* thus represents perhaps the most ambitious attempt so far to examine the media imperialism argument empirically from the perspective of audience response. In order to do this, they organised fifty 'focus groups' consisting of three couples each to watch an episode of *Dallas*. The idea of watching the programme in groups was essential to one of their guiding premisses, that the meanings of TV texts are arrived at via a *social* process of viewing and discursive interpretation. They believe, in common with other recent views,[45] that TV viewing is not essentially an isolated individual practice, but one in which social interaction – 'conversation with significant others' – is a vital part of the interpretative and evaluative process. This may be even more significant when the programme in question is the product of an alien culture and, thus, potentially more difficult to 'decode'.

The groups that Katz and Liebes arranged were all from similar class backgrounds – 'lower middle class with high school education or less' – and each group was 'ethnically homogenous':

> There were ten groups each of Israeli Arabs, new immigrants to Israel from Russia, first- and second-generation immigrants from Morocco and Kibbutz members. Taking these groups as a microcosm of the worldwide audience of *Dallas*, we are comparing their 'readings' of the programme with ten groups of matched Americans in Los Angeles.[46]

The groups followed their viewing of *Dallas* with an hour-long 'open structured' discussion and a short individual questionnaire. The discussions were recorded and formed the basic data of the study, what Katz and Liebes refer to as 'ethno-semiological data'.

The groups were invited to discuss, first, simply what happened in the episode – 'the narrative sequence, and the topics, issues and themes with which the programme deals'.[47] Even at this basic level Katz and Liebes found examples of divergent readings influenced, they argue, by the cultural background of the groups and reinforced by their interaction. One of the Arabic groups actually 'misread' the information of the programme in a way which arguably made it more compatible with their cultural horizon. In the episode viewed, Sue Ellen had taken her baby and run away from her husband JR, moving into the house of her former lover and his father. However, the Arab group confirmed each other in the more conventional reading – in their terms – that she had actually gone to live in her *own* father's house. The implications of this radical translation of the events of the narrative must at least be to undermine the notion that texts cross cultural boundaries intact.

More importantly, perhaps, Katz and Liebes found that different ethnic groups brought their own values to a judgement of the programme's values. They quote a Moroccan Jew's assessment:

> *Machluf*: You see, I'm a Jew who wears a skullcap and I learned from this series to say, 'Happy is our lot, goodly is our fate' that we're Jewish. Everything about JR and his baby, who has maybe four or five fathers, who knows? The mother is Sue

Ellen, of course, and the brother of Pam left. Maybe he's the father. . . . I see that they're almost all bastards.[48]

This sort of response, which seems to be not just a rejection of Western decadence, but an actual reinforcement of the audience's own cultural values, extended from issues of interpersonal and sexual morality to the programme's celebration of wealth: 'With all that they have money, my life style is higher than theirs.' However, here, at the 'real foundations', Katz and Liebes found a more typical response to be an agreement on the importance of money:

Miriam: Money will get you anything. That's why people view it. People sit at home and want to see how it looks.

[. . .]

Yosef: Everybody wants to be rich. Whatever he has, he wants more.

Zari: Who doesn't want to be rich? The whole world does.[49]

It scarcely needs saying that responses like these demonstrate no more than agreement with aspects of the perceived message of *Dallas* and cannot be taken as evidence of the programme's ideological effect. All cultures, we must surely assume, will generate their own set of basic attitudes on issues like the relationship between wealth and happiness. *Dallas* represents, perhaps, one very forceful statement of such an attitude, informed by a dominant global culture of capitalism. But it would be absurd to assume that people in any present-day culture do not have developed attitudes to such a central aspect of their lives quite independent of any televisual representations. We clearly cannot assume that simply watching *Dallas* makes people want to be rich! The most we can assume is that agreement here, as with disagreement elsewhere with the programme's message, represents the outcome of people's 'negotiations' with the text.

Katz and Liebes are careful not to draw any premature conclusions from this complex data. But they do at least suggest that it supports their belief in the active social process of viewing and demonstrates a high level of sophistication in the discursive interpretations of ordinary people. They also make the interesting suggestion that the social and economic distance between the affluent denizens of the Southfork Range and their spectators around the globe is of less consequence than might be thought: 'Unhappiness is the greatest leveller.'[50] This thought chimes with Ang's argument that it is the melodramatic nature of the narrative and its appeal to the 'tragic structure of feeling', rather than its glimpses of consumer capitalism at its shiny leading edge that scores *Dallas*'s global ratings.

The general message of empirical studies – informal ones like Ang's and more large-scale formal projects like Katz and Liebes's – is that audiences are more active and critical, their responses more complex and reflective, and their cultural values more resistant to manipulation and 'invasion' than many critical media theorists have assumed. If we take this empirical work as an adequate response to Fejes's call for investigation of the impact of the 'imperialist text' on 'the lives and human relations' of audiences, we might conclude that this impact has been seriously overstated in the polemics of writers like Schiller, Dorfman and the Mattelarts.

Laughing at Chaplin: problems with audience research

In accepting this, however, we have to bear in mind the inherent limitations of empirical research in this area. For the empirical study of audience reception of a text is notoriously problematic in that it involves the task of making public that which is, at some level, 'private': the 'effects' of a text on a consciousness, on the thoughts, attitudes and beliefs of a viewer, listener or reader. Katz and Liebes's work is actually quite well conceived in terms of the minimal constraints it imposes on the discursive articulation of these processes of consciousness. Their use of informal group discussions guided by 'open' questions at least helps to minimise the influence of the researcher on the data obtained. But the 'artificial' nature of *any* controlled viewing of a programme must always introduce an element of doubt about the validity of the findings. The very fact, for instance, of being *asked* to consider an episode of the programme in a 'critical' way might place the subjects in the perceived role of 'critics' rather than simply 'viewers' and thus produce more reflective and actively negotiated readings than might occur in everyday viewing.

Katz and Liebes defend their use of group viewings and discussions by suggesting that these probably approximate more to normal viewing practices than the individual isolated viewing of the programme. This is a fair point, but we must also recognise the difference in the discursive context established by this 'formal' group situation and the informal one of everyday domestic viewing. In relation to this difference, Richardson and Corner describe the difficulties of accounting for 'the variables of domination, inhibition and consensus introduced by group dynamics'.[51] People in any public social situation will be influenced in their discourse by the subtle pressures and constraints introduced by the situation itself. Researchers will of course display a greater or lesser sensitivity to these problems in their method-ologies. But the most sensitive ethnographic research can never entirely escape the problems that arise from placing people in the self-conscious situation of being investigated or of articulating their views in a public and inevitably power-bound discursive arena. What all this amounts to is that there will always be a gap between how people rehearse their views of a text in public – i.e. in any empirically available form – and how they might 'live' their experience of that text in the undisturbed and unmonitored flow of mundane existence.

Such issues of validity are only the baseline of the problems facing the empirical investigation of media imperialism. The problem of translating the 'phenomenological' data of the viewer's experience into empirical data is common to any investigation of audiences and is central to the debate over media effects generally. The critique of media imperialism is at one level simply a version of the 'ideological effects' argument advanced by many critical media theorists in the West.[52] But the cross-cultural nature of the investigation in the case of media imperialism means that another layer of difficulties is added: that of *interpreting* the empirical data. The point at stake here is whether researchers can correctly interpret responses from a different cultural context in terms of their own cultural understanding. Katz and Liebes seem to treat the responses of the groups they studied as relatively unproblematic at this level: that is, they seem to assume that everyone was speaking the same basic critical-discursive 'language'. Perhaps this was because the cultural horizons of the groups with whom they worked were sufficiently close to each other's and to their own for the normal assumptions of mutual intelligibility and common reference that apply *within* a culture to seem to operate. So, perhaps we could talk of a common 'meta-culture' uniting the different ethnic groups in their study? This 'meta-culture' might be defined, for example, by a common experience of television as a medium, common cultural touchstones such as concepts like 'justice', 'love', 'loyalty', 'personality', 'life style', a common experience of social *modernity*. It is general points of reference like these that narrow the gap between cultures and make the assumption of mutual intelligibility possible.

But we have only to imagine Katz and Liebes's study being carried out with, say, a remote Amazonian Indian tribe for these assumptions rapidly to fall away. How, for example, might such an ethnic group respond to this question, put by a researcher in Katz and Liebes's study to a Russian emigrant: 'Do you mean without emotion?' The interviewer was trying to clarify the speaker's reading of the personality and conduct of J.R., and the response to his question showed that the term 'without emotion' was a common point of reference between them – seen as both meaningful and relevant to the context. But 'emotion' in the sense tacitly recognised in this exchange is a relatively modern and, in fact, highly complex abstract psychological concept. It is probably only meaningful within the particular cultural configuration of European humanism (and its influence) since the nineteenth century. We cannot assume that the question would have the same (or necessarily *any*) meaning for someone outside this sphere of cultural influence. The point is that quite 'ordinary' terms in the critical discourse of televisual texts could present real hermeneutic problems once a certain point of cultural 'distance' is reached.

We don't even have to go so far in terms of cultural distance as the hypothetical 'primitive' to appreciate these interpretive problems, as an article by Irene Penacchioni, 'The Reception of Popular Television in Northeast Brazil', illustrates. Penacchioni's article, based on her work in the poorest and most underdeveloped region of Brazil, is largely a polemic

against the comfortable assumptions of media critics in the West. She tells
three stories which 'will hopefully confuse you as media academics'.[53] One
of these stories concerns her experience in the town of Teresina: 'the capital
of the most infamous, driest and poorest state in the Northeast . . . a tropical
town, surrounded by grey swamps . . . a dead-end town of the interior'.
Brought to this wretched unvisited place by the accident of an emergency
landing of the plane on which she was travelling, she explores the town:

> It is midnight. The streets are almost empty. We arrive at the only central square.
> Immediately we are attracted by a strange, faint ray of light which from far away
> seems to be surrounded by ghost-like silhouettes. The light comes from a
> television set. We hear laughter. A tall man from the Sertao, ie. from the
> countryside, is laughing so much that he has to hold on to his bicycle. And what
> do we see on the screen? Charlie Chaplin's bread dance from the *Gold Rush*. So
> all of us in the square are laughing at the same time about the same things.[54]

But are they? Penacchioni goes on to raise some doubt:

> How can we allow ourselves to talk about the influence of television, if we are not
> even capable of understanding this laughter which resounds across linguistic and
> cultural differences?[55]

Laughter here is the response which needs interpretation. How does the
European sociologist, with her stock of cultural referents (Chaplin – 'the
little man' – pathos-as-comedy – the classic silent movie) know that she
laughs 'about the same things' as the tall peasant from the tropical swamp-
land? Isn't all she can confidently say that they both see the image and
laugh?

Perhaps it seems perverse to press these uncertainties. Well let's look at
the consequences of ignoring them. The assumption that Chaplin evokes the
same response in the European intellectual and the Latin American peasant
can rapidly lead to the assumption that his humour has 'universal appeal',
that something in the antics of the little man touches a chord in a common
humanity which transcends cultural difference. Another media critic,
Michael Tracey, makes exactly this deduction. He links the incident
described by Penacchioni with the popularity of Chaplin among children in
his own home town of Oldham after World War I. The children sang a folk
song about Chaplin which Tracey had heard recorded by a modern folk
group, the Oldham Tinkers. An image of a vast web of connections across
time and space begins to form, with the 'common humanity' of the little man
bringing together the urchins of a northern English mill town, New York
movie audiences, Third World peasants, Parisian intellectuals, the 1920s and
the 1980s in one great family of humanity. Tracey lets himself be carried by
this image into what he admits is a 'terribly heretical' inversion of the
cultural imperialism thesis. Of the Oldham children's song he writes:

> Was that early evidence of the cultural influence of Hollywood, a primeval
> moment of the imperialism of one culture, the subjection of another? It seems

almost boorish to think of it that way. Was the little man not a deep well of pleasure through laughter, a pleasure that was simply universal in appeal? Was it not Chaplin's real genius to strike some common chord, uniting the whole of humanity? Is that not, in fact, the real genius of American popular culture, to bind together, better than anything else, common humanity?[56]

The appeal to 'common humanity' or, as we might say, to 'universalism' is a denial of essential cultural difference. Here it has two implications. First, it implies that hermeneutic difficulties are overstated, that there is 'common understanding' between cultures at some 'deep' level, thus, that we all laugh at the same thing. Second, it denies the possibility of cultural imperialism *because* it denies funadamental cultural differences: the ubiquity of a cultural form is thus separated from any question of domination since it can always be explained in terms of universal appeal. You will have noticed that both Ang and Katz and Liebes go in for a bit of universalism in their speculations on the appeal of *Dallas* – the notion of its appeal to a 'tragic structure of feeling' and so on. Tracey simply takes this notion slightly further. The logical conclusion can be seen in an argument deployed by a defender of the 'free market' in global communications, Ithiel de Sola Pool, who claims: 'The Americanization of world culture so often commented on and often deplored might be better described as the discovery of what world cultural tastes actually are.'[57]

What is wrong with the idea of universalism? Why shouldn't matters be as simple as Tracey suggests? What are the ideological and the hermeneutic grouses here? Let's take the ideological ones first. The main trap that Tracey falls into is that of discounting the significance of the power of the Western media simply to distribute their images. One major reason why Chaplin's humour can be plausibly seen as universal is that it is universally *present*. Quite obviously, if his films had never been distributed outside America, he would never have been a candidate. The force of this argument is seen when we think that no Mongolian or Balinese comedian has been suggested, by Western critics, as striking the chord of common humanity. We cannot sensibly separate this fact from the difference in global media power between these countries and the United States.

The representing of the particular as the universal is a very common ideological ploy: it is found in evangelical and missionary trends in religions such as Christianity that attempt to represent the human race as united at some deep level as, for example, the 'children of God'. This has the obvious implication of denying the claims of other religions. And Marx, of course, points out how the capitalist class tries to represent its interests as 'universal'.[58]

Roland Barthes explores the ideology of universalism in a penetrating short essay, 'The Great Family of Man'. The title refers to an exhibition of photographs staged in Paris, which aimed to show how certain themes and practices occur in all the cultures of the world. Barthes analyses the 'mythology' at work in this exhibition as the conjuring of a universal human community out of examples of cultural diversity:

> This myth functions in two stages: first the difference between human morphologies is asserted, exoticism is insistently stressed, the infinite variations of the species, the diversity in skins, skulls and customs are made manifest, the image of Babel is complacently projected over that of the world. Then, from this pluralism, a type of unity is magically produced: man is born, works, laughs and dies everywhere in the same way; and if there still remains in these actions some ethnic peculiarity, at least one hints that there is underlying each one an identical 'nature'.[59]

What is at work here, Barthes claims, is a suppression of *history* by the use of a discourse of 'nature'. The sentimentality of the notion that we are all brothers and sisters 'under the skin' disguises the historical facts, not just of cultural difference, but of domination and inequality: it is in these historical conditions, argues Barthes, that people experience birth, death, work and laughter, not in some blissful 'natural' human condition. Barthes objects to universalism's claim that all human beings are really the same, because this claim is invariably made by a dominant culture. 'Let us ask', he says, 'the north African workers in the Goutte d'Or district of Paris what they think of *The Great Family of Man*.'[60]

Claims to universality, in short, nearly always relate to some project of domination: it is very rare that the model of 'essential humanity' is taken from an alien culture

So talk of 'common humanity' always risks being ideologically compromised. The reason why Tracey seems to yield to it is that it offers a superficial explanation of popularity, of Penacchioni's 'shared laughter' with the Brazilian peasants. But the explanation is superficial precisely because it doesn't ask the difficult hermeneutic question: is this the *same* laughter? Communality – humanity breaking through the cultural divide – is only a comforting *inference* from the ambiguous phenomenon of laughter. So the hermeneutic grouse is that universalism simply ignores the problem of interpretation. Penacchioni tells another story involving laughter, which makes it plain why we have to treat it as ambiguous and requiring interpretation:

> In the third story we are watching the television news together with Juan who is 20 years old, who cannot read, and who hitherto has lived in the interior of the Sertao, the Northeast drylands. Suddenly on the screen there appears one of those horrifying sequences which are the speciality of the information Leviathan: a motor boat runs out of control up on the beach and into the bathers, hurling them into the air. A lot of them die – Juan bursts out laughing.[61]

This is clearly not the laughter that 'resounds across linguistic and cultural differences'. Penacchioni does not attempt to interpret it and from the details we are given, we certainly could not. Yet the only difference between this laughter and the laughter at Chaplin is our judgement of its appropriateness. What this should tell us is that it is dangerous to take any response at face value. Significance always has to be read *within* the signifying system of a culture. Reading audience responses to media texts in other cultures is thus potentially much more complex than has generally been allowed for in empirical projects. The problems of interpretation involved should make us cautious of drawing premature conclusions from empirical work, or at least of generalising from existing work to other, perhaps more 'distant' cultural contexts.

This thought brings us to the final problem facing empirical work. This is the question of whether it can, within the bounds of practicality, ever hope to grasp cultural imperialism at a sufficient level of generality. Katz and Liebes suggest that their groups – largely composed of immigrants to Israel – could be seen as 'a microcosm of the worldwide audience for *Dallas*'.[62] But all sorts of objections might be raised to this claim.

The attractions of the state of Israel for their study (apart from the convenience of its being the home of the main researchers) must have been its special nature as a sort of cultural 'melting pot' – a modern state with a diversity of ethnic groupings arising from recent immigration. Yet, this very convenience might argue against their claims that it offers a representative picture of the global situation. We have already mentioned the possibility that there is a higher degree of cultural proximity between these ethnic groups and a Western audience – that a common 'meta-culture' of social modernity might attenuate problems of cross-cultural understanding. The fact of having chosen to emigrate and of being resident in a modern developed state must in some way mark these groups out from their 'ethnicity'. It could be argued that they will have a different relationship to their cultural 'roots' – perhaps stronger, perhaps weaker – than those who stayed at home. In fact the sense of cultural identity is likely to be more complex and problematic for *all* the inhabitants of Israel – 'established' Israelis, Palestinians, or recent immigrants – than, say, for the average French or Chinese person. Reactions to texts like *Dallas* might clearly be different for groups already undergoing cultural upheaval, or with special problems of national identity, than for those in more stable cultural conditions. These thoughts must cast doubt on the claim that Katz and Liebes studied a 'microcosm' of the global *Dallas* audience.

None of this is intended as specific criticism of Katz and Liebes's study; it is meant simply to indicate how difficult would be the task of finding a true microcosm of the audience for the imperialist text. At one point in their article Katz and Liebes recognise, with some apparent exasperation, the limitations of their project and the cost and complexity of, for example, expanding it from *Dallas* to other genres of TV programme: 'What we are doing is complex enough.'[63] This is precisely the point I want to make. The global terms in which the cultural imperialism argument is couched by theorists like Schiller actually place it beyond the practical bounds of empirical research. Compromises like Katz and Liebes's study are probably the best we are likely to get and the large areas of doubt they inevitably leave will have to be lived with. So the cultural imperialism argument, when posed as an empirical question at the level of audience response to media texts, may well be an unanswerable question.

Recognising these difficulties – of methodology, interpretation and sheer scale – should help us form a judgement of the value of empirical studies of cultural imperialism. Their value, it seems to me, is limited to *problematising* the stronger versions of the cultural imperialism argument. What studies of the audience tend to suggest is that people are too active and complex in their responses to texts for the claims of widespread easy cultural manipulation to stand. This much is valid enough; but we need to recognise that empirical findings cannot actually *refute* the cultural imperialism argument, since problems of evidence ultimately defeat them. In a sense, the inherent limitations of empirical work make it almost bound to demonstrate the inconclusive nature of the debate. Katz and Liebes's final ironic comment makes this point well:

> Hegemonic theorists will find it easy to interpret the reactions of both acceptors and rejectors of the values in *Dallas* as establishment messages. If the money and muscle of the Ewings are an invitation to the fantasies of social mobility and the supposed 'American way', identification with the *Dallas* characters will serve the purpose. But what about those who see in *Dallas* only a reminder of how much better off they are without power? It takes only the slightest agility to see that this is even more hegemonic. It is a message to stay down, and enjoy the better of the possible worlds, letting the unhappy few take care of the rest.[64]

If it is possible to read either identification with, or rejection of, a media message (supposing such responses could be reliably adduced) as a form of hegemony, clearly the problem of cultural imperialism is beyond the reach of any simple empirical project, and has to be tackled at the level of reason and theory. The theoretical problems of deciding what actually is to count as cultural imperialism – is 'a message to stay down' the same sort of dominance as seduction towards the 'American way'? – are not empirical questions.

So what, finally, is the use of empirical research? As currently conceived and with its practical limitations, it seems to be more useful as a sort of exemplary aid to *thinking out* the problem than as a project with the ambition of conclusively solving it. For example, Katz and Liebes's use of discussion groups prompts us to think about the effects of TV viewing not in terms of the lonely encounter of an individual consciousness with a text, but as a *social encounter* in which the media message is itself mediated by a broader cultural context. Penacchioni's anecdotal evidence from Brazil supports this and even suggests that in this particular cultural context the social nature of viewing departs from that typical of the European context:

> We are dealing here with a cultural context in the widest sense where the European dichotomy does not exist between silence, concentration and solitude on the one hand, which are related to literature or to the watching of a film; and on the other, variety, noise and common distraction which relate to different cultural contexts. Here in Brazil . . . the television is integrated within a collective sound space in the midst of almost uninterrupted activity.[65]

To think out the issue of media imperialism in Brazil or Israel or anywhere else, then, we need to put matters in the broader context of the cultural 'environment' of the audience. But now the spectre of the ambiguity of 'culture' arises again. What do we actually mean by a cultural context? How is this separable from the moment of culture established in interaction with the media? These are complex, difficult questions and they will eventually take us beyond the established discourse of media theory.

Media and culture

It's worth pausing to take stock of the debate over research into media imperialism. Most of the discussion so far has cast doubt on the simple notion that 'imperialist media' have a direct manipulative effect on the cultures they gain access to. No one really disputes the dominant presence of Western multinational, and particularly American, media in the world:[66] what is doubted is the cultural implications of this presence.

We saw first how much of the research labelled 'media imperialism' is conducted at the level of political-economic or institutional analysis and how the specific moment of cultural domination constantly recedes. Cultural domination, though conceived (for example in the work of Herbert Schiller) as the object of analysis, constantly tugs back to economic domination.

We then noted how critics of this sort of 'macro' approach like Fejes, Tracey and Boyd-Barrett, have called for a demonstration of the cultural effects claimed in terms of the actual impact of media texts on an audience. Analysis of texts themselves, even relatively sophisticated ideological readings like Dorfman and Mattelart's, cannot demonstrate this impact. What is at stake is the more difficult task of judging how audiences *respond to* an 'imperialist text'. What little work has been done on this tends to suggest that audiences are more active, complex and critically aware in their readings than the theorists of media imperialism have allowed. This belief in the 'active audience' is supported by audience research within Western societies on the general issue of the supposed 'ideological effect' of media texts: people generally, it seems, are less deceived than critical media theorists have supposed.

At this point, the media imperialism case began to look a little shaky; but we had to add to this picture a number of criticisms of empirical work on audience response. Problems of access to the phenomenological data of the experience of TV programmes, problems of cross-cultural interpretation and problems of sheer scale and practicality all conspire to deny empirical work any final authority. We need, instead, to treat it as advisory and cautionary. This doesn't make the simple media imperialism case look any stronger, but it does mean that matters remain to some extent unresolved in relation to the impact of media texts.

However, the final point I made about empirical studies was their help in reformulating the problems we are dealing with. The stress that studies like that of Katz and Liebes place on the social context of viewing directs our attention away from the text–audience nexus and towards much broader questions of the location of media forms within a culture. Seen in this way, the media imperialism argument might be shown by (or rather, via) empirical studies to be not so much *wrong* as *wrongly formulated*. Thus the cultural 'impact' of the political-economic and institutional dominance that Schiller catalogues may be impossible to grasp in the interrogation of texts and audiences: it may involve a more complex form of cultural 'mediation' than the research programmes of media specialists have so far offered. The cultural imperialism of media imperialism may even lie beyond the conceptual range of media studies. This is a possibility I have hinted at several times: now we ought to look at what this implies.

The major implication is that the relationship between media and culture needs careful thought. There is an assumption shared both by proponents and critics of the media imperialism case that the media are somehow at the centre of cultural processes and that issues of cultural domination therefore turn on issues of media domination. For example, Schiller, predictably, claims that 'the public media are the foremost example of operating enterprises that are used in the penetrating processes' of cultural domination; but equally Boyd-Barrett, a severe critic of Schiller, states that media imperialism, 'is possibly the single most important component of cultural imperialism, outside formal educational institutions'.[67] There is a sense in which the media are the most obvious target, since the most public. But the danger of pursuing this obviousness is that we may take media issues as the substance of cultural imperialism, when they may be no more than indications of a more deeply structured cultural process. Lodziak warns against what he calls the 'media-centredness' of media theory, by which he means the tendency of people working in this area to assume the cultural and ideological processes they study are at the centre of social reality. This narrow perspective he argues, distorts the overall social significance of something like television:

> Television's power is so strongly assumed that, rather than being the object of analysis, it tends to prescribe research practices and theoretical reasoning. . . . Media-centred reasoning is unable either to explain why television has become the dominant leisure activity in a majority of Western societies or to grasp the social significance of this.[68]

Lodziak is in effect challenging media theorists to gain a sense of orientation by performing a sort of 'Copernican twist': by removing themselves from the centre of their cosmology. This is also sound advice for us. It is now worth interrogating the centrality generally assigned to the media in culture.

Let us begin with some of the strongest claims advanced by contemporary cultural theorists. These are found in the currently fashionable, though in many ways problematic, theories of 'postmodernity' associated with thinkers like Jean Baudrillard, Jean-François Lyotard and Fredric Jameson. I shall have something to say about these theories in the final part of this book; for the moment all I want to register is the tendency within this sort of cultural theory to claim a virtual identity between 'media' and 'culture' in contemporary societies. As an example of this we can consider a claim about television made by two Canadian social theorists, Arthur Kroker and David Cook:

> TV is, in a very literal sense, the real world, not of modern but of *postmodern* culture, society and economy – of society typified by the dynamic momentum of the spirit of technicisme triumphant and of real popular culture driven onwards by the ecstasy and decay of the obscene spectacle – and that [*sic*] everything which escapes the real world of TV, everything which is not videated as its identity-principle, everything which is not processed through TV as the technical apparatus of relational power *par excellence*, is peripheral to the main tendencies of the contemporary century. In postmodernist culture, it's not TV as a mirror of society, but just the reverse, *it's society as a mirror of television*.[69]

Behind the hyperbole of this lies a not uncommon perception that contemporary culture is so thoroughly saturated by the mass media that it is impossible to separate out an immediate 'real' cultural experience from those we experience through the flat surface of the television screen. Baudrillard, whom Kroker and Cook closely follow here, has been the most extravagant proponent of this idea, claiming that reality itself has given way to a media-produced 'hyperreality' in which 'the medium and the real are now in a single nebulous state whose truth is undecipherable'.[70] In fact in Baudrillard's discourse the very power attributed to them transforms the concept of 'the media'. They can no longer be seen as the *means* – the forms and institutions – through which communication occurs: they become a sort of *principle* of (post)modern cultural experience which dissolves the notion of meaningful communication. This view connects both with a general mistrust of the possibility of immediate 'lived reality' that is pervasive of the discourse of postmodernity, and with a very patronising stance towards the media audience – or as Baudrillard usually has it, 'the masses'.

Such claims are, of course, very easy to criticise from the perspective of orthodox media research, for writers like Baudrillard and Kroker and Cook simply fail to engage with any sort of empirical evidence or with the hermeneutic issues we have discussed in this chapter.[71] However it is possible to sympathise at least with what such theories are attempting to articulate: a shift in cultural practices that significantly alters the terms in which we can speak about cultural experience. For example, when Baudrillard speaks of the 'obscenity' of television images he is trying to grasp a situation in which 'the most intimate processes of our life become the virtual feeding ground of the media' (think of the lingering shots of private grief that seem obligatory in the coverage of any disaster), while at the same time, 'the entire universe comes to unfold arbitrarily on your domestic screen' (think of the vast range of disconnected images it is possible to conjure up by 'zapping' across the channels). All this, Baudrillard claims, 'explodes the scene formerly preserved by the minimal separation of public and private'.[72]

'Obscenity' is the state of extreme 'visibility' of all phenomena. There is thus a sense in which television may radically alter our sense of cultural 'boundaries', like the public and the private, making all experience equally visible but also equally 'flat' – robbing us of the differentiations that give events particular significances.

The hyperbolic rhetoric of postmodernist media theory can be seen as an attempt to grasp the *feel* of a culture in which, as Harvey reminds us, 'the average American is now reputed to watch television for more than seven hours a day'.[73] But the big question remains: *whose* 'feel of the culture' is being described? Does the average American actually experience the decomposition of cultural meanings that people like Baudrillard suggest are the concomitant of media practices? Or are we dealing with another example of the sort of gap between the world of the cultural critic and that of the media audience that Ang and others detect?[74]

We can pursue this by turning to a far less extreme, though still strong, argument about media centrality; that offered by Stuart Hall. Hall's analysis of the development of the mass media within Western societies leads him to suggest that:

> Quantitatively and qualitatively, in twentieth-century advanced capitalism, the media have established a decisive and fundamental leadership in the cultural sphere. Simply in terms of economic, technical, social and cultural resources, the mass media command a qualitatively greater slice than all the older, more traditional cultural channels which survive.[75]

This is to argue that the sheer enormous material presence of the mass media has marginalised other, older, means of social communication in modern societies in which people live 'increasingly fragmented and sectionally differentiated lives'. The mass media thus become the primary way in which people in massified, 'anomic', socially fragmented capitalist societies gain a sense of the social 'totality' and of their relation to it:

> This is the first of the great cultural functions of the modern media: the provision and the selective construction of *social knowledge*, of social imagery, through which we perceive the 'worlds', the 'lived realities' of others, and imaginarily reconstruct their lives and ours into some intelligible 'world-of-the-whole.'[76]

In Hall's view, then, the mass media are central to modern capitalist culture since they are the primary resource for the meaningful organisation and 'patterning' of people's experience. In this they are intimately related to the technico-economic and social processes of modern capitalism, since these latter produce both the 'bewildering complexity' of social modernity and the technical means for 'mediation' of this complexity of experience. The cultural centrality of the media is thus a function of the type of society which engenders it: modern capitalist societies generate social experience in all sorts of modes and at all sorts of levels: 'in regions, classes and sub-classes, in cultures and sub-cultures, neighbourhoods and communities, interest groups and associative minorities'[77] and, we may add, in familial, interpersonal and 'existential' modes. The media do not supplant this experience (as Kroker and Cook suggest), they provide a way of organising it into a coherent and intelligible 'whole' – it is in this sense of 'managing' experience that the media has 'leadership' in the sphere of culture.

Hall's argument is a strong one because it is cautious in its formulation – it doesn't suggest that the modern media have entirely swamped all forms of communication and cultural practice, merely that they have a unique managerial function. It is also plausible in terms of the routine social practices of people in advanced capitalist societies – for obvious instance, the way in which television viewing has tended to 'colonize' most people's leisure time.[78] Yet for all this, there is a danger that the importance of the media may be overstated even here. For all its evidential problems, audience research does suggest that the media cannot have the undisputed managerial function that Hall implies, since media messages are themselves mediated by other modes of cultural experience: this is what is implied by the notion of the 'active audience'.

The undeniably high profile of the mass media in contemporary cultural practices, set against the evidence that people bring other cultural resources to their dealings with it, suggests that we can view the relationship between media and culture as a subtle *interplay of mediations*. Thus, we may think of the media as the dominant *representational* aspect of modern culture. But the 'lived experience' of culture may also include the discursive interaction of families and friends and the material-existential experience of routine life: eating, working, being well or unwell, sexuality, the sense of the passage of time and so on. So the following relationship might suggest itself:

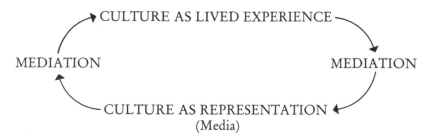

CULTURE AS LIVED EXPERIENCE

MEDIATION   MEDIATION

CULTURE AS REPRESENTATION
(Media)

The relationship implied in this is the constant mediation of one aspect of cultural experience by another: what we make of a television programme or a novel or a newspaper article is constantly influenced and shaped by whatever else is going on in our lives. But, equally, our lives are lived as *representations to ourselves* in terms of the representations present in our culture: our biographies are, partly, 'intertextual'. We can make matters less abstract by giving an illustration of each 'moment' in this interplay.

According to Hall's notion of the 'managerial' role of the media, the average inhabitant of the Midlands city where I write this organises her or his 'worldview' primarily in relation to the social knowledge furnished by television, newspapers, magazines and so on. On this account (which has the *prima facie* support of all the newsagents, video-hire stores, TV rental companies etc. in the city doing a healthy trade) what it is to be living in the late twentieth century in the capitalist West is made coherent by a perpetual flow of media images. Yet it is clear to me that the people I see around the city have a 'real' cultural experience in their everyday lives which has a certain priority over any experience provided by the media. This lived experience is very probably closer to people's sense of what their lives are about: it is, indeed, what people think of as 'real life' as distinct from the represented life of the media. So this mundane but existentially close level of experience – worrying about families, organising the routines of the day, having a headache, gossiping, daydreaming, sharing a joke – must itself 'manage' people's use and perception of media images.

Let us take the example of romantic love. During an average week, television offers a range of versions of what love is all about: from the 'realism' of soap operas to the 'romance' of old black-and-white movies. These images will be mediated by the 'real' experiences of viewers during that week: by their ongoing relations with their families or their lovers, by their knowledge of the problems or triumphs of friends and so on. What people come to judge as the cultural reality of 'love' will thus be, in some sort, the public representation which accords best with the personal evidence of lived reality. This is what is behind the common criterion applied to fictional representations: whether they are 'true to life' or not. This, then, is the moment of the dominance of lived reality over representation.

We can take the same example of romantic love to illustrate the other moment of dominance: that of representation over lived experience. The experience of 'being in love' may seem to be deeply personal and 'immediate': something we feel is unique to the person involved. In this sense we may think that *representations* of this experience are always derivative of the 'real thing': attempts to grasp and convey something that is essentially 'subjective'. So when Gustave Flaubert says that Emma Bovary 'was in love with' Leon Dupuis he is faced with the problem of representing this deeply personal feeling. This is how he describes the rather obsessive-neurotic nature of Emma's feelings of love:

> she sought solitude that she might revel in his image undisturbed. It marred the pleasure of her daydream to see him in the flesh. The sound of his step set her trembling. But in his presence, her agitation subsided, leaving nothing but an immense astonishment that worked itself out in sadness.[79]

If you respond to this, as I did, with enthusiasm for the psychological insight and the powers of emotional evocation – if this seems to strike some precise chord – you should ask, why? Is it that Flaubert manages to conjure up in language some particular aspects of 'the real thing'? Well, Flaubert rather debunks this idea when he tells us that Emma's feelings for Leon owe a lot to the romantic novels she has read:

They were all about love and lovers, damsels in distress swooning in lonely lodges, postillions slaughtered all along the road, horses ridden to death on every page, gloomy forests, troubles of the heart, vows, sobs, tears, kisses, rowing boats in the moonlight, nightingales in the grove, gentlemen brave as lions and gentle as lambs, too virtuous to be true, invariably well dressed and weeping like fountains.[80]

So this fictional experience of love is actually a product of other (fictional!) fictions. And when *we* read Flaubert, doesn't this add to *our* sense of the 'reality' of love? We don't need to go into all the complexities of discussing texts within texts to realise that the experience of love may be at least partly a product of representations. The implications are that every romantic novel we read, every soap opera we watch, may add to, shape or mediate our 'real' experiences. This is not to say that these experiences are, as a consequence, any less 'real': the point is that present 'reality' must always be partly a function of our past experiences which generally, in modern cultures, include experiences of media texts.

What this suggests is that the dialectical relationship between 'lived experience' and cultural (media) representations is one that cannot easily be analysed into its constitutive parts: of course people rightly discriminate between their own 'real life' and the things they see on the television or read about in books. But if we think about it, there must be a constant interchange between, and mediation of, these levels of experience. It is just as implausible to think of real life as absolutely immediate experience, entirely separate from cultural representations, as it is to think of television as 'the real world' (Kroker and Cook).

Where does this view of the constant mediation of one level of experience by another leave us in situating the role of the media in modern culture? The key to this is, I think, in keeping a firm grasp on the idea of *mediation* itself. Extravagant claims for media power seem to arise where theorists come to see the media as *determining* rather than as mediating cultural experience – that is, as at the centre of things rather than as related to other practices and experiences. First we must bear in mind that all cultures involve interactions between representations and 'lived reality' – even those 'traditional' cultures which we may think of in distinction from modern mass-mediated ones. Modern societies clearly involve much more routine interaction with media texts than 'traditional' societies, and, as Hall suggests, there are likely to be real historical differences between cultures subject to mass media(tion) and those less so. But this does not imply that the media are at the 'centre' of modern cultures in the sense that people live their cultural reality entirely through the media. People in modern societies are involved in all sorts of relationships and practices other than watching television, and to do justice to these it is necessary to 'decentre' the media from the position that they have gained in some cultural theories.

All this suggests that the most useful way to think about the effects of 'imperialist' media on another culture may not be in the narrow terms of media imperialism, where this concentrates exclusively on media institutions and media texts. It will probably be better to think of cultural imperialism as a much broader process of cultural change which involves the media among other factors. If we think of the significance of the spread of Western media into the cultural life of 'developing societies' it may be possible to think of this impact as a shift in the balance of forces in the 'dialectic' of culture-as-lived-experience and culture-as-representation: of people coming to draw more on media imagery in their constructions of reality. This process, however, proceeds as part of a whole range of other changes in the way in which people experience their lives: living in cities, being dependent on large-scale capitalist industry both for income and for the satisfaction of needs, experiencing their lives as divided into a number of discrete 'spheres' – work, consumption, 'private life' and so on. These changes in routine lived reality (which, in all sorts of ways, also involve the mediations of media representations) may be described as the impact of capitalist modernity. As I will argue in chapters four and five, it is in terms of the spread of capitalist modernity that the idea of cultural imperialism is best understood.

Notes

1. This literature can be found for example in the journals, *Media Development, Journal of Communication*, and *Media, Culture and Society*.
2. F. Fejes (1981) 'Media Imperialism: an Assessment', *Media Culture and Society*, Vol. 3(3), pp.281–9 (p.287).
3. Ibid. See also M. Tracey (1985) 'The Poisoned Chalice? International Television and the Idea of Dominance', *Daedalus*, Vol 114(4), pp.17–56.
4. Ibid.
5. See I. Wallerstein (1974) *The Modern World System*, New York, Academic Press.
6. See Chapter 4, pp.105–8. For discussions of 'dependency theory' see A. Webster (1984) *Introduction to the Sociology of Development*, London, Macmillan, and I. Roxborough (1979) *Theories of Underdevelopment*, London, Macmillan.
7. See R. Jenkins (1987) *Transnational Corporations and Uneven Development: The Internationalization of Capital and the Third World*, London, Methuen.
8. See the discussion of 'modernization theory' in Chapter 5, pp.143–44.
9. See J.O. Boyd-Barrett (1982), 'Cultural Dependency and the Mass Media', in M. Gurevitch et al. (eds) *Culture, Society and the Media*, London, Methuen, p.178. For a general critique of dependency theory see P. O'Brien (1975) 'A Critique of Latin American Theories of Dependency', in I. Oxaal et al. (eds) *Beyond the Sociology of Development*, London, Routledge and Kegan Paul.
10. H.I. Schiller (1979) 'Transnational Media and National Development', in K. Nordenstreng and H.I. Schiller (eds) *National Sovereignty and International Communication*, New Jersey, Ablex p.21.
11. Ibid., p.23.
12. Ibid.
13. One of the idiosyncratic features of Schiller's work is his tendency to suggest something *approaching* a 'conspiracy theory' linking multinational industries

with US strategic planning. See, for example, H.I. Schiller (1976) *Communication and Cultural Domination*, New York, M.E. Sharpe, pp.19–23.

14. Schiller (1979), op. cit., p.30.
15. Ibid., p.31.
16. See the discussions in Chapter 4, pp.126–31 and Chapter 5, pp.144–46.
17. H.I. Schiller (1985) 'Electronic Information Flows: New Basis for Global Domination?', in P. Drummond and R. Paterson (eds) *Television in Transition: Papers from the First International Television Studies Conference*, London, British Film Institute, p.11.
18. See, for example, A. Mattelart (1979) *Multinational Corporations and the Control of Culture*, Brighton, Harvester Press. The book by Dorfman and Mattelart that we will discuss in the following section is an exception to this general approach.
19. P. Golding and G. Murdock (1979) 'Ideology and the Mass Media: the Question of Determination', in M. Barrett et al. (eds) *Ideology and Cultural Production*, London, Croom Helm, p.222, (emphasis added). See also P. Golding (1977) 'Media Professionalism in the Third World: the Transfer of an Ideology', in J. Curran et al. (eds) *Mass Communication and Society*, London, Arnold.
20. R. Samarajiwa (1984), 'Third-World Entry to the World Market in News: Problems and Possible Solutions', *Media Culture and Society*, Vol. 6(2), pp.119–36, (pp.120–1; emphasis added).
21. Tracey, op. cit., p.45.
22. Fejes, op. cit., p.287.
23. A. Dorfman and A. Mattelart (1975) *How to Read Donald Duck: Imperialist Ideology in the Disney Comic*, New York, International General Editions. See also A. Dorfman (1985) *The Empire's Old Clothes*, London, Pluto Press, and Mattelart's discussion of the American educational television programme, *Sesame Street*, in Mattelart (1979) op. cit.
24. M. Barker (1989) *Comics: Ideology, Power and the Critics*, Manchester, Manchester University Press, p.279.
25. J. Berger, quoted in introductory pages to Dorfman and Mattelart, op. cit., p.3.
26. D. Kunzle (1975) 'Introduction to the English Edition', Dorfman and Mattelart, op. cit., p.11–21 (p.14).
27. Dorfman and Mattelart, op. cit., p.78.
28. Barker, op. cit., p.287.
29. Ibid., p.299.
30. Dorfman and Mattelart, op. cit., p.97.
31. Ibid.
32. Ibid.
33. Ibid., p.98.
34. Boyd-Barrett, op. cit., p.193.
35. I. Ang (1985) *Watching Dallas: Soap Opera and the Melodramatic Imagination*, London, Methuen, pp.1–2.
36. M. Mattelart, quoted ibid., p.2.
37. G. Lealand quoted in Tracey, op. cit., p.36.
38. See particularly, D. Morley (1980) *The 'Nationwide' Audience: Structure and Decoding*, London, British Film Institute.
39. Ang, op. cit., p.4.
40. Ibid., p.96.
41. Ibid., p.113.

42. See the critique in D. Webster (1988) *Looka Yonder: the Imaginary America of Populist Culture*, London, Routledge/Comedia, p.202. The main fault Webster finds is that Ang overstates the 'spontaneous' nature of the populism she describes, failing to acknowledge, for instance, the way in which the tabloid press may *organise* a populist discourse around television.

43. E. Katz and T. Liebes (1985) 'Mutual Aid in the Decoding of *Dallas*: Preliminary Notes from a Cross-Cultural Study', in Drummond and Paterson, op. cit., p.187.

44. Ibid, p.190.

45. See, for example, D. Morley (1986) *Family Television: Cultural Power and Domestic Leisure*, London, Comedia, and D. Morley and R. Silverstone (1990) 'Domestic Communication – Technologies and Meanings', *Media, Culture and Society*, Vol. 12(1), pp.31–55.

46. Katz and Liebes, op. cit., p.188.

47. Ibid., p.190.

48. Ibid., pp.193–4.

49. Ibid., p.194.

50. Ibid., p.197.

51. K. Richardson and J. Corner (1986) 'Reading Reception: Mediation and Transparency in Viewers' Accounts of a TV Programme', *Media, Culture and Society*, Vol 8(4), pp.485–508 (p.488).

52. For a critique of these arguments, see C. Lodziak (1986) *The Power of Television: A Critical Appraisal*, London, Frances Pinter.

53. I. Penacchioni (1984) 'The Reception of Television in Northeast Brazil', *Media, Culture and Society*, Vol 6(4), pp.337–341 (p.338).

54. Ibid., p.339.

55. Ibid.

56. Tracey, op. cit., p.40.

57. I. de Sola Pool (1979) 'Direct Broadcast Satellites and the Integrity of National Cultures', in Nordenstreng and Schiller, op. cit., p.145.

58. See, for example, the well known claim that 'the ideas of the ruling class are in every epoch the ruling ideas', K. Marx and F. Engels (1970) *The German Ideology*, London, Lawrence and Wishart, p.64. See Giddens's interpretation of this passage as a claim about 'the representation of sectional interests as universal ones' – A. Giddens (1979) *Central Problems in Social Theory: Action, Structure and Contradiction in Social Analysis*, London, Macmillan, p.193.

59. R. Barthes (1973) *Mythologies*, London, Paladin, p.100.

60. Ibid., p.102.

61. Penacchioni, op. cit., p.339.

62. Katz and Liebes, op. cit., p.188.

63. Ibid., p.189.

64. Ibid., p.198.

65. Penacchioni, op. cit., p.339.

66. But see Tracey's discussion of the complexity of TV distribution around the world, and his point that these flows do not fit neatly into the model of 'total domination of international television by the United States' – Tracey, op. cit., p.23.

67. Schiller (1976), op. cit., p.9, and O. Boyd-Barrett, (1977) 'Media Imperialism: Towards an International Framework for the Analysis of Media Systems', in J. Curran et al., op. cit., p.119.

68. Lodziak, op. cit., pp.2–3.
69. A. Kroker and D. Cook (1988) *The Postmodern Scene: Excremental Culture and Hyper-Aesthetics*, London, Macmillan Education, p.268.
70. J. Baudrillard, quoted in D. Kellner (1989) *Jean Baudrillard: From Marxism to Postmodernism and Beyond*, Cambridge, Polity Press, p.69.
71. See the critique in Kellner, ibid., pp.73–6.
72. J. Baudrillard (1985) 'The Ecstasy of Communication', in H. Foster (ed.) *Postmodern Culture*, London, Pluto Press, p.130.
73 D. Harvey (1989) *The Condition of Postmodernity: An Enquiry into the Origins of Cultural Change*, Oxford, Basil Blackwell, p.61.
74. Cf. Kellner's critique of Baudrillard's 'theoreticism', Kellner, op. cit., pp.74–5. See also Lodziak, op. cit., Chapter 4, 'The Maligned Audience'.
75. S. Hall (1977) 'Culture, the Media and the "Ideological Effect" ', in Curran et al., op. cit., p.341.
76. Ibid., pp.340–1.
77. Ibid.
78. See H. Sahin and J.P. Robinson (1981) 'Beyond the Realm of Necessity: Television and the Colonization of Leisure', *Media, Culture and Society*, Vol. 3(1), pp.85–95.
79. G. Flaubert (1950) *Madame Bovary*, Harmondsworth, Penguin, p.120.
80. Ibid., p.50.

3

Cultural Imperialism and the Discourse of Nationality

In this chapter we turn from the (deceptively) self-contained and concrete discourse of the media, to a more generalised discourse of culture. In many of the media imperialism arguments what seems to be at stake is the threat to 'national cultures'. For instance, Nordenstreng and Schiller entitle their collection on media imperialism, *National Sovereignty and International Communication* and speak in their introduction of 'advocating respect for the cultural and political sovereignty of all nations'. Now as we saw in the previous chapter the real target of Schiller's critique is the 'world capitalist system', and his discourse is to a large extent the Marxist discourse of class domination. But clearly anyone discussing global issues cannot avoid speaking in terms of nations and nationality. This is, however, a difficult discourse for Marxists. As Pool puts it:

> Nationalism is the doctrine of the right wing that most easily coopts the left. Historically, liberals and radicals have been internationalists. Marx's statement, 'the workers have no fatherland', epitomizes that view. Liberal intellectuals have fought for freedom of movement, freedom from censorship, world cultural exchange, and condemned ethnocentrism and prejudice.[1]

The defence of 'national cultures' is thus in certain senses ideologically problematic for the general left-wing perspective from which critiques of cultural imperialism arise. But it is also, as we shall see, *conceptually* problematic. What this chapter will try to do is to set out some of the problems involved in this very general way of speaking about cultural imperialism: as the domination of one national culture by another. These problems are complex and interrelated, but we can organise them roughly into four categories.

First, there are the problems which arise in relation to the specifications of a national culture. 'Cultures' – in the sense of the communal practices, values and shared meanings of social collectivities – do not map neatly on to the political grid of nation-states. There is obviously some sense in which we can speak of a 'national culture' but we have also to realise that within nation-states, and even possibly across national boundaries, there exist patterns of cultural identification which are quite different from, and often in direct conflict with, the 'national culture'. The frequent mismatch between these diverse 'cultural identities' and 'national cultural identities' in the modern world is the first problem we will address. In section one, we will notice the contradictions and ambiguities this produces in the discourse of cultural domination within UNESCO. Section two will extend this discussion to consider how the idea of the invasion of a national culture fares in the context of the cultural plurality of modern nation states.

The most general implication to be drawn from these considerations is that 'national identity' is one among several ways in which people may experience a sense of cultural belonging, but that it has a special political and ideological significance. The fact that the nation-state is the most significant political-economic unit into which the world is divided means that there is often a good deal of deliberate 'cultural construction' involved in the making of national identities. However it would be a mistake to see 'national identity' as a purely ideological construct. There is something about the experience a person has of belonging to a nation which cannot be grasped simply as ideology. The second set of problems we shall probe – in sections three and four – concerns the complex ideological-psychological processes through which a sense of 'national identity' may arise.

Here, however, an important subtext emerges. For the discussions of national identity that we will consider tend to stress that this form of cultural identification can only be understood in terms of broader historical processes – and specifically those which have brought about the conditions of social *modernity*. The nation-state system itself needs to be seen as a phenomenon of modernity. The underlying argument of the chapter – and my third point here – will thus be that we need to shift our conceptualisation of the issue of cultural imperialism from one primarily on the plane of *space* to one primarily on the plane of *time*. All social phenomena – all phenomena – take place, of course, simultaneously in both time and space. But what I am thinking of is the tendency we might have to think about cultural imperialism in predominantly *spatial* terms. Talk of 'national sovereignty' is essentially spatial talk: it invokes images of national boundaries. There is therefore a tendency in this discourse to think geographically and synchronically: that is as if the processes we are dealing with were spread out across space and 'frozen' in time. Thus, United States cultural domination of some Latin American country will usually be expressed in the 'now' and in terms of place. For example we might think of the centres of cities looking the same, or in metaphors of cultural proximity and distance, or of the dominated country being a tourist venue for North Americans, or of domination as cultural 'invasion' with its territorial connotations, or of Western electronic media crossing national boundaries and penetrating cultural space.[2] All these ideas operate predominantly on the plane of space, though, of course, if we pause to think about it, the processes all take time – we should, for example, speak of 'the centres of cities *coming to look* the same'. But we don't commonly think of time and space together and by thinking in a spatial vocabulary we tend to ignore the element of time. One implication of this is to think of cultural identity as something 'static', frozen in time – 'Englishness', 'the American way' – rather than, as it must be, something constantly changing and developing. To recognise the dimension of time in cultural identity is immediately to problematise the idea of cultural imperialism as we shall see in section five.

The final problem is a question of value. It is the question of how domination is conceived in this discourse. We saw that the idea of domination in relation to 'imperialist' media texts is highly problematic. Here we will consider a different formulation of the idea of cultural domination: that in which it is asserted that the *autonomy of a culture* is threatened by the influence of an alien culture. This formulation, common within the discourse of nationality, raises problems in the understanding of what 'a culture' actually *is*.

Cultural identity: the UNESCO discourse

One way into the issue of national cultures is to consider how the concept has been used in the institutional discourse of UNESCO. Here a discourse of cultural imperialism exists within the parameters imposed by an 'international' institutional setting. Definitions of cultural identity within the discourse of UNESCO will be shaped by the underlying need to reproduce the discursive structure of UNESCO itself: that is by the need constantly to assert the legitimate superordinacy of nation-states over other agencies within the global conversation. For UNESCO discourse is primarily the global conversation of nation-states. The implication is that talk of cultures and the need to protect them as it occurs in the setting of UNESCO will tend to privilege the nation as a site of cultural identity – cultural identity will tend to be elided with national identity. So when people speak in UNESCO of the need to defend cultural identity from cultural imperialism they are usually speaking of the need to defend national cultures.

However, as Philip Schlesinger has noted,[3] the simultaneous existence of a 'pluralising tendency' which asserts the equality of *all* cultural configurations (not only those belonging to nation states) sets up interesting ambiguities and tensions within the UNESCO discourse. To put it simply, UNESCO is forced in its pronouncements to vacillate between the assertion and denial of national identity as (definitively) cultural identity.

We can observe this tendency at work in the report of UNESCO's World Conference on Cultural Policies held in 1982 in Mexico City. The broad purpose of this conference, one of a series begun in Venice in 1970, was the discussion of the nature and significance of culture in international affairs and the formulation of a set of policy recommendations in the cultural field. In the words of the opening address to the conference by Fernando Solana: 'A fundamental item on our agenda is respect for the cultural identity of all people.'[4]

So here UNESCO sets itself the task of debating cultural identity in the name of 'all people'. This is significant: the discourse is constructed initially in terms of 'people' rather than 'nations':

> Most delegates emphasised people's growing awareness of their cultural identity, of the pluralism stemming from it, of their right to be different and of the mutual respect of cultures one for another, including those of minorities.[5]

This is the *pluralist* rhetoric of UNESCO, repeated constantly throughout the 200-odd pages of the final report: the assertion of the right to peaceful coexistence of cultural differences: 'a point on which all were agreed – recognition and respect for others, tolerance, a spirit of brotherhood and the acceptance of differences'.[6] It is worth noting in passing the reference to 'a spirit of brotherhood', for this involves another ideological commitment of UNESCO (though couched in unfortunately sexist language): a commitment to a unifying discourse of 'humanism'. It is only because of the assumption of an underlying sameness – 'brotherhood', a common humanity – that differences come to be tolerated: 'Culture belongs to man – all of men. Culture was universal but not one.'[7]

The rhetoric of a universal humanism – which holds that we are all the same at some 'basic' level[8] – underwrites the UNESCO commitment to defence of cultural difference. Pluralism here derives from humanism. Though it forms part of the seamless web of diplomatic rhetoric of such reports, this link between pluralism and humanism is a curious one. For the assertion of an underlying sameness of all people is used as an answer to the difficult question: why *should* different cultures tolerate one another? The UNESCO answer is that they should, and should live together in harmonious difference, because something binds them together at a much deeper level. It is this something which, it is implied, makes *cultural* difference tolerable. The metaphor of the family – 'brotherhood' – is used here to suggest these deeper 'ties'. In effect, recognition of legitimate difference is only bought with an assertion of a deeper 'sameness'. This curious paradox stems almost entirely from the need to provide some ideological backstop to the institutional role of UNESCO. Pluralism is a necessary part of UNESCO's existence as an institution for the conduct of the global conversation, so pluralism cannot be contested within its rhetoric: it is a given of UNESCO discourse. A 'humanism' which is so general and abstract as to be unexceptionable provides a convenient rhetorical 'grounding' for the values of pluralism: the values of difference, tolerance, forbearance, peaceful coexistence. But this rhetoric does not bear too much examination: why, after all, *should* being human mean we should tolerate other people's cultural practices? Would this apply, for example, to canibalism, or, more immediately relevant, to female circumcision, or the stockpiling of nuclear weapons? But here we draw close to the abyss, for we glimpse the possible 'groundlessness' of *any* values, even big friendly modern ones like tolerance and so on. Let us retreat, for the present, from this depressing implication. Pluralism, however derived, is an essential part of the UNESCO discourse.

This pluralism is disciplined by the other main institutional determinant of UNESCO rhetoric, its composition on the level of nationality. Thus: 'Many delegates . . . considered that one could not speak of cultural identity without reaffirming the fundamental concepts of national sovereignty and territorial independence.'[9] In the recommendations of the report there are constant references to cultural identity as national identity – 'national spiritual values . . . ethics, habits and customs of the nation as a whole'.[10] Cultural autonomy is similarly associated with national sovereignty – 'The Conference . . . declares that cultural autonomy is inseparable from the full exercise of sovereignty.'[11]

National culture is the mould into which, by the very nature of UNESCO as an inter-national body, cultural identity tends to be squeezed. Thus cultural domination – to which the conference devoted two specific sets of policy recommendations – is conceptualised predominantly in national terms, for example as 'one of the most severe dangers which threatens the cultural identity of the nations'.[12]

But pluralism in its most general form also inevitably reasserts itself:

> A number of delegates insisted, however, that cultural identity could not be defined solely in terms of national identity. Cultural identity, that of individuals and that of groups, communities or classes, was in fact multidimensional in nature . . . thus national identity could be rooted in a wider identity – a regional one for example . . . while pluralism could apply equally to conditions within a given national identity and to the specific characteristics of each minority group or social class.[13]

The UNESCO discourse seems doomed to a diplomatic inconsistency. On the one hand it has to assert pluralism at all levels, but on the other it must assert cultural defence in terms of the status quo of national divisions. This forced ambiguity leads to conceptual confusion. The report recognises, for example, the centrality of language to culture, but as Schlesinger has observed:

> Clearly, if language is central to cultural identity, *cultural* identity cannot be equivalent to *national* identity, as various linguistic groups may inhabit a given nation-state or be otherwise linked beyond its confines.[14]

The UNESCO discourse cannot negotiate this complexity with any coherence. In its recommendations on the issue of cultural domination it urges member states to:

> – strengthen national languages with a view to affirming cultural identity and helping it to recover its natural role which is that of expressing the different aspects of activity and life and thereby furthering national development.[15]

The UNESCO discourse of cultural identity is, in short, intrinsically ambiguous and contradictory, and these difficulties derive in large part from its discursive position as an 'inter-national' body. This is an important point, for it reminds us that the issue of 'who speaks' is always a crucial one in discourses of cultural imperialism.

Not all the ambiguities of the UNESCO discourse are 'diplomatic' ones. There are genuine conceptual difficulties in articulating cultural identity and these contribute to a tendency to elide cultural with national identity. For 'the nation' *appears* to be a more concrete, 'identifiable' entity than 'a culture' and there is often a common-sense assumption that nations and cultures more or less go together. What the UNESCO discourse reveals is the rhetorical possibility of recognising the non-equivalence of nation and culture whilst speaking of cultural domination as though they *were* equivalent.

The reason why we must engage with this difficult distinction between national identity and cultural identity is that a majority of the discourses of cultural imperialism, and certainly those with the most prominence – the UNESCO discourse, that thematised by the term 'Americanisation', much of the talk of media imperialism – treat the issue as one of domination of national culture by national culture. But this conceptualisation can only be strictly coherent where we can speak of a unified national cultural identity in the supposedly 'invaded' culture. Where we cannot – where, for example, there is struggle between ethnic or regional cultures within a nation – this discourse of cultural domination will be compromised. This is because the claim to a 'swamping' or an erosion of national culture might mean imputing a cultural unity where none exists. The political effect of this may be to abet one form of cultural domination by contesting another. The construction of a discourse in which the cultural 'other' (or even 'enemy') lies beyond national boundaries may lend a spurious legitimacy to whatever cultural forces can assert themselves as representative of 'the nation' or whichever culture manages to speak as the national culture.

Clearly this problem will present itself with greater or lesser urgency from one nation to another: France's national culture at present is the site of less struggle than, say, that of Sri Lanka or the Lebanon. But we would be misled if we thought of the relatively unified national culture as the rule in the modern world. As Anthony D. Smith reminds us, quite the opposite is the case:

> Today, more and more people are realising that the world is 'plural'; that is to say, the so-called 'nation-state' is rarely a true appellation, for few states have ethnically homogeneous populations. On the contrary: most are composed of two or more ethnic communities, jostling for influence and power, or living in uneasy harmony within the same state border.[16]

Most nations then are not homogeneous cultural entites, and in a great many active struggle and contestation is a significant feature of contemporary politico-cultural life. This is not a residual phenomenon, having to do with a few ethnic conservative factions surviving in predominantly unified nations but, as Smith argues, a significant *developing* trend in nations in the period roughly since the end of World War II: what he calls 'the ethnic revival'. It is worth quoting Smith's list of contemporary states, 'with fairly large minorities':

> Canada, the United States, Mexico, Brazil, Peru, Trinidad, Bolivia, Guyana, Paraguay, Ecuador; Britain, France, Belgium, Switzerland, Spain, Yugoslavia, Rumania, Czechoslovakia, the Soviet Union, Cyprus, Iraq, Israel, Jordan, Syria, Lebanon, Saudi Arabia, Egypt, Turkey and Iran; Pakistan, Afghanistan, India, Burma, Sri Lanka, China, Malaysia, Indonesia, Vietnam, Laos, the Philippines, Australia and New Zealand; and in Africa: Morocco, Algeria, the Sudan, Ethiopia, Kenya, Uganda, Tanzania, Zambia, Zimbabwe, South Africa, Namibia, Angola, the Congo, the Camaroons, Nigeria, Ghana, Ivory Coast, Sierra Leone, Senegal, and many other new states.[17]

If smaller minorities are included the list can be extended so that, on Smith's reckoning, only a handful of modern states – including Portugal, Greece, Iceland, Norway, Malta and, with qualifications, West Germany and Japan – can claim to be ethnically homogeneous. In the light of this, it is difficult to resist his claim that 'the very term "nation-state" is a misnomer',[18] and the implication that the world's divisions should properly be conceived as between states 'containing' cultural diversity and those with potential or actual cultural struggle.

The above list shows how fully each continent of the world is represented and how ethnic diversity characterises both 'Third World' and 'First World' societies including, of course, those of the assumed cultural imperialists. It is often observed that ethnic diversity is a particular problem in Third World nations, those whose colonial pasts had landed them at independence with the problem of forging a national identity out of a territorial-administrative contrivance: 'lines drawn on a map'. This is quite true, but it should not lead us to think of the 'developed' world as having 'mature' unified cultural identities. Think, for example, of the blacks in the United States, the French Canadians, the Northern Irish in the United Kingdom – and, of course, of all the ethnic divisions in the Soviet bloc now gaining attention as a result of the policies of *perestroika*.

The recognition of the cultural diversity of the units we know as nation-states seems set to fragment the cultural imperialism argument in its 'national' formulation along two main fault lines: not only may there be difficulty in identifying a unified national cultural identity in the 'invaded' country, but the same might be said of the putative 'invader'. What, then, *is* the 'American way' that threatens global hegemony? To these problems we may add the complications introduced by recognising cultural identifications which transcend national boundaries, the most obvious being those of religion. Although we need to be careful about the misleading sense of unity implied by such expressions as 'the Islamic World' or 'the Christian World',[19] there are religious practices and observances which are significant for cultural identity and which do not map easily on to the political grid of nation-states.

Given all these qualifications, how much wind remains in the sails of the argument about cultural imperialism typically raised in the discussions of UNESCO – the idea of the domination of one national culture over another?

'Yanquíes afuera'

Let us begin with the question of the cultural plurality of the 'imperialist' nations, and take the obvious example of the arch-imperialist, the United States. Granted, the States are not as united in cultural terms as they advertise themselves: the famous 'melting pot' has not formed a homogeneous nation out of the world's huddled masses.[20] This does not prevent us from identifying 'the American way' as a hegemonic culture (or at least one aspiring to hegemony) within the contested terrain of United States culture. It is clear that, for example, black, Hispanic or American Indian cultures are in real senses dominated by a mainstream white (WASP?) American culture. It is reasonable to think of this 'hegemonic' culture, this dominant 'version' of America, as that exported by corporate capitalism, such that this will appear to other nationalities as American culture pure and simple. The slogan, 'Yankees go home' recognises no subtleties of cultural variation in the Yankees. What it recognises are the bearers of cultural practices which are dominant at home and abroad: dollar power and its manifestation in cultural goods; Madonna and McDonald's. A 'phenomenology' of cultural invasion grasps the salient features. In this sense, McDonald's *is* American culture in a way that no New York clam house, pizza parlour, Jewish deli or chop suey restaurant can ever be. So we can reasonably speak of a hegemonic American national culture as experienced from outside. This experience may relate to certain symbolic materials: denim, celluloid (at one time, chromium), and symbolic forms and dimensions: high-rise buildings, multi-lane highways, shopping malls (at one time, 'streamlining').[21]

Clearly, such aspects of *perceived* American culture may be distinguished from a more complex 'reality' in which the symbolic images exist in a contested or contradictory form, or at least alongside other 'versions' of American culture. These images exist as what Barthes might have called the *myth* of America.[22] But this 'mythical' nature does not mean they do not exist as a *real* cultural threat: McDonald's restaurants have, after all, a real concrete existence that materially affects the built environment and the routine practices of a culture. All that can be said is that there remains a gap between the perception of McDonald's as America and the plurality of cultural instances which make up 'real' America. We may ultimately decide that it makes more sense to think of McDonald's as instancing cultural domination in temporal terms ('modernity') rather than spatial terms

('America'). But we must allow, for the present, that there is at least a certain coherence in a discourse of cultural imperialism which sees McDonald's as America: that is as the salient feature of a hegemonic version of America which has 'imperialist' intent.

The other side of the relationship presents rather more problems. Does ethnic plurality prevent us from speaking of the impact of cultural imperialism on a 'national culture'? Perhaps the best way into this complex question is to consider one nation.

In November 1985 there were demonstrations in all the major Spanish cities urging the withdrawal of Spain from NATO, which it had joined under the 'transitional' centre-right administrations of Adolpho Suarez and Leopoldo Calvo Sotelo following the death, in 1975, of General Franco. These demonstrations were taking place under a socialist administration and were part of a campaign leading up to a referendum promised for the following spring by the socialist prime minister, Felipe González. The demonstrations tied in the referendum on NATO with the issue of the substantial American military presence in Spain, which had been established under a treaty between the United States and Franco in 1953. Removal of Spain from NATO was urged along with removal of the US bases from Spain.

The demonstrations were clearly anti-American. In one which took place in Seville, banners reading 'NO AL IMPERIO YANQUÍ' were paraded past wall slogans, 'FUERA YANQUÍES DE CENTROAMERICA' ('Yanks out of Central America'). The culmination of the demonstration was the ceremonial dropping of four large banners, each in the shape of the Stars and Stripes, spelling out the initials OTAN (NATO), from the Triana bridge into the river Guadalquivir. The demonstration was good natured and festive in Andaluz fashion: but here, nonetheless, were anti-American political sentiments which were mixed with anti-American cultural sentiments. How did these relate to Spanish national identity?

In fact, quite problematically. The red banners of the Communist Party mingled in the crowd with the green flags of the Andaluz region. Of the red and yellow of the Spanish national flag there was no sign – except, defiantly, on the building of the local Franquista political headquarters, outside which the procession paused to deliver some extra choruses of protest. These anti-American demonstrations were held primarily in the name of a *regional* identity, not a national one. The aim was, indeed, the withdrawal of Spain from NATO and of the US bases from Spain and this, of course, had a motivation in class-political, as well as in geopolitical terms. But in so far as the protesters spoke for their 'country' they spoke for Andalucía as much as, and probably more than, for Spain.

Regional identity is a prominent feature of modern Spanish society. Andalucía, though not the most fiercely independent of the regions, has a strong sense of its separateness from 'Spain', seen as the central administration of Madrid. It was one of the four regions – the others being Catalonia, Galicia and the Basque region – which were in the process of achieving political autonomy (Catalonia actually achieved it) in the 1930s when the Spanish civil war broke out. After the war Franco systematically suppressed this regionalism and imposed an authoritarian centralist rule from Madrid which, in all sorts of ways, fabricated a 'unified Spain'. One of the main cultural forms this suppression took was restrictions on regional languages: in effect Castilian was imposed as the language of Spain and the quite distinct languages of Catalan, Galician and Euskara (the Basque language) were forbidden. Since these languages, collectively, form the 'mother tongues' of about one quarter of the Spanish population, there is a strong case for calling Franco's regime one of internal cultural imperialism.[23]

To appreciate this, we can focus on one image of the Franquista 'imperialist' presence in the regions of Spain, that of the military. The military barrack in most provincial towns of any size is a clear sign of the power of the centre over its regions. Over it flies the Spanish national flag, the armed guards at its gates are most probably conscripts from another region, and above its gates, in Castilian, is the army motto 'Toda por la Patria'. This phrase is powerfully constructive of a sense of national history. It does not simply mean 'All for the Fatherland' – to mean this the word *por* would have to be replaced by *para*. Instead, *por* has a sense of 'on account of', 'because of' or 'through'. The motto thus contrives to constitute an historical 'Spain' which makes the national army – and, indeed, everyday life as it passes by the barrack gates – a possibility. 'Toda por la Patria' is thus less an exhortation to national unity than an insistence on its inescapable historical reality, a conjuring of a long, unbroken Spanish national past.[24]

It is in such images, and in the distinct political context to which they refer, that we can appreciate the potential force of regionalism in a country like Spain. Where cultural matters – language, history – are brought into such close proximity with images of force – the military presence – they will clearly be thrown into high relief. The British military presence in Northern Ireland presents, to some extent, an analogous situation. With the liberalisation and democratisation of the Spanish state after Franco, the regions have gained considerable political autonomy; but the barracks, a reminder of the continuing political power of the military – and hence of the centre – remain. Moreover, the continuing separatist struggle of ETA in the Basque region demonstrates that devolution of power is not an instant solution to problems of regionalism. There is a chronic *structural* tension built into nation-states like Spain – and, arguably, the United Kingdom – which 'contain' distinctive cultural identities within their borders.

To return to the NATO demonstrations, we can see that their anti-imperialism was quite a complex one: it recognised America as the imperialist, but it also had a strong flavour of anti-centralism as anti-imperialism, a deep-seated distrust of the Madrid government.[25] This can be further illustrated at a cultural level by quoting one of the popular chants of the demonstration. The main chorus went:

Que salgan, que salgan, que salgan
Que salgan los Yankíes de aquí
No queremos estar en la OTAN
De la OTAN queremos salir

(Let them go, let them go, let them go
Let the Yankees go from here
We don't want to stay in NATO
We want out of NATO)

A second verse elaborated on the anti-American theme in an interesting
way:

Que salgan, que salgan, que salgan
Que salgan los Yankíes de aquí
No queremos beber Coca-Cola
Cruzcampo queremos beber

(We don't want to drink Coca-Cola
We want to drink Cruzcampo)

The specification of the *local* Sevilla beer, Cruzcampo – not, say, Aguila
from Madrid – is, in its own small way, significant. Other verses preferred
the local Andaluz *mantequa color'a* (dripping coloured with paprika) to
mantequilla amarilla, the 'sophisticated' butter of the north. The implicit
popular critique of cultural imperialism is interesting in that it operates on a
spatial plane which does not need to recognise national boundaries: metro-
politan tastes can be just as alien as 'foreign' ones in this discourse.

These examples show just how slippery the concepts of national and
cultural identity are, and how complex matters can become within this
discourse. But they do at least show how, against the background of the
ethnic diversity of most nation-states, it is possible for people to reject the
cultural imperialism of an alien nation without in the process affirming the
unity of the nation which they inhabit. The nation, then, is not the only
possible referent against which the cultural imperialist can be set as the
cultural 'other': 'Americanisation' may be perceived coherently as a threat to
the culture of a region, a city, 'this side of the mountain' and so on.
Moreover, cultural identification seems possible on *several* such levels. No
doubt there were people on the anti-NATO demonstration who thought of
themselves at different times (and even, conceivably, simultaneously) as
Sevillanos, *Andaluces* or *Españoles*. It is perfectly intelligible to wish to
preserve one's cultural identity in any or all these forms against the threat of
cultural invasion.

This has implications for the concept of national identity for we can say,
as a first approach, that national identity is just one form of 'belonging'
amongst others, and one which can, in principle, coexist with others. The
problem is of course, as separatist struggles like that of the Basques
demonstrate, that it generally doesn't. National identity is nearly always a

vexed form of identification. This is because it is one 'constructed' in relation to a territorial-administrative category – the nation-state – which is the most significant (and hence most contested) 'container' of political and economic power in the modern world.[26] National identity is a distinctive form of cultural identity owing to the high political and economic stakes involved. Since there is more riding on the continued identification of a populace with its nation than, say, with its city, there is likely to be more deliberate ideological 'work' involved in the construction of national identity at a symbolic level.

A discourse of cultural imperialism at the level of national identity will often be ideologically problematic since it may take as its reference cultural elements – the flag and its rituals, the national anthem, state ceremonials – deliberately intended by the administrative institutions of the nation-state to enlist identification. However, these ideological elements seem unlikely to exhaust the content of national identity. As Giddens suggests, people's feelings of 'national belonging' are probably rather more complex, in general, than, 'a set of symbols and beliefs force-fed to an unwilling or indifferent population'.[27] In all probability, the sentiments involved in national identity will be common to other forms of cultural identity.

To get any further in understanding the discourse of cultural imperialism which takes the nation-state as its focus we need a clearer understanding of the idea of national identity. As the case of Spanish regionalism shows, national identity cannot simply be read off from nationality – that is, the political sense of belonging to a nation-state, of holding a passport. If cultural imperialism is a threat to national cultural identity, it must be a threat to the *experience* of belonging. What exactly is involved in the experience of belonging to a nation-state – and how does this experience come about?

Nation and culture as 'imagined community'

Discussions of national identity are mostly found in the literature of the politics of nationalism but, as Schlesinger observes, little of this is 'purpose built' for interrogating the more general ideological-psychological complex of collective identity.[28] Most commonly the aim in accounts of nationalism is to locate its historical origins in the nation-state and other phenomena of modernity, such as capitalism, industrialism and mass communications. In such accounts the concept of national identity is often treated as the outcome of certain developments, for instance, in Ernest Gellner's argument, of the pressure of industrial society to produce 'large, centrally educated, culturally homogeneous units'.[29] Yet the specific psychological contents, the 'phenomenology', as it were, of national identity is rarely probed in detail.[30] But this experience of national identity is precisely what is at stake in the discourse of cultural imperialism, for it is often claimed that the sense of belonging to a specific (national) culture is under threat. Recently some discussions of nationalism have tried to illuminate this experience. We shall consider two such: the work of Benedict Anderson and that of Anthony Giddens.

Benedict Anderson's book, *Imagined Communities* is an essay on the historical origins of nationalism, but one that makes a useful attempt at conceptual definition at the outset. Anderson defines the nation as an 'imagined political community':

> It is *imagined* because members of even the smallest nation will never know most of their fellow-members, meet them, or even hear of them, yet in the minds of each lives the image of their communion.[31]

This is a fairly obvious thought yet a most important one, for it immediately locates national identity at a certain level of abstraction. National identity is here seen as a 'communion' which can *only* be one of the imagination: if I feel I belong to the English nation it cannot be because I have concrete relations with more than a tiny handful of them. Furthermore, I would be more likely to identify with these people in most contexts as family, friends, neighbours and so on, than as fellow English nationals. And yet, as Anderson goes on to say, there is an undeniable 'reality' to this imagined communion:

> [The nation] is imagined as a *community* because, regardless of the actual inequality and exploitation that may prevail in each, the nation is always conceived as a deep, horizontal comradeship. Ultimately, it is this fraternity that makes it possible, over the past two centuries, for so many millions of people, not so much to kill, as willingly to die for such limited imaginings.[32]

Anderson adds two more specifications to his definition of the nation: that it is imagined as *limited* – 'has finite, if elastic boundaries, beyond which lie other nations' – and as *sovereign*, that is as autonomous from other states with regard to its internal legislative authority. The virtue of Anderson's approach for us is that it represents, in Schlesinger's words, 'the sense of nationhood as one looks outward from within',[33] that is, how nationhood is liable to be *experienced* by people. This experience, which we could call the sense of national identity, is of an imagined community limited by territorial boundaries and offering certain freedoms to its nationals in respect of the sovereign power of the nation-state. (A good instance of this last point is the freedom from the judgment of Ayatollah Khomeini offered to Salman Rushdie by his British nationality.)

National identity for Anderson, then, is something which exists in the imagination of people. But he is quick to say that this doesn't imply that it is a *false* imagining, nor, by implication, 'that "true" communities exist which can be advantageously juxtaposed to nations'. Anderson argues that:

> In fact, all communities larger than primordial villages of face to face contact (and perhaps even these) are imagined. Communities are not to be distinguished by their falsity/genuineness, but by the style in which they are imagined.[34]

This is an important point for our purposes for it suggests that all cultural identities – be they national, regional, local – are, in one way, of the same order. They are all representations (in the sense that imagination is a representative faculty) of belonging. Anderson is quite right to say that nationalist sentiments are no less 'true' than identifications with a region or even a small 'organic' community. Where people think beyond the immediate presence of others, which is today almost everywhere, they 'imagine a community' to which they belong.

Anderson's reference to the style in which communities are imagined relates to his central argument about the origins of nationalism. Essentially he argues that a certain convergence of historical events towards the end of the eighteenth century made 'nation-ness' imaginable. Foremost of these events was the rise of 'print capitalism' in Europe. The commodified and mechanised production of books and, more importantly, of newspapers had, he argues, a decisive role in the production of a national consciousness. The increasing capacity for the dissemination of printed material made possible by the dynamics of capitalism and the development of print technology had two major consequences. It 'fixed' a vernacular language as the 'national' language, and it made possible a new apprehension of national 'community' by the convergence of time and space that it created in its representations.

The first of these points is easy to understand. The initial market for print capitalism was 'literate Europe', a relatively small 'bilingual' elite of Latin readers and vernacular speakers. Once this market was saturated, the pressure of capitalist expansion meant that 'the potentially huge markets represented by the monoglot masses' would soon be sought out and printing in the vernacular would become the norm.

The drive of capitalism, in conjunction with other developments such as the Protestant Reformation's preference for the vernacular over the Latin of Catholicism, Anderson argues, produced print languages which represented 'unified fields of exchange and communication below Latin and above the spoken vernaculars'.[35] For the first time it was possible for the mass of speakers of different vernaculars within a particular country to understand each other via a common print language. Not only could speakers of the many different 'Frenches' or 'Englishes' understand one another in writing, they could also think of themselves as united under their common print language:

> In the process, they gradually became aware of the hundreds of thousands, even millions, of people in their particular language-field, and at the same time that *only those* hundreds of thousands, or millions belonged. These fellow-readers, to whom they were connected through print, formed, in their secular, particular, visible invisibility, the embryo of the nationally-imagined community.[36]

For Anderson, 'national imagining' is a phenomenon of modernity, a form of experiencing which is only possible within the context of the technological and economic changes that produced modern capitalist societies. The 'style' of imagining nation-ness is essentially a mass-mediated style, one achieved in literate societies with well-developed communication structures. It is an imagination encouraged by reading the national newspapers.[37]

This brings us to his other main contention about the effects of mass vernacular printing: its capacity to co-ordinate the imagination of social time and space. The modern novel and, in particular, the newspaper, he suggests, encourage people to imagine the simultaneous occurrence of events which are spatially distant. Daily newspapers co-ordinate discrete events happening across a country or even across the globe – a murder here, a strike in this region, an earthquake on another continent – according to the single principle of their occurrence at the same time, that is on the same calendrical date. Anderson argues that this implies a modern apprehension of time as 'empty homogeneous time': time as a universal medium, measurable by clock and calendar, through which societies 'move'. It is this view of time, which encompasses the significantly modern concept of 'meanwhile', that allows people to think their relation to others across the spatial spread of large nation-states. Again, this apprehension of time is a function of a broader process of modernity, connected particularly, he says, with the development of secular science. But newspapers are the prime cultural carriers of this apprehension, daily reproducing for us the 'meanwhile' of our cultural-historical imagination. Of the mundane practice of reading the daily newspaper he says:

> The significance of this mass ceremony – Hegel observed that newspapers serve modern man as a substitute for morning prayers – is paradoxical. It is performed in silent privacy, in the lair of the skull. Yet each communicant is well aware that the ceremony he performs is being replicated simultaneously by thousands (or millions) of others of whose existence he is confident, yet of whose identity he has not the slightest notion. Furthermore, this ceremony is incessantly repeated at daily or half-daily intervals throughout the calendar. What more vivid figure for the secular, historically-clocked, imagined community can be envisioned?[38]

Anderson's approach has the virtue of offering an account of the processes by which identification with the rather abstract notion of a 'nation' becomes *possible*. It becomes possible because of a complex of technological and representational changes which mark off 'modern' cultural imaginings from those of 'traditional' societies. The rise of the modern nation-state corresponds to these changes. But there is also an account of why the cultural imagining of nationality becomes *necessary* or, rather, of why it becomes the dominant form of cultural identification. This is because the processes of social modernity arise out of the decay of other cultural practices which offered their own general orientation to people. Anderson discusses here, particularly, the 'sacred script languages' of Christianity or Islam, which united people in 'the great transcontinental sodalities of Christendom, the Ummah Islam and the rest'; the belief in the natural organisation of societies under dynastic monarchs whose authority derived from 'divine right'; and the conception of 'sacred time' (as opposed to modern calendrical time) in which 'cosmology and history were indistinguishable, the origins of the world and of men essentially identical':

> Combined, these ideas rooted human lives firmly in the very nature of things, giving certain meaning to the everyday fatalities of existence (above all death, loss and servitude) and offering, in various ways, redemption from them.[39]

The breakdown of these certainties of existence under capitalist secular rationalism created a sort of vacuum in cultural orientation: 'the search was on, so to speak, for a new way of linking fraternity, power and time meaningfully together'.[40]

To summarise Anderson's position, he argues that national identity is a particular style of 'imagining the community' made possible by and also, in a sense, *required by* the processes of social modernity: secular rationalism, a calendrical perception of time, capitalist-driven technological development, mass literacy and mass communications, political democratisation, the modern nation-state. All these features combined in complex ways to promote identification with the nation as the dominant form of cultural identity.

As a way of making the phenomenon of identification with the abstract notion of the 'nation' intelligible, Anderson's account has much to commend it. It might be argued that he relies too much on 'the rather overworked Catholic metaphor of general communion in collective representations',[41] and that this tends to suggest a misleading homogeneity of cultural identification within the boundaries of the nation-state. As we saw earlier, regional and ethnic divisions (complexly articulated with class divisions) are a chronic feature of most modern nation-states. But to be fair to Anderson, his aim is to account for nationalist sentiments where they exist – in the imaginings of those who do identify with the nation. There is no reason to suppose that national imaginings always exclude other forms of identification, nor, as we shall presently see, that they are always at the forefront of people's minds. And it is possible to argue that some of those elements of modernity which Anderson discusses in relation to national identity may also be relevant to an explanation of modern regional identity. A sense of belonging to a region like Andalucía surely requires the same 'distant imagining' as that involved in the sense of Spanish nationality, and probably derives from similar social developments (mass literacy, regional media, and so on). The contingent fact of the power of the capitalist nation-state to police its cultural boundaries is enough to account for the dominance of nationalism over regionalism, but it seems that quite similar psychological processes are at work in both types of identification.

The attraction of Anderson's account, then, is its linking of national identity with the processes of social modernity. National identity is a highly mediated imaginary belonging which, in a sense, replaces earlier forms of cultural belonging. There is thus a connection between the phenomenon of national identity (and, we might add, the search for competing cultural identities like regionalism) and the general breakdown of existential certainties that characterises modern social life.

Thinking about national identity in this way problematises the simple view of cultural imperialism as the eclipse of one national identity by another more powerful one. This is because we can now recognise that national identities are not cultural belongings rooted in deep quasi-natural attachments to a homeland, but, rather, complex cultural constructions that have arisen in specific historical conditions. There is a 'lived reality' of national identity, but it is a reality lived in representations – not in direct communal solidarity. Furthermore, national identities are, paradoxically, the cultural outcome of the very same processes – expanding capitalism, Western rationality, the breakdown of 'tradition', the 'mediatisation' of cultural experience – that are said, in other discourses, to constitute cultural imperialism itself!

All this seems to point to the need to understand cultural imperialism *primarily* in historical rather than in 'spatial synchronic' terms. We shall now look further at the context of cultural modernity in which national identities arise, drawing on the account of nationalism offered by Anthony Giddens.

National identity as a consequence of modernity

Giddens's reflections on nationalism form part of a much broader social-theoretical analysis conducted often at a rather daunting level of abstraction.[42] Nevertheless, the relevance of his views on nationalism to what we are here calling national identity, though they ought really to be read in the context of his larger theoretical project, is quite easy to grasp.

Giddens sees nationalism as, in large part, a psychological phenomenon, and he distinguishes this psychology from the strictly *institutional* issues having to do with the nation-state. Much of what he discusses as 'nationalism' involves just those processes of attachment which might be called 'national identity'. He also stresses, like Anderson, that nationalism is a phenomenon of modernity, a form of psychological 'belonging' specific to societies organised on the scale and with the technological resources deriving from capitalism and with the nation-state as the most significant 'power container'. An important part of his analysis of nationalism is an attempt to explain the psychology of this particular form of cultural attachment in terms of the transformations of human experience brought about by the social processes of modernity.

The feeling of belonging to a nation, Giddens claims, represents, 'an attentuated form of those "primordial sentiments" of which Clifford Geertz speaks in tribal societies and village communities'.[43] The sense of belonging that these pre-modern cultural contexts provided was based on what Giddens calls 'high presence availability', that is to say contexts in which relations are based on direct face-to-face contact with others (the parallel with Anderson's argument is, again, clear). In such contexts, feelings of belonging are grounded in the structures of kinship, religion and 'tradition'. Such structures provided the meanings and the moral contexts in which people found their general existential orientations: they provided what Giddens, following R.D. Laing, calls 'ontological security', a sense of the stability of human 'being' in relation to the natural and created world.[44]

In modern mass-capitalist societies this security dissolves:

> The dissolution of the foundation of society in relations of presence substantially replaces the grounding of those primordial sentiments in tradition and kinship by a more routinized, habitual round of 'everyday life'. . . . In the spheres of 'everyday life' created by the expansion of capitalism the areas of 'meaningful' existence retreat – to the intimacy of personal and sexual relations on one side – and to the arenas of mass ritual on the other (as in spectator sports and in political ceremonial). In such conditions of social life, the ontological security of the individual in day-to-day life is more fragile than in societies dominated by tradition and the meshings of kinship across space and time.[45]

'Everyday life in the modern world' consists largely of routine practices – labour under capitalism being the most significant – in which 'the moral bindingness of traditionally established practices is replaced by one geared extensively to habit against a background of economic constraint'.[46] Giddens argues that, in these conditions, the rise of nationalist sentiments can be explained as one way in which ontological security is maintained. The gap created by the 'morally meaningless' routine practices of modernity is to some degree filled by feelings of belonging to the same national language community. However, Giddens doesn't argue that nationalist sentiments are a constant and abiding form of collective identity. It is just the tendency of nationalism to 'surge and decline', to vary with varying conditions of social and political stability, that his theory seeks to explain. For the most part, ontological security simply remains fragile in modern societies; it is in circumstances in which it threatens to break down altogether – as in the disruption of routine life brought about, for instance, by mobilisation for war – that nationalist sentiments tend to emerge most strongly.

Giddens goes on to offer an explanation of the force and volatility of nationalist sentiments in psychoanalytic terms derived from Freud and Le Bon. In times of crisis, he argues, 'regressive forms of object identification come to the fore'. People will tend to become more vulnerable to the ideological offensives of national leaders and, indeed, to invest emotional attachment in them and in the symbols of the nation which they invoke:

> Regressive identification with a leader-figure and with the symbols represented by that figure or comprised in his or her doctrines, carries with it that essential feature of nationalism, whether benign or militant, a strong psychological affiliation with an 'in-group' coupled with a differentiation from, or rejection of, 'out-groups'.[47]

What Giddens is trying to account for here is the genuinely puzzling phenomenon of 'passionate' nationalism as it occurs in secular-rationalist societies. The example of the Falklands/Malvinas war and the upsurge of nationalism that accompanied it is one striking example of such a puzzle, which often catches liberal and progressive thinkers on the hop. As this sort of 'extreme' national identification arises it becomes difficult to resist the idea that some sort of sedimented psychological processes like the ones Giddens describes are at work, for how else to explain the frequent resistance of nationalist sentiments to rational argument?

But is this 'extreme nationalism' the same phenomenon as 'national identity'? Philip Schlesinger thinks not, and that Giddens has missed an important distinction:

> One of the oddities of this account is that Giddens nowhere makes an explicit distinction between nationalism and national identity, but rather conflates the two. . . . Nationalism, one may agree, is a particular kind of doctrine, but the term tends to carry the sense of a community mobilized (at least in part) in the pursuit of a collective interest. National identity may be invoked as a point of reference without thereby necessarily being nationalistic. . . . once the political boundaries of the nation-state have been achieved, a national identity, with all the accompanying mythico-cultural apparatus, may be in place and is not necessarily identical with nationalism as such.[48]

This is an important criticism: Schlesinger wants to argue for a sense of national 'belonging' which is distinct from the 'passionate attachments' of nationalism, and is presumably a part of routine life. Making this distinction, he claims, 'allows us to accommodate a range of variation which is otherwise obscured by a single concept' (that of nationalism).[49] It is a fair point that there may be significant psychological and political distinctions to be made between the national identifications involved in, say, rising to the harangues of the nationalist leader, or cheering 'our boys' off at the quayside, or standing for the national anthem or, simply, sensing the 'at homeness' of arrival back from another country. A 'phenomenology' of national identification that could discriminate between these experiences would probably tidy up some of the political problems critics on the left feel when faced with the issue of nationalism. To this extent, Schlesinger's criticism of Giddens is justified.

However, to argue for a sense of national identity at the *routine* level of modern social experience is implicitly to make a stronger challenge to Giddens's overall claims about the experience of modernity, and this is rather more contentious. For Giddens's major claim here is that routine existence in capitalist modernity is such as to replace any strong 'public' cultural attachments with habitual practices relating to the general 'commodification' of social experience under capitalism. 'Routine' is an important part of human life in all societies, but Giddens's claim is that, in capitalist modernity, a morally vacuous 'habit' governs most of routine. What has been lost with the coming of modernity is the 'meaningful' element of routine practices afforded by 'tradition'.[50] 'Tradition' is another very slippery term, but what Giddens means by it here is 'the "purest" and most innocent mode of social reproduction'[51] in which people act as they do in their daily life because such action is authorised by repetition across generations and tied to consensually held moral and existential beliefs within a community. Traditional routine practices are, for Giddens, meaning sustaining; (modern) habitual routine practices are not.

Now the realm of the 'public' in modern societies is, largely and for most people, the realm of habitual routine practices: commuting, working, shopping and so on. And this context is not one out of which significant cultural identities are likely to be formed. These are more likely to arise in the 'marginal' realms of meaning of the 'private' sphere of family and sexual relations, or the essentially representational sphere of 'mass ritual'.[52] The implication of this is that modern everyday life is a life drained of meaningful immediate *public* cultural identities. My statement, earlier, that I am less likely routinely to identify with other English people as fellow nationals than as family, friends and so on may be taken as a reflection of this attenuated public cultural realm. On this interpretation, Giddens's argument about modern social experience moves against the notion of an abiding routine sense of national identity as it does against any form of immediate cultural identity in 'habitual routine'. The elision of national identity and 'nationalism' of which Schlesinger complains may now be seen as a more principled one. For Giddens, nationalism is a 'distant imagining' in two senses: it involves the essentially mediated apprehension of belonging to a spatially spread 'community', and it is generally 'distant' from mundane existence. For most people, most of the time, their national identity is not at the forefront of their lived experience.[53]

We can now bring the argument back to the question of cultural imperialism. If what Giddens says about the nature of routine life in modern societies is correct, then we might expect most people's mundane concerns to be quite distant from their sense of national cultural identity. In everyday activities like working, eating and shopping people are likely to be concerned with their immediate needs – their state of health, their family and personal relations, their finances and so on. In these circumstances the cultural significance of working for the multinational, eating lunch at McDonald's, shopping for Levis is unlikely to be interpreted as a threat to national identity, but in terms of how these practices mesh with the meaningful realm of the private: McDonald's as convenient for the children's birthday party; jeans as a dress code for leisure-time activities.

The same reasoning might be applied to the habitual-routine consumption of media products, though here the situation can be rather more complex. If most people's focus of meaning is in the family and personal-sexual relations, then their reception of programmes like *Dallas* is likely to be shaped by these concerns. So the implications of Giddens's arguments[54] tend to chime with the empirical findings of critics like Ang (see Chapter 2, pp. 46–47) who stress the pleasure derived from the interpersonal drama of these texts over any images of cultural imperialism they may contain. It should not be surprising then that, as Ang found, ordinary people are less exercised than 'professional intellectuals' on the question of TV imports. On the other hand, as Anderson points out, the media are probably the primary carriers of a sense of national identity. Whatever (background? dormant?) sense of national belonging people have from day to day probably derives from such things as national news broadcasts. The media, then, are *potentially* the source of strong national identification, as when they act as 'the arenas of mass ritual' of spectator sports and political ceremonials.[55] But the 'depth', the endurance and the political significance of such mediated identification will probably depend on factors external to the media itself, for example the general state of social and political stability in the country.

All this suggests that we may have to discriminate between different orders of reaction to the threat of cultural imperialism to national identity. In societies and at times in which habitual routine governs most social experience – what we might call the 'stable mode' of capitalist modernity – national identities tend to be at the background of consciousness and so the routine reception of alien culture goods may proceed in the same manner and according to the same needs as the consumption of any other cultural commodities. By contrast, in societies and at times in which there is uncertainty, dissent, or active struggle over national or regional identity, or where the nation is under external threat, the 'distant imaginings' of national or regional identity may become foregrounded in consciousness and the threat of cultural imperialism become more immediate. This might explain, for example, the more marked antipathy towards 'los Yanquíes' voiced in the context of political demonstrations like that in Seville in contrast with the mundane reception of American cultural products (watching American films on Spanish TV) in the habitual-routine 'flow' of modern social experience. This is not to say that reactions to cultural imperialism are always tied to fervant nationalism, but it is to suggest, with Giddens, that the general sense of cultural belonging is replaced, in the 'stable mode' of capitalist modernity, by a 'commodified' habitual social experience in which all 'identities' become, effectively, submerged. The 'us' of 'in-group identification' becomes increasingly difficult to fill with a content, other than those specifically invoked in the ideology of nationalism – language and 'national history' – in the increasing 'sameness' of commodified modern life.

Anderson's and Giddens's discussions of nationalism suggest some useful ways of thinking about national identity and its implications for this particular discourse of cultural imperialism. Both stress the 'imagined', essentially mediated, nature of this belonging, and the fact of its being peculiar to the broader social conditions of modernity, in particular the 'convergence of social space and time' brought about by technological advances in communications and so on. Both also argue that identifying with the nation somehow replaces cultural identities formed around the cultural 'givens' that supplied the existential certainties and ontological security of pre-modern societies.

Where Giddens substantially departs from Anderson is in his arguments concerning the impermanence of nationalist sentiments, their tendency to 'surge and decline'. In focusing on this, and on nationalism in the context of the European nation-state (Anderson draws his models from both Europe and post-colonial societies) Giddens tends to construct a theory relevant to what I have called the 'stable mode of capitalist modernity'. In such modes, which we may say represent the mainstream cultural experience of the developed capitalist West, the implication of his argument is that we need to see national identity as a potentially powerful sentiment, but one usually 'backgrounded' in consciousness and remote from the needs and concerns of habitual-routine modernity. The normal 'foreground' of people's cultural imagination in capitalist modernity is likely to be the realm of the private (family, personal-sexual relations) or the 'public-representational' realm of the media, or the complex interplay of these two realms (*vide* the attraction of domestic soap operas – what we might call the symbolic private sphere lived publicly through the media). As a consequence largely of the habitual-isation of experience in the economic spheres of commodity production (work) and consumption, people's sense of identity is much less likely to be lodged in the 'public' sphere of immediate communal culture, which most theorists of modernity agree is in decline. Capitalist modernity emerges as the massive general homogenising principle of social experience in the 'developed' world, and arguably (though in an 'uneven', unstable, economically corrupt and 'superexploitative' fashion[56]) in the 'developing' world. To pay attention to the central significance of modernity, then, means to abandon the idea that the 'artificial' ideologically created identities of nationalism mask some 'core' of real cultural-communal identities in developed societies.

Of course, we must immediately qualify this by allowing for all the actions of human agents which resist, oppose, compete with or chafe against the tendencies of modernity. One of the most significant of these competing tendencies is, as we have already noted, the evidence of increasing regional and ethnic struggle in most modern nation-states. Where this occurs, clearly, cultural identities will be more foregrounded. But we must resist the notion that ethnic or regional struggle always represents a challenge to the social principles of modernity. Some aspects of some struggles may contain 'anti-modern' tendencies, for instance those associated with strong religious sentiments. But others may be grounded in economic and political struggles which largely accept the 'terms' of capitalist modernity. The situation from case to case is obviously highly complex and demands the sort of particular empirical examination which is beyond our scope. What we can say in general terms is that the context of modernity is that within which all these particularities and complexities occur.

The implication is that the most useful general way of thinking about cultural imperialism may not be in terms of the elusive notion of the 'national culture' but precisely in terms of the spatial-historical spread of modernity itself. We can make a distinction between two possible discourses of cultural imperialism as they have emerged in this chapter. The first, with which we began, is the familiar discourse of cultural imperialism as the attack on national/cultural identity, a discourse conducted around the binary opposition of 'us and them' and on the 'synchronic-spatial' plane. It is the discourse of 'Americanisation' and so on. In so far as this discourse centres on notions like 'national identity', it is a distinctly modern discourse. We are probably justified in calling it an imaginary discourse since it counterposes the 'imagined community' of 'our nation' with the 'imperialist nation' and invokes the 'myths' of, say, 'Spanishness' against those of 'Americanness'.

But underlying this is the broader discourse of cultural imperialism as *the spread of the culture of modernity itself*. This is a discourse of historical change, of 'development', of a global movement towards, among other things, an everyday life governed by the habitual routine of commodity capitalism. One reason for calling this discourse a broader one is that the 'imaginary' discourse of cultural identity only arises *within* the context of modernity. It is within this broader discourse that we can locate, for example, Herbert Schiller's critique of the cultural domination of multi-national capitalism. As we saw in the previous chapter, Schiller's 'totalising' analysis is not subtle, but it does at least raise deeper issues of structural change that have significant implications for global cultural experience. Whether these deeper structural issues and their cultural implications can be grasped in the critique of capitalism alone, or in a broader critique of modernity is a question which will exercise us in Chapters 4 and 5.

Culture and time

Most of the arguments in this chapter have suggested that the conceptual (and, indeed, the political) problems which attend this discourse arise from the tendency to think in an exclusively *spatial-synchronic* mode and to ignore the essentially historical nature of cultural processes.

By this I mean that the imagined opposition is of two cultures, spatially divided but 'frozen in time': cultural imperialism is conceived as 'how we live' threatened by the imposition of 'how they live'. What this leaves out of account is the essentially dynamic nature of culture. How we live' is never a 'static' set of circumstances, but always something in flux, in process. The political discourse of national culture and national identity *requires* that we imagine this process as 'frozen' and this is done via concepts like the 'national heritage' or our 'cultural traditions'. This 'freezing' conceals a complex historical process in which sorting out the definitive features of 'our culture' becomes highly problematic. Here I want to note the implications of taking the dynamic nature of cultural processes seriously.

There are two points to be made. First, that the contents of 'our culture' continually shift with the passage of time, as Schlesinger has it, 'the elaboration of national [or other cultural] identity is a chronic process'.[57] What we take to be 'our culture' at any time will be a kind of 'totalisation' of cultural memory up to that point. This totalisation will be a particular and selective one in which political and cultural institutions (the state, the media) have a privileged role. Second, and as a consequence, 'our culture' in the modern world is never purely 'local produce', but always contains the traces of previous cultural borrowings or influence, which have been part of this 'totalising' and have become, as it were, 'naturalised'.

The first point can be briefly illustrated in relation to some of the cultural practices referred to by the historian Eric Hobsbawm as 'invented traditions'. For Hobsbawm, an invented tradition means:

> a set of practices normally governed by overtly or tacitly accepted rules and of a ritual or symbolic nature, which seek to inculcate values and norms of behaviour by repetition, which automatically implies continuity with the past. In fact, where possible, they normally attempt to establish continuity with a suitable historic past.[58]

Hobsbawm and his collaborators are concerned with the consequence for historians of the curious fact that many of the 'traditions' of modern societies, while having the appearance of long established and invariant practices 'hallowed' by their deep roots in national history, are, really, of recent origin. Not only this, they are often the deliberate *invention* of the institutions of the nation-state. One example Hobsbawm gives is 'the deliberate choice of a Gothic style for the nineteenth-century rebuilding of the British parliament, and the equally deliberate decision after World War II to rebuild the parliamentary chamber on exactly the same basic plan as before';[59] another is the fact that 'the Flemish taught in Belgium today is not the language which the mothers and grandmothers of Flanders spoke to their children: in short it is metaphorically, but not literally a "mother tongue" '.[60] There are countless other examples: the Festival of Nine Lessons and Carols from King's College Cambridge, broadcast throughout the world on Christmas Eve and emblematic both of 'traditional' English Christmas and the customs of an ancient university, dates only from 1918.[61]

These 'invented traditions' function, according to Hobsbawm, in the same ways as all traditions, that is in providing a sense of *invariance*. The cultural illusion is fostered by invented traditions, particularly those associated with national identity (national anthems date at earliest from the mid-eighteenth century), that the practices representing 'us now' embody an invariant past reaching back to 'time immemorial'. The 'authenticity' of such practices – the authority attributed them in respect of their supposed deep roots in the culture – is often questionable.

But the point is not just that some aspects of a nation's 'cultural heritage' turn out to have surprisingly recent origins. More significantly, invented traditions can be seen as a phenomenon of modernity. There is a sense in which simply *recognising* a practice as 'traditional' marks it off from the routine practices of proper traditional societies. As Giddens puts it:

> The sloughing-off of tradition in a certain sense begins with its understanding *as* tradition: tradition has its greater sway when it is understood simply as how things were, are (and should be) done. The encapsulation of certain practices as 'tradition', however, undermines tradition by placing it alongside other modes of legitimating established practices.[62]

When we think of preserving 'traditional' practices within modern societies we are really speaking of something quite different from defending or 'protecting' the traditional practices of some primitive tribal culture. The invented traditions that Hobsbawm describes, and arguably even 'traditional' observances that have genuinely ancient roots, seem to function in modern societies as representations – cultural constructions – of a stable past. It is not as though cultural imperialism threatens the continuity of cultural patterns in modern societies: rather it poses a threat to our collective imaginings of a culturally definitive past.[63]

Yet we might say that one consequence of the 'imagining' of such a stable past is the obscuring of the essentially dynamic and often 'hybrid' nature of cultures. Now, this has fairly obvious implications for the notion of cultural imperialism as it is conceived on the 'us now'/'them now' model of the synchronic-spatial plane. For our sense of 'us now' generally leaves out of account all the previous (and often recent previous) interaction between us and them. This is a point that Ithiel de Sola Pool, a libertarian critic of the cultural imperialism thesis, makes:

> National cultures when they are lauded by their eulogists, are generally described as age-old traditions. . . . But to a very large degree, the claims to a hoary past are mythology. Each generation sees its culture as that with which it grew up. Its hallowed values and traditions are those it learned in childhood. Many elements that it values as its culture were controversial foreign imports a generation or two ago.[64]

What Pool wants to do with this argument is to suggest that resistance to cultural imports is really just a resistance to change as it is experienced across the span of a human life: the 'natural human impulse' to 'freeze change at one's youth'. This argument, like any that invokes a universal fact of 'human nature', needs to be treated with some caution. This is particularly so when it is used, as it is here, to recuperate cultural resistance in terms of 'understand-able' though reactionary emotional ties.

But Pool does have a point about the fairly rapid assimilation of imported cultural practices. This is well illustrated in a story which appeared in the *Guardian* newspaper documenting a curious New Year custom from Japan: the mass performance by hundreds of amateur choirs of Beethoven's Ninth (Choral) Symphony. The story describes how Japan's NHK television network even carries programmes on how to sing the chorus parts of the symphony, a conductor drilling viewers in the German words of Schiller's *Ode to Joy*. How can we make sense of this in the discourse of cultural imperialism? The 'tradition' is thought to date from just after World War I, though the practice of performing Western classical music dates from a deliberate policy of cultural 'modernisation' pursued by Japan in the nineteenth century. But in what sense is this still an 'alien' cultural practice? The story suggests that the performances have become thoroughly 'Japanese' in their cultural significance:

> Many Japanese call the annual Beethoven spectacle a celebration of understanding and friendship. . . . To the Mainichi Shimbun newspaper's music critic, Kazuyuki Toyana, it has become a mental form of misogi, a Shinto ritual of purification.[65]

What makes it difficult to read this situation as one of cultural imperialism is the sense we have of the *incorporation* of these practices into a culture over time. This is a particularly striking example, but the process of incorporation, is, of course, very common. Staying with the example of music we can think of the European appropriation of first jazz (British 'trad' as an especially successful 'naturalisation') and then rock 'n roll from America; or of the peculiarly complex interaction between European and Latin-American dance music.[66] In all such examples the interactions are complex, with influences flowing back and forth over time (think for example, of American rock re-exported from the UK in the 1960s by groups like the Beatles). The sort of discourse which freezes cultural identities historically will not be able to cope with these complexities. Language is a prime example: full of imported idioms which eventually, and often quite quickly, become 'naturalised' and taken as part of the standard against which future 'invasions' come to be criticised. And when we think of the cultural history of post-colonial nations like those of Latin America the situation becomes more complex still. For a discourse of cultural 'authenticity' here is vexed by the problem of deciding between the claims of a 'Latin' culture organised around the nation-state built by the original European colonisers and an indigenous, if residual, 'American' one.

Recognising the relatively short span of cultural memory, which allows us to forget previous cultural appropriations, does not invalidate the *experience* of 'invasion' by new practices and products where it occurs: pointing out the historical inconsistency of a British jazz fan's objection to the 'swamping' of popular music by American rock will probably cut little ice. But recognising the complex chronic nature of cultural interaction and change and hence the constant reconstitution of cultural identities does pose problems for the logic of the defence of 'authentic cultures'. What, in the light of the 'diachronic' analysis of cultures, could be meant by an 'authentic culture'? And once this sort of notion is problematised, the political and 'ethical' grounds for objection to cultural imperialism become rather hazy. If change is a constant feature of modern cultures, why object to it? The next section will examine one common approach to these questions of value: the idea that what is at stake is the 'autonomy' of a culture.

The discourse of nationality is only one way of speaking about cultural imperialism and, though perhaps the most common, by no means the most significant. There is an elegant twist to the story about the Japanese Beethoven celebrations. The article suggests that the maximum playing time for compact discs of 72 minutes, set by the Japanese manufacturers as a world standard in the 1970s, was intended to ensure that a performance of Beethoven's 'Ninth' would fit on to one disc. Perhaps this curiously derived standardisation – rather than the idea of the threatened authenticity of a national music – has wider cultural implications in the long run.

Domination and cultural autonomy

We now turn to the problem of how domination is conceived in this discourse of cultural imperialism. In what sense are collectivities conceived as 'national cultures' thought to be exercising domination?

The notion of domination implied is a fairly straightforward one, resting on the idea that alien cultural products and practices are *imposed* on a culture. But we have already met the major problem with this notion. It is the fact that often people don't seem to object to the importation of these products and practices: they don't perceive them as an 'imposition'; hence it is difficult to see where domination at a specifically cultural (rather than an associated economic) level is occurring. We saw this in relation to the research into audiences for television imports like *Dallas*. Of course some people will object and struggle in relation to national/regional cultural identity may intensify such objection. But even then it is likely that the objections and the perceptions of cultural invasion will be mostly restricted to a small sector of intellectuals – what Ang calls 'professional cultural critics' – and, perhaps, political activists. For most people, in developed societies at least, the conditions of cultural reception described by privatised routine modernity do not encourage strong cultural identification, except in the very particular circumstances of 'orchestrated' nationalism. These are difficult generalisations to make with any certainty, but we can safely say that a substantial number of people in developed societies are willing recipients of 'imperialist media texts' such as *Dallas*. This is not to say they are consequently the dupes of their ideological messages and values. There is also *prima facie* evidence that plenty of people in the 'underdeveloped world' are enthusiastic about the cultural products of the West though, again, the uses and meanings attached to them cannot be easily assumed.

The upshot of this is that, at the level of individual responses, it is quite difficult to attribute cultural domination: domination is only there where it is perceived: there only needs to be some element of division in individual perceptions within a cultural community for the attribution of cultural imperialism to be undermined. The temptation is strong for intellectuals who do feel cultural imperialism as a threat to 'speak for' the culture by attributing a form of 'false consciousness' to the masses who don't. Here the critique of cultural imperialism comes up hard against the same problems and risks facing many left critiques of 'consumer culture': the problems of access to other people's cultural consciousness and the risks of a paternalist politics.[67]

But there may be another way of formulating the domination involved in cultural imperialism. Instead of on the level of individual responses, it might be thought of in terms of the culture as a whole. The argument would run something like this: whatever the divergence in individual responses to cultural imports, domination is occurring where the 'autonomy' of a culture – roughly speaking, its right to develop along its own lines – is threatened by external forces. It is this 'holistic' formulation of cultures that is usually implied in claims made by critics of cultural imperialism about the 'swamping' of indigenous cultures by alien ones. I should say now that I have no objection to the 'holistic' view of culture – the view that it is 'more than the sum of its parts'. A culture, like a society, has to be conceived as in some sense existing in structures and representations (language, again, being the prime example) which have 'ontological independence' from the individual members of the culture, though the precise nature of this conception is a major and long-running problem in social theory.[68] It is not this view, but the associated belief in the idea of 'cultural autonomy' as a moral-political principle that I want to probe. The principle of cultural autonomy holds, roughly, that a culture has the right to 'self-legislation' and freedom from heteronomous control. Domination here is the exercise of such heteronomy: manipulation or control of the culture from outside.

To assess this claim we need to examine the concept of autonomy. Autonomy is used as a description of a certain condition of action and as a moral-political principle both at the level of individuals and of collectivities. It is used in the analysis of individual actions to describe the exercise of free moral agency. As Lindley puts it:

> An autonomous person is not someone who is manipulated by others, or forced to do their will. An autonomous person has a will of her or his own, and is able to act in pursuit of self-chosen goals.[69]

The concept of autonomy is also used widely in political analysis in relation to the 'actions' of institutions, notably nation-states. Here it is associated with the concept of 'sovereignty' to indicate the right to self-legislation and freedom from external interference within a bounded political-geographical domain. We saw a good example of this usage in relation to the UNESCO discourse, in which the UNESCO conference declared that 'cultural autonomy is inseparable from the full exercise of [national] sovereignty.'

Two features of the concept of autonomy are common to both these usages:

1. The idea of freedom from external control, constraint or manipulation (Heteronomy).
2. The idea that it applies to 'agents'. That is, only entities to which actions can be ascribed can be autonomous. This condition applies without

difficulty to human individuals and can be plausibly extended to social institutions like political parties, governments or nation-states.

It makes sense, then, to talk of individuals as potentially autonomous (or, more properly, as having potential degrees of autonomy) and of social institutions acting for collectivities (nations, regions etc.) having or aspiring to autonomy. In the case of institutions we have to recognise that the sense in which they 'act' is a more abstract one: at a more basic level of analysis it involves the actions of individuals within these institutions. Nonetheless, most people would find intelligible statements involving corporate actions such as 'The Bank of England intervened to stop further falls in the value of the pound.' There are some tricky problems for social-theoretical analysis in such formulations, but these do not directly concern us at the moment.

We are concerned with the idea of 'cultural autonomy', and for this to be a meaningful notion we could have to be able to apply both features of autonomy to 'cultures'. Cultures would need to be things that could be free of external control and things that could be said to *act*, that is, to be agents. Typical discussions of 'cultural autonomy' in political analysis tend to gloss over this issue. For example, Anthony Smith writes: 'Cultural autonomy implies full control *by representatives* of the ethnic community over every aspect of its cultural life, notably education, the press, the mass media, and the courts.'[70] What this represents is a definition in which the 'holistic' view of culture is lost: autonomy is here referred not to cultures as such, but to the *representatives* of cultures – individuals or institutions. It is these to which agency, and thus control, is ascribed. But the problem with this approach is clearly that the now familiar problem of 'who speaks' arises. For the representatives of a culture may demand autonomy for their actions on behalf of the culture, but this does not imply that they speak 'for the culture' as a whole. 'Representatives' of a cultural community may oppose cultural imports while other members of the community welcome them: we are returned to the individual level of analysis with all its problems.

What is at stake is the sense in which a culture in the holistic sense may be said to be capable of autonomy. And the real problem here is that cultures in this sense *cannot be seen as agents*. Cultures don't 'act' even in the rather abstract sense in which social institutions like governments act. Cultures in this sense are simply descriptions of *how people act* in communities in particular historical situations. They are totalisations of individual and group practices: how people live. Clifford Geertz puts a similar view: 'culture is not a power, something to which social events can be causally attributed; it is a context, something within which they can be intelligibly . . . described.'[71]

Geertz's view has rather stronger implications than I would want to press. I would not want to deny that a culture may, reasonably, be said to exercise influence over individual actions, as is supposed in the notion of the effect of cultural 'norms' of behaviour. But this sort of influence is not the same thing as 'action', since it does not suppose the intentionality implied in the notion of an agent. The influential or determining character of a culture is a function of the 'weight' of its historical totalisation of appropriate ways of behaving, not a function of any deliberate aims or intentions by which we could describe it as 'acting'.

If we accept that cultures are not agents it then becomes difficult to speak of 'cultural autonomy'. This is not just a theoretical quibble: recognising cultures as totalisations of collective practices makes it plain that, as people begin to act differently in sufficient numbers, so cultures change. In modern societies at least, people come and go from cultural communities and cultural commodities are imported and consumed, constantly shifting the balance of 'what we do'. Cultures are therefore protean entities; their boundaries are shifting and permeable. They don't have the characteristics of 'permanence', 'integrity' or 'selfhood' that we ascribe to agents. The right of cultures to exercise autonomy – freedom from external control and so on – cannot then really be applied to the 'holistic' view that cultures are 'ontologically distinct' from individuals, more than the sum of their parts. The moral criterion of autonomy logically restricts us to the analysis of agents and their actions. Individual members of 'a culture' may complain about cultural imperialism impinging on their autonomy or they may not. 'Cultural representatives' in institutional settings (for example UNESCO) may 'speak for' the culture and its autonomy, but here they are really speaking on behalf of individuals. But what doesn't speak, doesn't act, and therefore can't be said to have autonomy is the culture itself.

So the criterion of autonomy applied to cultures in the holistic sense fails to provide us with a basis for an ethical-political critique of cultural imperialism. Autonomy can apply to individuals in this context, but this doesn't help the critics of cultural imperialism with the (substantial) cases in which individuals don't object to cultural imports.

There may be other, quite independent, grounds for a critique of cultural imperialism and I shall mention two such: one, in passing, to illustrate a critique that doesn't rest on the idea of domination, and another that suggests the movement to other aspects of cultural imperialism – its relation to capitalism and to modernity – that will occupy us in the following chapters.

An interesting point about the autonomy principle is that it is quite indifferent to the *outcomes* of cultural practices and processes: so long as these take place free from heteronomous control the autonomy principle is entirely satisfied. The implication of this is that autonomy would not necessarily be at issue if all cultures came to resemble one another. If all restaurants looked like McDonald's or Pizza Hut, all music became variants of Western electronic rock, all cities concrete and glass clones of Milton Keynes, all television programmes blandly 'international', if identical parades of shops were to be found in every shopping centre in the world – defenders of autonomy could not grumble, so long as this homogeneity was the outcome of autonomous choices. For autonomy is *only* concerned with freedom of action, not with the outcomes of actions.

Often (negative) judgements about the 'homogenising' function of cultural imperialism become mixed up with critiques of domination in relation to autonomy. But they are quite distinct issues: to object to global homogenis-ation has no *necessary* connection with autonomy, nor even with domination. For why should we object if everything came to look the same? We might argue that richness, variety and difference are goods in themselves, but then, under other considerations, so are order, uniformity and universality. Babel and Esperanto both have their enthusiasts. It is difficult to object to global homogenisation (supposing, of course, that this is occurring) without falling back on the simple intuition that it is a good thing that there is variety in cultures. But then we have to ask, a good thing for whom? Who is to enjoy the range of cultural difference? It is not difficult to see how this preference for variety might become that of the Western global-cultural tourist as much as of the concerned anthropologist. There are probably much stronger arguments for uniformity of cultures in the broad sense, where uniformity implies, for example, the maximisation of health care, nutritional technology, housing provision, education and so on across all cultures. Clearly there are other major issues of value here which relate to the cultural processes of modernity itself. Not all objections to 'cultural imperialism' – 'homogeneity' being a good example – are grounded unambiguously in what the left would call the critique of domination. To risk labouring the point, we need to ask 'who speaks?'.

The problems of value raised in this section point us, like the earlier arguments, away from the analysis of the interaction of cultures across spatial, geopolitical boundaries, and towards the analysis of cultural change across *time*. The 'liberal' line I have been taking in relation to the claims of autonomy will not satisfy those radical critics who insist that cultural imperialism does involve domination in that it invariably means the spread of a 'capitalist culture' characterised by the increasing 'commodification' of everyday life. For such critics, the broad processes of capitalist modernity represent an essential attack on personal autonomy in that the 'locus of control' of cultural processes is increasingly shifted from individuals and 'public collectivities' towards the institutions of corporate capitalism and the state. Cultural imperialism is thus to be criticised in historical terms: it spreads a capitalist modernity which is inherently dominating and opposed to the 'emancipatory interests' of human beings. This is a rather crude encapsulation of some complex and powerful arguments. But in it we can glimpse the problems such arguments must confront. What is 'capitalist culture'? Is capitalism the major determinant of 'modernity' as cultural experience, or is modernity itself the governing principle – and need this involve domination? So . . . what is modernity?

Notes

1. I. de Sola Pool (1979) 'Direct Broadcast Satellites and the Integrity of National Cultures', in K. Nordenstreng and H.I. Schiller, *National Sovereignty and International Communication*, New Jersey, Ablex, p. 139.
2. See, for example, the notion of a Latin American 'audiovisual space' in A. Mattlelart, X. Delacourt and M. Mattelart (1984) *International Image Markets: In Search of an Alternative Perspective*, London, Comedia.
3. P. Schlesinger (1987) 'On National Identity: Some Conceptions and Misconceptions Criticized', *Social Science Information*, Vol. 26 (2), pp. 219–64. I am grateful to Professor Schlesinger for making this paper available to me – I have found it extremely helpful in thinking through the issues in this chapter.
4. UNESCO (1982) *Final Report of World Conference on Cultural Policies*, Mexico City and Paris, UNESCO, p. 179.
5. Ibid., p. 8.
6. Ibid.
7. Ibid.
8. See the discussion of Barthes on 'universal humanism' in Chapter 2, pp. 53–54.
9. UNESCO, op. cit., p. 22.
10. Ibid., p. 59.
11. Ibid., p 61.
12. Ibid., p. 60.
13. Ibid., p. 23.
14. Schlesinger, op. cit., p. 227.
15. UNESCO, op. cit., p. 60.
16. A.D. Smith (1981) *The Ethnic Revival in the Modern World*, Cambridge, Cambridge University Press, p. 9.
17. Ibid.
18. Ibid., p. 10.
19. See, for example, Edward Said's criticism of Western perceptions of a homogeneous 'world of Islam': E. Said (1978) *Orientalism*, London, Routledge and Kegan Paul.
20. See Smith's discussion of 'assimilation': Smith, op. cit., Chapter 8.
21. On the perception of symbolic American forms in the UK see D. Hebdige (1988) 'Towards a Cartography of Taste 1935–1962', in *Hiding in the Light*, London, Comedia/Routledge.
22. See R. Barthes (1973) *Mythologies*, London, Paladin.
23. This oversimplifies a complex political situation. For accounts see R. Carr (1982) *Spain 1808–1975*, Oxford, Oxford University Press, and P. Preston (ed.) (1976) *Spain in Crisis: the Evolution and Decline of the Franco Régime*, Brighton, Harvester Press.
24. I am grateful to Dr Anny Jones for advice on these points of Spanish language and culture.
25. One banner in the Seville demonstration read 'Felipe: Dime con quien pactas y te dire quien eres' (Felipe: Tell me who you make pacts with an I'll tell you who you are). The socialist prime minister, Felipe Gonzáles, is here taunted with the image of himself re-enacting Franco's pact of 1953. The ironies go deeper in that González is a native of Andalucía.
26. See A. Giddens (1985) *The Nation-State and Violence: Volume Two of A Contemporary Critique of Historical Materialism*, Cambridge, Polity Press, p. 13.

27. A. Giddens (1981) *A Contemporary Critique of Historical Materialism, Volume One: Power, Property and the State*, London, Macmillan, p. 192.

28. Schlesinger, op. cit., p. 236. Schlesinger provides a very useful critical review of this literature.

29. E. Gellner, (1983) *Nations and Nationalism*, Oxford, Basil Blackwell, p. 35.

30. Gellner claims that 'nationalism does not have any very deep roots in the human psyche': ibid., p. 34. Cf. Giddens's discussion of the need for a psychological account: Giddens (1985), op. cit., pp. 214–15.

31. B. Anderson (1983) *Imagined Communities: Reflections on the Origin and Spread of Nationalism*, London, Verso, p. 15.

32. Ibid., p. 16.

33. Schlesinger, op. cit., p. 247.

34. Anderson, op. cit., p. 15.

35. Ibid., p. 46.

36. Ibid., p. 47.

37. Schlesinger points out how little attention Anderson gives to the electronic media and 'the implications of their easy crossing of national boundaries' (op. cit., p. 249). This is surely a major omission in Anderson's account.

38. Anderson, op. cit., p. 39.

39. Ibid., p. 40.

40. Ibid. Compare with this the discussion of Castoriadis's idea of the 'social imaginary' in modern societies: see Chapter 5, pp. 156–63.

41. Schlesinger, op. cit., p. 249.

42. See, Giddens (1981) op. cit.; (1985), op. cit. and (1984) *The Constitution of Society*, Cambridge, Polity Press.

43. Giddens (1981), op. cit., p. 193.

44. For Giddens's most detailed discussion of 'ontological security' see A. Giddens (1979) *Central Problems in Social Theory: Action, Structure and Contradiction in Social Analysis*, London, Macmillan, p. 219ff. Laing's original formulation of the idea is found in R.D. Laing (1965) *The Divided Self*, Harmondsworth, Penguin, Chapter 3.

45. Giddens (1981), op. cit., pp. 193–4.

46. Ibid., p. 154.

47. Ibid., p. 195.

48. Schlesinger, op. cit., p. 253.

49. Ibid., p. 260.

50. Giddens is sensitive to the possibility that he may be read here as 'proposing a romantic view of the past, in which people lived in the local community and in harmony with one another and with nature'. Replying to these criticisms, he recognises that 'social life in traditional communities was often a fraught and dangerous affair'. The point he stresses is: 'Many of the routines we follow in day to day life are materially safe and secure, but psychologically and morally unrewarding': A. Giddens (1989) 'A Reply to my Critics', in D. Held and J.B. Thompson *Social Theory and Modern Societies: Anthony Giddens and his Critics*, Cambridge, Cambridge University Press, pp. 278–9. See also the discussion of Giddens on the 'crisis of moral legitimacy' in modern societies in my conclusion.

51. Giddens (1979), op. cit., p. 200.

52. Giddens (1981), op. cit., p. 194.

53. See Giddens (1985), op. cit., p. 218.

54. See also the concept of 'privatism' in, for example, J. Habermas (1976) *Legitimation Crisis*, London, Heinemann; R. Williams (1983) *Towards 2000*, London, Chatto and Windus; C. Lodziak (1986) *The Power of Television: A Critical Appraisal*, London, Frances Pinter.
55. Giddens (1981), op. cit., p. 194.
56. See the discussion in Chapter 4, pp. 106–8 and Chapter 5, pp. 143–4.
57. Schlesinger, op. cit., p. 261.
58. E. Hobsbawm (1983) 'Introduction: Inventing Traditions', in E. Hobsbawm and T. Ranger (eds) *The Invention of Tradition*, Cambridge, Cambridge University Press, p. 1.
59. Ibid., p. 2.
60. Ibid., p. 14.
61. See also D. Horne (1986) *The Public Culture*, London, Pluto Press, p. 8ff. on 'creating nations'.
62. Giddens (1979), op. cit., p.200. I discuss these points in more detail in Chapter 5.
63. The same might even be said of 'developing societies': see Chapter 5, pp. 149–51 and particularly the reference to Peter Berger.
64. Pool, op. cit., pp. 145–6.
65. J. Burgess (1987) 'In Japan New Year Means the Ninth', *The Guardian*, 2 January.
66. See Hebdige, op. cit., and D. Laing (1986) 'The Music Industry and the "Cultural Imperialism" Thesis', *Media, Culture and Society*, Vol. 8 (3), pp. 331–41.
67. See the discussion in Chapter 4, pp. 126–31.
68. See Giddens (1979), op. cit. (Chapter 2) on these problems in relation to societies.
69. R. Lindley (1986) *Autonomy*, London, Macmillan Education, p. 6.
70. Smith, op. cit., p. 16 (emphasis added).
71. C. Geertz (1973) *The Interpretation of Cultures*, New York, Basic Books, p. 14.

4

The Culture of Capitalism

We must remember that the discourses of cultural imperialism as media imperialism or as the attack on national cultural identity or, here, as the spread across the globe of a culture of capitalism do not 'totalise' to a coherent thesis. They are 'ways of talking' about processes which have been loosely and sometimes contradictorily 'organised' by the concept 'cultural imperialism'. So the chapters of this book do not unfold a progressive argument that exists neatly and coherently in the 'cultural imperialism thesis'.

But there is a progressive argument in the criticisms I have offered so far. Cultural imperialism cannot be fully understood within the terms of reference of 'media imperialism': it generates deeper questions about cultural identity. Cultural identity cannot be fully understood in the spatial-synchronic terms of the arguments about national domination but requires attention to *historical* processes of cultural change, and in particular to the processes of *modernity*. At this point the critique bifurcates. The connections between the cultural aspects of capitalism and of 'modernity' are so close that they can only be artificially separated out in analysis. The purpose of treating them separately is to engage with the critiques of cultural imperialism which have cast capitalism as the main cultural enemy. However, in doing this we shall find that issues arise which cannot be resolved within the problematic of 'capitalist culture' alone, but which suppose other socio-cultural changes. 'Capitalist modernity' is the real issue. This is why the argument bifurcates. This and the next chapter must be considered as parallel discussions.

First we will examine one of the most common arguments linking cultural imperialism to the spread of capitalism. This argument is found in writers we have already encountered – Herbert Schiller, Armand and Michelle Mattelart, Ariel Dorfman – among others. But the link is also implicit in a lot of other, particularly neo-Marxist, discourses about cultural imperialism. The distinctive feature of this approach is that it sees cultural imperialism as somehow in the *service* of capitalism, as a set of practices enabling the spread of capitalism as an economic system. This involves a certain 'functionalism' which is problematic in its own right (that is, as a theory of socioeconomic change) but which also fails to grasp capitalism as a cultural totality.

The stronger and more interesting claims belong to this latter view. The spread of capitalism must be seen as the spread of a distinctive 'cultural dominant' in its own right. Thus we will examine further the claim that the nature of multinational capitalism produces a homogenised global culture. Although there is evidence that an unprecedented cultural convergence seems to be occurring at certain levels, this cannot be read in the self-evidently negative terms that the critics of 'cultural homogenisation' assume.

We must ask what it is about capitalist culture that makes the prognosis of its uniform spread across the globe such a gloomy one, and here we must limit the discussion severely. Clearly it would be possible to characterise capitalist culture in many different ways. Some would have to do with the class structure it creates and some with other aspects of 'modernity' that accompany it – for example the increasing tendency towards a separation of the 'public' and the 'private' spheres of cultural action. I shall focus on just one approach, by far the most common one in cultural criticism. This is the idea that capitalism produces a *consumer culture* within which all cultural action and experience become 'commodified'. We will examine arguments which relate 'consumerism' as a consequence of capitalist expansion to the 'developing' societies of the Third World. These arguments have little force on their own, but demand a coherent critique of *Western* capitalism as a 'consumer culture'. Finally we must ask what would constitute such a critique, and what might be the grounds for considering the spread of capitalism as a form of cultural imperialism.

Cultural imperialism: pioneer of capitalism?

Writers who link cultural imperialism closely to capitalism frequently fall into a sort of functionalist argument, in which the cultural products of the developed capitalist world are used to lure other cultures into the world capitalist system or even to 'condition' workers for expanding multinational capitalist enterprise. We saw in Chapter 2 that Herbert Schiller's analysis dwells on the use of communications and media technology as agencies for 'the promotion, protection and extension of the modern world [capitalist] system'. Elsewhere, Schiller has defined cultural imperialism, in a much quoted passage, as:

> the sum of the processes by which a society is brought into the modern world system and how its dominating stratum is attracted, pressured, forced, and sometimes bribed into shaping social institutions to correspond to, or even promote, the values and structures of the dominating center of the system.[1]

There is a sense here of cultural imperialism as being simply in the service of the capitalist system. The suggestion is that the 'good life' of capitalist consumerism is displayed as a lure to the powerful in developing countries to get them on to the hook of the capitalist world system, much as Marx in his early work describes the consumer lured like 'the fly onto the lime-twig'.[2] This view is sometimes expressed in terms like 'the demonstration effect' of media imports. Schiller's writing even slides, on occasion, towards a deeper functionalism in which it almost appears that cultural imperialism can be explained by the mere requirements of the 'system' itself: 'The cultural-communications sector of the world system necessarily develops in accordance with and facilitates the aims and objectives of the general system.'[3]

Schiller has rightly been criticised for this functionalism – systems do not have aims and objectives.[4] But his analysis is not limited to a view of cultural imperialism as recruiting sergeant for the capitalist economic order. As I suggested in chapter two, Schiller's view of the capitalist world system itself seems sometimes to be of a cultural totality, 'a developmental path'. Viewed this way, cultural, imperialism appears as the spread of a *culture of capitalism*. However, it must be said that the nature of capitalist culture is never really probed in Schiller's work.

An important distinction exists between arguments which merely want to convict cultural imperialism of preparing the ground for capitalism and those that see it as the cultural concomitant of capitalism as a socioeconomic system. The first view generally tends towards crude, reductive analyses of cultural practices. A better example of this than Schiller's slightly ambiguous 'systems' argument is found in an article by Flora and Flora, 'The *Fotonovela* as a Tool for Class and Cultural Domination'. The authors argue that the *fotonovela* – 'a love story told in photographs with balloon captions presenting the dialogue . . . omnipresent among the masses in Latin America, Northern Africa, France and Italy' – fulfils various ideological functions, 'necessary to reinforce capitalist relations':

> The first serves to break down primary ties and integrate workers and peasants into an urban lifestyle. The second provides a mechanism of escape from real problems. The third encourages consumption of middle-class items.[5]

Flora and Flora's argument is deeply problematic in all sorts of ways: it constantly attributes 'false consciousness and passive acceptance of the larger socio-politico-economic context' to the 'masses'; it entirely ignores the active meaning-constructive nature of the reading process; and it is littered with functionalist explanations in terms of the 'needs' of the capitalist system. These problems stem precisely from the way the authors approach their cultural material, that is, simply as the ideological *tool* of the capitalist system. Discussing their first claim about the function of the *fotonovela* in the disintegration of peasant culture and the reintegration of workers into urban lifestyles, they write:

> Capitalist development depends on a highly mobile and inter-replaceable work-force (Braverman 1974). A first step in the creation of mobile workers is to

separate the individual from his or her primary group and accentuate his or her importance and adaptiveness over group cohesion and group solutions. Once the removal from a group setting occurs, integration and acceptance of values consistent with capitalism or monopoly capitalism can take place. The *fotonovela* stresses such a shift in values both directly and indirectly.[6]

This strikes me as implausible both as analysis of the intentions of the producers of *fotonovelas* (by what conspiratorial system are the plots 'a direct result of the multinational capitalistic industry which produces and sells the volumes to the working classes')[7] and of their likely effects. It also seems superfluous as an explanation of the acceptance of a capitalist work discipline amongst workers in developing countries. What Marx once called 'the dull compulsion of the economic' – the sheer need to survive by selling one's labour time – would appear an adequate explanation in the conditions of scarcity that characterise all developing countries. This implausibility derives, in part, from the crude functionalist view of cultural practices implicit in the analysis. Seeing cultural imperialism as a capitalist 'tool' tends to misrepresent both the dynamics of the capitalist process itself (for example, as conspiracy or as self-regulating system) and the nature of cultural practices.

This misrepresentation is not just a question of a particularly crude or undertheorised approach. It can be seen in relatively sophisticated theoretical analyses such as that of Salinas and Paldán's paper, 'Culture in the Process of Dependent Development: Theoretical Perspectives'. Working from within the perspective of Latin American 'dependency theory' these authors attempt an outline of how 'the state of dependent development is created and expressed in the cultural sphere of societies subjected to an external domination system'.[8] In line with the neo-Marxist complexion of most of dependency theory, their analysis stresses the interdependence of exogenous and endogenous processes in the development of Third World societies: the 'dependent development' of the economies of these countries is seen not simply in terms of *external* domination by the nations of the developed West or the multinational corporations, but also by the domination of the internal class structure. Salinas and Paldán view capitalism in both its national and multinational manifestations as the major principle of cultural imperialism and this shapes their view of the nature of cultural practices:

> Culture, as both a specific sphere of ideal reflections and a system of meanings attributed to the existing reality, cannot be separated from the basic socioeconomic structure of a given society. Culture is always an historically specific phenomenon, conditioned by the class structure of the society. . . . In a capitalist society the conflictive class structure gives birth to a cultural sphere predominantly divided along class lines.[9]

This expresses a fairly fundamental premiss of Marxist cultural theory, namely that cultural practices are related, somehow, to the class structure of capitalist societies. The problem with Salinas and Paldán's analysis – and in this they are typical of many Marxist approaches – is that they tend to focus on the implications of cultural practices for the class struggle, rather than probing the nature of capitalist culture itself. In doing this they slide towards a view of cultural imperialism as the 'tool' of capitalism, viewed here as the socioeconomic dominance of one class over another. This is clear from the section of their paper, 'Cultural expressions of the dependent development', in which they describe four 'distinct effects in the cultural sphere' of the situation of dependent nations in the world capitalist system. In only one of these cases does their discussion touch substantially on an element of what may be described as 'capitalist culture'.

First they comment on the way in which both ruling and subordinate classes in dependent countries are 'incorporated' into the dominant 'internationalized' sector of the economy. On the one hand, the bourgeois class welcomes the penetration of the national economy by multinational companies, since they are able 'to share patterns of consumption and thereby life-styles and cultural affinities similar to those sustained by the dominant sectors of developed economies'.[10] On the other hand, the working class, or a certain 'privileged' number of them, find their living dependent on the same penetration by the multinationals and thus their interests are incorporated into the general process of economic penetration. This argument is really part of a more general one common in dependency theory,[11] to the effect that the dependent structure of Third World economies tends to divide the class structure of these countries into two sectors: one economically tied to the 'modernising' industrial sector dominated by multinationals and one, based in 'traditional' indigenous industry and agricultural production, which becomes 'marginalised' and excluded from the processes of economic 'growth'. The existence of this second sector is Salinas and Paldán's second instance of an 'effect' of dependent development.

So far, all the stress is on the impact of economic imperialism on class structure. What are the 'cultural expressions' of these two instances? Well, they are barely mentioned. The 'incorporated' sectors are said to 'fall under the influence of the normative elements that are transferred [from the developed world] together with the technology'. Indigenous subcultures of the dominated class 'are shaken, both by the change of their objective situation in the sphere of material production as well as by the cultural-ideological elements imported from the metropolis'.[12] What this amounts to is simply the claim that capitalism changes the cultural practices of those who come into its orbit. This is something few would deny, but Salinas and Paldán offer no evidence, at this point, of *how* these changes are felt (what is the culture of capitalism?) or, indeed, of why they should be viewed as 'domination'. Their claim about the influence of 'normative' and 'cultural-ideological' elements is subject broadly to all the objections that have been raised to Flora and Flora's claims about the ideological effects of the *fotonovela*. It raises all the problems involved in attributing an ideological effect to the mass media that we met in Chapter 2.

One point at which Salinas and Paldán do avoid the problems of the attribution of ideological incorporation is where they refer, in passing, to the cultural effects of economic dependency on the 'marginalised' sectors of Third World nations. Here they argue that a cultural effect can be traced directly to the impoverishment of this sector. While some groups fall 'under the influence of foreign cultural models',

> Others are submitted to levels of existence that prevent them from exercising minimal cultural rights, because of the imperatives that poverty poses to their survival. [This represents] a 'poverty of the culture', understood as the incapacity for the elaboration of a more complex vision of the relations between men and women and their circumstances, which is the result of the necessity of focusing all attention on physical survival.[13]

If unproblematic connections are to be made between economic and cultural imperialism it seems to me that it is at this very basic *material* level. The evidence of the impoverishment and immiseration of vast numbers of people in dependent countries as a direct result of 'combined and uneven development',[14] that is as a result of capitalism's exploitation of labour power and material resources on a world scale, is clear, massive and well documented. Here Salinas and Paldán refer to the impoverishment of a marginalised sector excluded from multinational employment, yet there is plenty of evidence to show that such impoverishment, what André Gunder Frank calls 'super-exploitation', extends in many instances to those employed by multinational capitalism.[15] Where such degrees of poverty exist there can be no doubt that the cultural horizons of those affected shrink in the way that Salinas and Paldán claim.

It was a basic premiss of Marx's materialism that 'culture' can only be established on the material 'base' of the adequate provision for human needs and it was for this reason that Marx saw capitalism as, in a certain sense, 'progressive': the technological changes it gave rise to promised liberation from the low cultural horizons imposed by the continual struggle against nature for survival. Now where capitalism in its unequal growth across the world creates contexts in which people are forced back into a struggle for material survival – where it creates, in Frank's words, 'the development of underdevelopment' – then it can quite clearly and unambiguously be charged with a malign cultural effect: it denies people access to cultural experience, inhibiting the growth of what Marx saw as the 'radical needs and powers' of human beings.[16]

However true this may be, it is not the issue people tend to dwell upon when they charge capitalism with cultural imperialism. It is not the *denial* of cultural experience through poverty that is generally seen as the problem. Salinas and Paldán devote only one paragraph to this. Instead it is precisely the imposition of a way of life characterising the 'successes' of capitalism – the values and habits of a consumer culture and so on – that is criticised. This is the source of much confusion, for critics of capitalism are often accused of wanting to have their cake and eat it. On the one hand capitalism is seen as guilty of denying its material benefits to some but on the other it is guilty of spreading a shallow, 'materialist culture' predicated precisely on its material achievements: 'delivering the goods'. The reason for this confusion is, I think, the failure of critics of cultural imperialism to grasp fully the ambiguous gift of capitalist modernity, that is, to probe the contradictions of capitalist culture.

This failure derives, partly, from the 'functionalist' view I have described of cultural imperialism as the 'tool' of an advancing capitalist system. Salinas and Paldán's third instance of a cultural 'effect' reverts to just such a view. They claim that the cultural institutions, for instance the educational and media systems, of dependent societies are shaped to adapt to 'the requirements of dependent industrialization'. As in their other arguments, there is nothing here about the actual substance of capitalist culture; cultural institutions are seen simply as serving the 'requirements' of an economic system. It is only in their fourth and final point of discussion that anything descriptive of a culture of capitalism is proposed. And here the single claim that is made is the familiar one that capitalism produces a cultural homogenisation: 'In effect, dependent industrialization, accompanied by accelerated urbanization . . . can be seen as a drive toward cultural homogenization'.[17]

As we have seen, the notion of cultural homogenisation is far from simple. It may be a significant feature of the culture of capitalism, but this significance is not self-evident: it is not, for example, transparently a negative feature. But here there is no real attempt to probe the significance of cultural homogenisation in itself: it too is seen simply as an instrument for the spread of capitalist hegemony, 'for the reproduction of the whole society as a system of domination'.[18] Here again, the substance of a cultural phenomenon is subordinated to an analysis of its supposed function and thus, in effect, ignored. The effect is the same eternal retreat of the moment of the cultural that we saw in the discussion of media imperialism in Chapter 2.

The shortcomings of this 'functional' tendency in the neo-Marxist literature should now be apparent: we can move on to the difficult question of how to characterise the culture of capitalism.

Multinational capitalism and cultural homogenisation

In the discussion of autonomy we saw that this principle is quite indifferent to cultural outcomes. So if the choices made by cultural communities worldwide tend to converge, so long as these choices are autonomously made the enthusiast for autonomy can have no grumbles. Yet critics of multinational capitalism frequently do complain of its tendency towards cultural convergence and homogenisation. This is the major criticism made in the discourse of cultural imperialism which takes capitalism as its target. A good example is Cees Hamelink's book, *Cultural Autonomy in Global Communications*. Hamelink, who acknowledges the co-operation of both Schiller and Salinas,[19] places the issues of cultural autonomy and cultural homogenisation – or what he refers to as 'cultural synchronization' – at the centre of his analysis. He is broadly correct in identifying the processes of 'cultural synchroniz- ation' (or homogenisation) as unprecedented in historical terms and in seeing these processes as closely connected to the spread of global capitalism. But he fails to show why cultural synchronisation should be objected to and, specifically, he fails to show that it should be objected to on the grounds of cultural autonomy.

In his opening chapter Hamelink lists a number of personal 'experiences of the international scene' to illustrate his thesis. For example:

> In a Mexican village the traditional ritual dance precedes a soccer match, but the performance features a gigantic Coca-Cola bottle.

> In Singapore, a band dressed in traditional Malay costume offers a heart-breaking imitation of Fats Domino.

> In Saudi Arabia, the television station performs only one local cultural function – the call for the Moslem prayer. Five times a day, North American cops and robbers yield to the traditional muezzin.

> In its gigantic advertising campaign, IBM assures Navajo Indians that their cultural identity can be effectively protected if they use IBM typewriters equipped with the Navajo alphabet.[20]

The first thing to note about these examples is precisely their significance as *personal* observations – and this is not to make any trivial point about their 'subjective' nature. Hamelink expresses the cultural standpoint of the concerned Westerner confronting a perplexing set of global phenomena. We have to accept, at the level of the personal, the sincerity of his concern and also the validity of this personal discourse: it is valid for individuals to express their reaction to global tendencies. But we need to acknowledge that this globe-trotting instancing of cultural imperialism shapes the discourse in a particular way: to say 'here is the *sameness* that capitalism brings – and here – and here . . .' is to assume, however liberal, radical or critical the intention, the role of the 'tourist': the problem of homogenisation is likely to present itself to the Western intellectual who has a sense of the diversity and 'richness' of global culture as a particular threat. For the people involved in each discrete instance Hamelink presents, the experience of Western capitalist culture will probably have quite different significance. Only if they can adopt the (privileged) role of the cultural tourist will the sense of the homogenisation of global culture have the same threatening aspect. The Kazakhstani tribesman who has no knowledge of (and, perhaps, no interest in) America or Europe is unlikely to see his cassette player as emblematic of creeping capitalist domination. And we cannot, without irony, argue that the Western intellectual's (informed?) concern is more valid: again much hangs on the question, 'who speaks?'.

This said, Hamelink does draw from these instances an empirical conclu- sion which is, I think, fairly uncontroversial:

One conclusion still seems unanimously shared: the impressive variety of the world's cultural systems is waning due to a process of 'cultural synchronization' that is without historic precedent.[21]

For those in a position to view the world as a cultural totality, it cannot be denied that certain processes of cultural convergence are under way, and that these are new processes. This last is an important point, for Hamelink is careful to acknowledge that cultures have always influenced one another and that this influence has often enriched the interacting communities – 'the richest cultural traditions emerged at the actual meeting point of markedly different cultures, such as Sudan, Athens, the Indus Valley, and Mexico'.[22] Even where cultural interaction has been in the contxt of political and economic domination, Hamelink argues, there has been, in most cases a 'two-way exchange' or at least a tolerance of cultural diversity. There is a sharp difference for him between these patterns and modern 'cultural synchronization':

> In the second half of the twentieth century, a destructive process that differs significantly from the historical examples given above threatens the diversity of cultural systems. Never before has the synchronization with one particular cultural pattern been of such global dimensions and so comprehensive.[23]

Let us be clear about what we are agreeing. It seems to me that Hamelink is right, broadly speaking, to identify cultural synchronisation as an unprecedented feature of global modernity. The evaluative implications of his use of the word 'destructive', however, raises larger problems. It is one thing to say that cultural diversity is being destroyed, quite another to lament the fact. The latter position demands reasons which Hamelink cannot convincingly supply. The quotation continues in a way that raises part of the problem: 'Never before has the process of cultural influence proceeded so subtly, without any blood being shed and with the receiving culture thinking it had sought such cultural influence.'[24] With his last phrase Hamelink slides towards the problematic of false consciousness. As we have seen more than once before, any critique which bases itself in the idea that cultural domination is taking place 'behind people's backs' is heading for trouble. To acknowledge that a cultural community might have thought it had sought cultural influence is to acknowledge that such influence has at least *prima facie* attractions.

This thought could lead us to ask if the process of cultural homogenisation itself might not have its attractions. It is not difficult to think of examples of cultural practices which would probably attract a consensus in favour of their universal application: health care; food hygiene; educational provision; various 'liberal' cultural attitudes towards honesty, toleration, compassion and so on; democratic public processes etc.. This is not to say that any of these are indisputable 'goods' under any description whatever, nor that they are all the 'gifts' of an expanding capitalist modernity. We shall have cause, in the next chapter, to question both these issues. But it is to say that there are plenty of aspects of 'culture', broadly defined, that the severest critic of cultural homogenisation might wish to find the same in any area of the globe. Critics of cultural homogenisation are selective in the things they object to, and there is nothing wrong in this so long as we realise that it undermines the notion that homogenisation is a bad thing *in itself*. But then we enter a quite separate set of arguments – not about the uniformity of capitalist culture, but about the spread of its pernicious features – which require quite different criteria of judgement.

Engaging with the potentially attractive features of homogenisation brings us to see, pretty swiftly, the problems in its use as a critical concept. But there are other ways of approaching the issue, and one of Hamelink's arguments seems on the surface to avoid these problems. He argues that cultural synchronisation is to be deplored on the grounds that it is a threat to cultural autonomy. I have argued against both the notion of autonomy as applied to a 'culture' in the holistic sense and against any logical connection between the concept of autonomy and any particular *outcome* of cultural practices. Autonomy, as I understand it, refers to the free and uncoerced choices and actions of agents. But Hamelink uses the notion of autonomy in what strikes me as a curious way, to suggest a feature of cultural practices which is necessary, indeed 'critical', for the actual survival of a cultural community.

Hamelink's reasoning appears to be based on the idea that the cultural system of any society is an *adaptive* mechanism which enables the society to exist in its 'environment', by which he seems to mean the physical and material features of its global location: 'Different climatic conditions, for example, demand different ways of adapting to them (i.e., different types of food, shelter and clothing).'[25] Again, there is nothing particularly controversial about this, except in the obvious sense that we might want to argue that many of the cultural practices of modernity are rather more 'distanced' from the function of survival than those of more 'primitive' systems. But from this point he argues that the 'autonomous' development of cultural systems – the freedom from the processes of 'cultural synchronization' – are necessary to the 'survival' of societies. Why should this be so? Because 'the adequacy of the cultural system can best be decided upon by the members of the society who face directly the problems of survival and adaptation'.[26]

There are a number of difficulties arising from this sort of argument. First, what does Hamelink mean by the 'survival' of a society? In his reference to very basic adaptations to environmental conditions he seems to trade on the idea that a culture allows for the actual physical survival of its members. At times he explicitly refers to the physical survival of people. For example, he claims that the intensive promotion of milk-powder baby food in the Third World by companies like Nestlé and Cow and Gate is a practice that can have life-threatening consequences:

> Replacing breast-feeding by bottle feeding has had disastrous effects in many Third World countries. An effective, adequate, and cheap method has been exchanged for an expensive, inadequate and dangerous product. . . . Many illiterate mothers, unable to prepare the milk powder correctly, have not only used it improperly but have also inadvertently transformed the baby food into a lethal product by using it in unhygienic conditions.[27]

There *are* important issues having to do with the 'combined and unequal development' produced by the spread of capitalism of which this is a good example: we referred to these, briefly, in the previous section and we shall return to them in the following section. But the incidence of illness and death Hamelink refers to here, deplorable though it is, will obviously not carry the weight of his argument about cultural synchronisation affecting the physical survival of whole populations in the Third World. He cannot, plausibly, claim that cultural synchronisation with capitalist modernity carries this direct threat. It is probably true that capitalist production has long-term consequences for the global environment, thus for physical survival on a global scale, but this is a separate argument.

At any rate, Hamelink's notion of survival seems to slide from that of physical survival to the *survival of the culture itself*. But this is a very different proposition, which cannot be sustained by the functional view of culture he takes as his premiss. For the failure of a culture to 'survive' in an 'original' form may be taken itself as a process of adaptation to a new 'environment' – that of capitalist industrial modernity. A certain circularity is therefore introduced into the argument. Hamelink claims that unique cultures arise as adaptive mechanisms to environments, so he deplores heteronomy since it threatens such adaptation. But what could cultural synchronisation mean if not an 'adaptation' to the demands of the social environment of capitalism?

The incoherences of this account arise, I believe, from the attempt to circumvent the problems of autonomy in cultural terms by referring the holistic view to a functional logic of adaptation. As I argued in the last chapter, autonomy can only apply to agents, and cultures are not agents. Hamelink seeks to bypass these problems with an argument that reduces the ethical-political content of 'autonomy' to make it a mere indicator of social efficiency – the guarantor of the 'best' form of social organisation in a particular environment. His argument is incoherent precisely because autonomy cannot be so reduced: in cultural terms, 'best' is not to be measured against a simple index of physical survival. Things are far more complicated than this. Cultural autonomy must address the autonomous choices of agents who make up a cultural community; there is no escaping this set of problems by appeal to functionality. Hamelink gives the game away in his reference, cited earlier, to a form of cultural 'false consciousness' and elsewhere where he speaks of cultural synchronisation as cultural practices being 'persuasively communicated to the receiving countries'.[28]

I do not believe the appeal to autonomy grounds Hamelink's critique of cultural synchronisation. Even if it did, this would be an objection to the inhibition of independence by manipulation, not to the resulting 'sameness' of global culture. But Hamelink does want to object to 'sameness': this is implicit in his constant references to the 'rich diversity' of cultures under threat. What are the grounds for such an objection?

Adaptation to physical environments has, historically, produced a diversity in cultural practices across the globe. However the *preservation* of this diversity – which is what Hamelink wants – seems to draw its justification from the idea that cultural diversity is a good thing in itself. But this depends on the position from which you speak. If the attractions of a uniform capitalist modernity outweigh the charms of diversity, as they well may for those from the outside looking in, it is difficult to insist on the priority of preserving differences. Indeed, the appeal to variety might well be turned back on the critic of capitalism. For it might be argued that individual cultures making up the rich mosaic that Hamelink surveys are lacking in a variety of cultural experience, being tied, as Marx observed, to the narrow demands of the struggle with nature for survival.[29] Cultural synchronisation could in some cases increase variety in cultural experience.

It must be said immediately that arguments exist that the *nature* of such experience in capitalist modernity is in some sense deficient – shallow, 'one-dimensional', 'commodified', and so on. But this is not a criticism of homogenisation or synchronisation as such: it is a criticism of the sort of culture that synchronisation brings. It is quite different to object to the spread of something bad – uniform badness – than to object to the spread of uniformity itself. This demands quite separate arguments about capitalism as a culture, and it is to these that we will now turn.

It is worth making explicit the connection Hamelink sees between the processes of cultural synchronisation and the spread of capitalism. As with Schiller, it is the transnational corporations who are the major players: 'The principal agents of cultural synchronisation today are the transnational corporations, largely based in the United States, which are developing a global investment and marketing strategy.'[30]

Transnational firms are enormously significant in the organisation of capitalism worldwide. This significance in terms of economic domination is not to be contested. But what are the *cultural* implications of multinational capitalism?

Rum and Coke: capitalism, consumerism and the Third World

One reason why the threat of homogenisation has been perceived as so central to the spread of capitalism has been the presumed logic of multi-national markets: uniformity spread through the marketing of cost-efficient uniform products – 'world brands'. Yet the available evidence suggests that, though a move to uniform world brands may be an ideal from the multinational capitalist's point of view, it is likely to be realised in only a few instances. Sinclair, for example, suggests that transnational advertising must consider the 'cultural defences' of its target market and adapt the strategy accordingly:

> Indeed an awareness of cultural differences may become decisive in oligopolistic markets of the kind which transnational consumer goods manufacturers have already created in many countries of the world. As one economist points out, 'When global competition is driven by scale economies, at a certain point everyone gets equalized . . . the competitive advantage will go to the companies that are sensitive to individual market developments'. . . . Accordingly, we can find very few products which are true world brands, 'manufactured, packaged and positioned in roughly the same manner worldwide, regardless of individual economies, cultures and life styles'.[31]

The logic of capitalist competition may therefore point to other cultural outcomes than homogenisation in the crudest form. As Sinclair argues, even the most aggressively international brands like Coca-Cola, Marlboro and McDonald's take trouble to identify with the salient cultural features of their target markets. The results of these marketing strategies may be to insert the messages of advertisements into the connotational strings which make up the (already problematic) stocks of knowledge that constitute 'national cultural identity'. As an example of this, Sinclair cites the slogan of a campaign in the 1970s by General Motors to sell their Holden cars in Australia, by appealing to their essential 'Australianness': 'Football, meat pies, kangaroos and Holden cars. They go together under southern stars.' This slogan was merely an 'expedient translation' of one for General Motors in the United States: 'Baseball, hot dogs, apple pie and Chevrolet. They go together in the good old USA.' Sinclair comments:

> This example illustrates how audiences have no way of knowing when an appeal which seems to address them in their own national vernacular is in fact just a version of a global campaign, and makes it clear that there are more insidious strategies in global marketing than the world brand.[32]

If we ask why this sort of 'colonisation' of national cultural identity by commodities should seem dangerous – remembering the 'imaginary' nature of such identity in the first place (Chapter 3) – it is probably because some deeper transformation of the culture is supposed. The cultural practices of 'consumerism', rather than simply the 'commercialisation' of national symbols, are the supposed threat.

So, what is wrong with consumerism? Before we can answer this we need to see that the threat can be posed in two ways. One way is simply to take consumer culture as it exists in the West and subject this to criticism: if our consumer culture is deplorable, it is plainly wrong that it should be spread via the spread of capitalism. This argument, which sounds a lot simpler than it turns out to be, will be the subject of the following section. Another set of arguments refers to the *uneven* way in which the culture of capitalism spreads around the globe. We saw that the dependency theorists point to the divisive effects of multinational capitalism on dependent economies in the Third World. These include the creation of an 'incorporated' sector tied to multinational production and enjoying some of the benefits of 'consumerism', and a 'marginalised' sector doomed to poverty. These arguments remain largely on the economic level, though the cultural consequences of this economic imperialism are at least clear for the 'culture of poverty' of the marginalised sector. But there are other more directly 'cultural' arguments about combined and uneven development, for example Hamelink's discussion of the promotion of milk powders in the Third World. Though his main argument concerns 'cultural synchronisation', Hamelink provides a good general example of arguments about the *differential* effects of 'consumer culture' and in particular about the effects of transnational advertising in the Third World.

Among Hamelink's objections to the advertising practices of the transnational corporations are (a) that they aim to exploit economically; (b) that they deliberately deceive and manipulate their audience in the Third World; and (c) that they introduce commodities which are undesirable in themselves and in the process suppress better 'traditional' products. There is an element of truth in all these charges, but there is also a danger, in pressing them incautiously, of sliding towards the 'paternalist' position of the critique of 'false consciousness' or, worse, of a romanticised 'anti-modernism'.

Hamelink argues his case in relation to a limited number of consumer products but, to his credit, he chooses some – pharmaceuticals, baby food – that might appear to be undisputed 'goods'. Pharmaceuticals cannot plausibly be seen as the frivolous indulgences of a consumer culture. They seem, superficially at least, to be some of the major fruits of capitalist development, commodities which address basic human needs. They are also clearly an important category since they represent huge potential profits for Western multinationals in the markets of the Third World. One immediate criticism is that these products exploit this market at a basic economic level. Hamelink suggests that not only are the branded products of the multinationals often grossly overpriced, but advertising for them makes misleading claims about their effectiveness over 'generic' drugs:

> Supported by extensive advertising campaigns, products are sold that falsely claim to have a quality superior to products lacking trademarks. As a consequence of these campaigns, the primary target audience, the medical doctors, get very little objective, reliable information.[33]

The aggressive marketing of expensive branded pharmaceuticals that have a much cheaper 'generic' equivalent is a familiar practice in the developed world and one which has pretty clear ethical implications, related in the last instance to the question of whether health care should be in the domain of the capitalist market. The situation in the Third World is more problematic, given the more immediate threats of serious illness often present, and the relative (sometimes absolute) poverty of the mass of the population. There is more at stake in the deceitful 'hyping' of drugs where their cost represents a much higher proportion of personal income. Hamelink is quite correct in criticising the practices of advertising for sheer misinformation aimed at profit. But there are other arguments about the 'vulnerability' of Third World populations to advertising, some of which avoid the imputation of false consciousness while others don't. Sinclair summarises some of these:

> A number of plausible reasons have been suggested as to why we might expect the marginalised of the Third World to be particularly at risk from the influence of advertising: the vulnerabilities arising from their illiteracy and poverty, their lack of experience with consumer goods, and the absence of legal controls on marketing.[34]

The last case – lack of legal controls on marketing – seems a convincing one: it would take a pretty determined libertarian to argue that no legal constraints should be made on advertising, and in the West there are elaborate insitutional arrangements to try to ensure that advertising claims are 'legal, decent, honest and truthful', in the well-known words of the British Advertising Standards Authority. Whatever one's view of the final significance of such institutional-legal arrangements to consumer culture as a whole, it cannot be denied that the relative absence of such constraints in Third World states puts the consumer at a disadvantage, if only in terms of the risk of deliberately false claims by advertisers. Similarly, the argument about the vulnerability arising from illiteracy has an obvious force when understood in terms of the lack of direct information about the qualities and effective uses of commodities.

But the claim about the lack of experience with consumer goods introduces some problems. It could be argued that what is at stake here is simply another dimension of potential 'misinformation': generations of experience of consumer capitalism in the West have taught us to be suspicious of the more enthusiastic claims of advertisers, perhaps to expect less than is promised, to have a certain resistance to the 'hard sell'. It could be claimed that Western culture has built up stocks of common knowledge which enable its members to handle advertising in a more 'informed' way. The claim about lack of experience in Third World cultures could be interpreted as simple lack of 'practice' in interacting with advertising. If the relationship between advertiser and target audience is imagined as a 'struggle' over definitions of needs, it could be argued that the cultural resources are less fairly distributed in this struggle in the Third World than in the West. Nor should this surprise us, since it follows a similar pattern of unequal distribution of all other resources between the First and Third World. So relative lack of experience of consumer culture can be seen as producing 'vulnerability'. But there is the risk of paternalism if we stretch this claim to an argument that we in the West 'know better' the needs of other cultures than the members of those cultures.

There are points in Hamelink's argument which risk just such a paternalism. For example, in his discussion of the marketing of pharmaceuticals, he claims that advertising has lured people away from more effective 'traditional remedies':

> In Bolivia, for example, advertising for Alka-Seltzer has increased sales, even though there are more effective and cheaper alternatives, such as mint tea. In many areas of Peru, the population is thoroughly convinced that anything bought in the pharmacy has to be better than natural products. Every self-respecting family has Aspro, which they use with less knowledge and more unpleasant side effects than they do the naturally occurring medicines.[35]

The danger with this sort of argument is that it can easily slide from the (valid) critique of misinformation by the advertisers towards the view that populations in the Third World need 'protection' since they are unable to recognise their own true interests. After all, the majority of Westerners probably prefer products like Aspro and Alka-Seltzer to 'natural remedies', so why should these choices be thought odd or 'mistaken' when made by people in the Third World? There are two answers implicit in Hamelink's argument: first, that such choices are economically less rational for the Third World – 'consumption patterns are being created that lead to a wasteful spending of what little is available';[36] and second, that the ready availability of equal or better natural alternatives make choice of manufactures unnecessary. But the problem with both answers is that they unavoidably impute a degree of 'irrational' false consciousness, not simply lack of information, to the Third World consumer. For one must presume that the continued choice of manufactured pharmaceuticals has some relation to the experience of their effects – if not, one really is imputing irrationality! So it would seem that the reason Third World consumers prefer manufactures is that they experience them as being more effective – that is, their experience is precisely the same as the common one in the West. This does not imply that the manufactures *are* more effective: the experience may be simply in terms of the *speed* of effect, and the argument about side effects may well be a valid one. Nevertheless no real distinction can be made between the perception of interests here in the case of Third or First World consumers.

The general problem with Hamelink's argument here – and it is one typical of concerned criticism of cultural 'exploitation' in both the developed and the 'underdeveloped' world – is that it exceeds a legitimate criticism of an agent's understanding of her or his true interests. This is the sense in which it imputes an irrational false consciousness. What can we say about an agent's true interests? The range of knowledge involved here has been discussed by Raymond Geuss in relation to the general claims of the 'critical theorists' of the Frankfurt School, with whom the elaboration of an ideology-critique in relation to true and false interests is most closely associated. Geuss argues that one way of conceiving of an agent's true interests is as those desires she or he would develop and choices she or he would make in the hypothetical condition of 'perfect knowledge':

What does this 'perfect knowledge' comprise? Presumably it must include at least all empirical knowledge of the kind that can be provided by the sciences, but does it include such things as the kind of self-knowledge acquired in psychoanalysis, or knowledge of what would satisfy me? Do I know my real interests if I have available 'perfect' empirical knowledge, but have not used it to reflect correctly on my present wants and interests so as to make them consistent? If the Marquis de Sade had had the final Intergalactic edition of the Encyclopaedia Britannica at his disposal would what he then pursued have been his 'true' interests?[37]

Geuss's conclusion is that 'perfect knowledge' would have to include more than simple empirical knowledge: it would have to run to all the subjective insights and value judgements that comprise an agent's sense of 'the good life'. As Geuss admits, to invoke the hypothetical condition of 'perfect knowledge' is 'already to enter the realm of science fiction',[38] which is to say that none of us is ever in a position fully to know our own interests. The point is that knowing one's true interests always involves more than simple 'empirical knowledge'.

Taking Hamelink's instance of the overpricing of branded pharmaceuticals, we could safely say that it is in the interests of an agent not to buy such goods where an equal, cheaper alternative is available. What is central is simply *information* about the products, and the critic can legitimately say that the agent may not understand her or his own interests if she or he lacks this information. Hence the critique of misinformation in advertising is valid. This does not mean that the agent necessarily acts against her interests in every case where, possessing the information on pricing, she chooses the more expensive version, for there may be other factors involved. The convenience in obtaining the branded product, for example, or the disinclination to 'shop around' (although the second is more likely to arise in more affluent cultures). So the critic needs to take into account quite a wide range of factors before attribution of false consciousness (misunderstanding of true interests) can be made on the observation of behaviour.

Hamelink's discussion of the consumption of Aspro or Alka-Seltzer ignores just this range of factors and implies an irrationality in these choices which is difficult to sustain. For here we are not dealing with simple questions of information as in the case of pricing, but with much more complex 'knowledge' of the effects of these products. In what conditions could it be said that the agent choosing Alka-Seltzer as against mint tea does not understand his own interests? Well, perhaps in the case that the mint tea is cheaper, equally or more effective, and readily available. But all this hangs on the issue of 'effectivity' which, as I suggested, involves a complex 'psychosomatic' experience which is extremely hard to untangle.

Hamelink oversimplifies the case by implying that agents' interests follow from conditions we can identify empirically. For example, he claims that the needs of poor people in the Third World are somehow 'empirically' distinct from the satisfactions offered by the multinationals:

A cultural system which would be adequate for the poorest people in that system would mean a set of instrumental, symbolic and social relations that help them to *survive* in meeting such fundamental needs as food, clothing, housing, medical treatment and education. Such needs are not met if they are identified with the consumption of Kentucky Fried Chicken, Coca-Cola, Aspro, or Peter Stuyvesant cigarettes.[39]

What is being claimed here is that the 'needs', and hence the interests, of poor people in the Third World are obvious – so obvious that we can identify them from the outside and declare that 'they are not met if they are identified with the consumption of Kentucky Fried Chicken', etc. What is *intended* is an attack on the aggressive marketing of the multinationals, but what necessarily follows from this is the imputation of irrationality or at the very least the excessive malleability of the consumer, for this is what it means to say that people identify their needs with inappropriate consumption choices. Hamelink falls into this trap because he does not allow for the range of reasons why people should choose the products of the multinationals even in the face of their 'objective conditions' of poverty. To give just one instance, the social cachet of smoking American cigarettes may outweigh for some people the 'prudential' choice of spending limited resources on a 'healthy diet', if the latter means just an extension of life at subsistence level while the former brings with it the immediate rewards of some form of social regard. What are involved are simply different conceptions of 'the good life': Hamelink may disagree with one of these conceptions but, speaking from outside, he is in no position to judge it mistaken.

I need to stress that I am not contesting Hamelink's view of the 'objective' material conditions of people in the Third World. These I think are obvious, as is their connection with the exploitative arrangements of global capitalism. But I am contesting the idea that an 'adequate cultural system' can be identified for people in these material conditions of poverty in the sense he employs – that is, one that 'protects' them from their own 'misguided' choices. We can agree that people in the Third World may be more 'vulnerable' to marketing pressure in that they have few legal constraints on misinformation and less experience of the particular 'language game' of advertising. But what we can't do, without risking paternalism, is legislate on the 'true interests' of people in the Third World. This is particularly so, given that the choices we might judge 'misguided' are precisely those routinely made by agents in the West who have much more general experience and background knowledge at their disposal: pharmaceuticals in preference to 'natural' remedies, 'junk food', tobacco etc. What this latter consideration should suggest and what I shall presently argue, is that the critique of consumerist penetration of the Third World cannot be separated from the critique of consumerism in the West.

I do not for a moment think that Hamelink's intention is to impute irrationality to agents in the Third World. Part of the reason why he ends up doing this is bound up with the logic of arguments about the manipulative power of advertising – which are of the same order as arguments about the ideological power of the media generally (Chapter 2). There is another reason why his well-meaning critique is pushed in this paternalist direction, and that is the underlying sense that what the West has to offer is not, generally, worth having: junk food, junk television, tobacco, a routine dependence on manufactured analgesics, bottle-feeding as against breast-feeding, and so on. The implication is that we should criticise modern capitalist culture as it exists in the West: that is in terms of its claim, to quote Herbert Marcuse, 'to deliver the goods'. But this isn't really what Hamelink does; instead he conflates these criticisms with his claims about the 'adequate cultural system' of Third World societies and this conflation tugs towards a sort of 'anti-modernity' by proxy. It is as though the Third World is attributed with a special need and even a special *responsibility* to resist the enticements of an ersatz commodified culture. They have mint tea and the 'natural' cultural practices of breast-feeding; they are, somehow, closer to the 'basic needs' that we have lost with affluence. Therefore we should look to their 'innocence' as the hope of our own cultural salvation – *this* is why they need 'protection'. This is the thin end of a wedge which ends in the romanticism of the Western counter-cultural identification with the Third World in the 1960s and 1970s, the view, as Sinclair describes it,

> that Third World countries should defend the natural innocence of their traditional values against corrupting incursions by Western 'materialism'. To the extent that this view romanticised wretchedness, conflated all non-Western cultures and patronised genuine Third World aspirations for material improvement, we would not regard it as tenable today.[40]

I am not accusing Hamelink of 'romanticising wretchedness' but I do think that we need to be very careful in the formulation of critiques of the impact of consumerism on 'underdeveloped' cultures if we are to avoid the unfortunate 'romantic' implications of the polarisation of the natural and traditional with the artificial and modern.

There is a constant temptation for the Western cultural critic to displace their own cultural dilemmas on to concern for other cultures. This was something identified, in a slightly different context, by Claude Lévi-Strauss in a chapter of his book *Tristes Tropiques* which he entitled 'A Little Glass of Rum'. Lévi-Strauss is concerned here with the problem of the anthropologist's ambiguous relation to his own culture and the one he chooses to study. The enthusiasm for the values of alien cultures which he says is common amongst anthropologists is often 'a function of his distain for, and occasionally hostility towards, the customs prevailing in his native setting'.[41] If this is true of anthropologists, how much more so for Western critics of cultural imperialism! Lévi-Strauss tells a story about his visits to the rum distilleries of Martinique and Puerto Rico:

> In Martinique I had visited rustic and neglected rum-distilleries where the equipment and the methods used had not changed since the eighteenth century. In Puerto Rico, on the other hand, in factories of the company which enjoys a virtual

monopoly over the whole of the sugar production, I was faced by a display of white enamel tanks and chromium piping. Yet the various kinds of Martinique rum, as I tasted them in front of ancient vats thickly encrusted with waste matter, were mellow and scented, whereas those of Puerto Rico were coarse and harsh. We may suppose, then, that the subtlety of the Martinique rum is dependent on impurities the continuance of which is encouraged by the archaic method of production.[42]

Lévi-Strauss takes this contrast as a metaphor for the 'paradox of civilisation':

> its charms are due essentially to the various residues it carries along with it, although this does not absolve us of the obligation to purify the stream. By being doubly right, we are admitting our mistake. We are right to be rational and to try to increase our production, and so to keep manufacturing costs down. But we are also right to cherish those very imperfections we are endeavouring to eliminate. Social life consists in destroying that which gives it its savour.[43]

We do not have to agree with every implication of Lévi-Strauss's parable to see that there are contradictions in capitalist modernity which are difficult to escape for those who enjoy its conveniences whilst lamenting its lack of 'savour'. The contemplation of a different culture allows us the sense of escape from these contradictions:

> We ourselves are caught up in the evolution of our own society and are, in a sense, interested parties. We are not in a position not to will those things which our situation forces us to carry into effect; when we are dealing with foreign societies, everything is different: the objectivity which was impossible in the first instance is freely granted to us. Since we are no longer agents but spectators in the transformations which are taking place, we are all the better able to compare and evaluate their future and their past, since these remain subjects for aesthetic contemplation and intellectual reflection, instead of being brought home to us in the form of mental anxiety.[44]

The significant sense in which we are 'interested parties' in our own society's evolution is that of our ambiguous relation to our own 'consumer culture'. The critique of it cannot extend to a complete rejection of it either theoretically (since we are part of it and it of us) or practically, since we depend on it for our survival and for many of our satisfactions. Even the most dedicated anti-modern movements of the counter-culture of Western societies are caught up in contradictions. As Cornelias Castoriadis has observed: 'There is scarcely any community without taped music; and a tape recorder implies the totality of modern industry'.[45] We need to avoid the critique of cultural imperialism becoming a *pretext* for a certain disingenuous critique of our own culture, a critique which wants to have its cultural cake and eat it.

All these considerations suggest certain limits on the critique of consumerist penetration of the Third World. While we can agree that there are genuine material-cultural effects arising from the combined and uneven development of global capitalism – the most important being the poverty it inflicts on vast numbers in dependent societies – we are simply not in a position to deny the attractions consumer culture may have for other cultures unless and until we have established a coherent critique of our *own* consumer culture.

Consumer culture in the West: 'euphoria in unhappiness'

For about the last forty years, analyses of the culture of capitalism have placed the cultural practice of *consumption* at the centre. This is easy to understand, for in a sense the production of more and more goods to be consumed is all capitalism is about. 'Delivering the cultural goods' in a capitalist society is essentially about placing as many cultural experiences as possible in the market-place, putting a price on them and generating profits from them. This is not widely disputed: even defenders of the capitalist system agree that consumption is the cultural *telos* of capitalism as an economic system. To give just one example, in *The Stages of Economic Growth*, an influential text of the modernisation theory school of development studies of the 1960s, W.W. Rostow referred approvingly to the final stage of development of capitalist modernity – a development he saw as the common future of all societies – as 'The Era of High Mass Consumption'.[46]

The point is not the simple fact of a high level of consumption in developed capitalist societies, but the cultural significance of this. If we want to maintain some distinction between the levels of analysis of the 'economic' and the 'cultural' we might say that generally the activities of production and consumption belong to the former and the phenomenon of 'consumerism' belongs to the latter. The virtue of such a distinction is that it allows us to focus on one set of arguments whilst 'bracketing' some rather closely connected ones.

Critics of capitalism who stress its economic inequities (its differential access to consumption) or who object to the damaging ecological consequences of its drive towards 'growth' (the consequences of mass consumption) are speaking, broadly, on the level of the economic. This level addresses the control, concentration, distribution, and use of material resources. Critics speaking on the level of the cultural are those whose concern is more directly with the *experience of living* in capitalist society – with the meanings people attach to the practices of consumption, and with the significance of such practices for people's sense of purpose, happiness, identity, and so on. This rough and ready distinction fails to account for a lot of difficult issues, but it allows us to focus on some of the most significant arguments about capitalist culture as the ambiguous 'gift' offered to the developing world. All human beings in all cultures consume: what is at stake in the idea of 'consumer culture' or of 'consumerism' is a culture whose *central preoccupation* seems to be that of consuming.

Why do cultural critics object to consumerism? Even with the distinction I have made between economic and cultural arguments, this is still a long and complicated story. Rather than attempting to summarise all the arguments, I shall organise the discussion around a number of general objections that might be raised against a hypothetical 'traditional culture' following the path of development that Schiller speaks of (Chapter 2) towards the 'consumer culture' of capitalism.

'Moralising criticism'

In his book *The Minimal Self*, Christopher Lasch refers to a speech made by President Carter in 1979 in which the president 'attributed the national "malaise" to the spirit of self-seeking and the pursuit of "things" '.[47] As Lasch says, this is to treat consumerism as 'a kind of moral lapse' rather than as a set of cultural practices intimately related to the capitalist production in which we are all caught up. Carter's 'moralistic indictment' was, of course, from the liberal-right of politics. As such it was open to the criticism of being either hypocritical or contradictory in attacking the culture of consumerism whilst defending the economic system that encourages it. But Carter did express, and probably in good faith, a conventional attitude with deep cultural roots – that there is something *essentially* wrong with the pursuit of consumer goods. In what sense could this moral intuition be true?

I think it could be true in so far as the absorption with buying and possessing things might make people less concerned with the needs of others, in a word, more selfish. It by no means necessarily follows that an affluent consumer culture will be more selfish than any other sort of culture. One famous example of a 'culture of selfishness' suggests that, just the reverse of affluent consumerism' a state of extreme material deprivation may lead to general patterns of selfishness. This is the description given by the anthropologist Colin Turnbull of the Ik people living on the Uganda/Kenya border.[48] Living in a state verging on starvation, the Ik developed habits and attitudes which would seem to most people in affluent capitalist culture almost inexplicable in their extreme selfishness. They not only jealously guarded their own food, but stole it from children, the old (including their own parents) and the ill. They also seemed to find amusement in the hunger and suffering of others.

What does this example suggest? That deprivation rather than affluence is a more likely cause of a generalised selfishness in a culture? Saying this places us in a rather tricky moral position, for we may end up by claiming that we in the affluent West are better people – less selfish – than the Ik, simply because of our better material circumstances. If we resist this rather self-satisfied conclusion, as I think we should, then the most we could say is that we are 'morally luckier' than the Ik, in not being placed in the way of extreme selfish behaviour of the Icien variety by force of material circumstances.

But where does this leave the idea of 'selfishness'? Surely as behaviour which has to be assessed *relative* to the material circumstances of a culture. We can recognise selfish behaviour within our own culture, according to our own cultural standards. But we normally think of something which stops short of laughing at the plight of dying relatives – this we would call not selfish but pathological. And we might shrink from calling the behaviour of the Ik 'pathological' when seen in the context of their extremes of deprivation. So it is very difficult to speak of a society, affluent or deprived, producing more or less 'general selfishness'. Are the capitalist cultures of the West more generally selfish than those of the Third World or of the (fast disappearing) planned economies of the East? It's very difficult to say. The claim that a consumer culture is one that encourages selfishness is rather hard to uphold.

This does not mean that no moral judgement can be made about consumer cultures. For example, the objective situation of the affluence and waste of the capitalist West in the face of the poverty and need of the Third World seems to me to be obviously morally wrong. But I can make this moral judgement without being drawn into difficult speculation about comparative selfishness.

There are other aspects to the moral intuition that the 'pursuit of "things" ' is wrong in itself, and one of these is the moral suspicion of 'material' over 'spiritual' satisfactions. This is an intuition with its roots (in the West) in certain versions of Christian theology. Now some people do take a moral attitude towards consumption practices which is directly informed by religious conviction. This sort of attitude may lie on a continuum from the rational-ethical at one end to the puritanism of strict fundamentalist sects at the other. But what is behind most of these particular (and limited) attitudes is a broader sense of the transcendent value of the spiritual over the material aspects of human life. It is this which is more widely and shallowly distributed across the largely secular culture of the West. The traces of a mistrust of the satisfactions of the body over the 'spirit' are to be found in the common accusation that capitalist culture is too 'materialistic'. For what does it mean to be 'materialistic' in this sense, other than to be concerned, in a way judged morally wrong, with the satisfactions and comforts of the body? Materialism should not be (though it frequently is) confused with other moral judgements like greed or 'selfishness'. It is explicitly concerned with the rectitude of an *ontological* preference: summed up in the Christian claim that 'Man does not live by bread alone.'

It becomes plain, then, why the moral charge of excessive materialism presents big problems for Marxist critics of capitalist culture. For (most) Marxists claim to be 'materialists' in the sense of rejecting religious and other 'spiritual' views of the human condition as mere ideology – as 'idealism' in a similar pejorative sense as (some) Christians use the term 'materialism'. This point is summed up nicely by the Marxist critic Raymond Williams:

It is often said that our society is too materialist, and that advertising reflects this. We are in a phase of a relatively rapid distribution of what are called 'consumer goods', and advertising, with its emphasis on 'bringing the good things of life', is taken as central for this reason. But it seems to me that in this respect our society is quite evidently not materialist enough, and that this, paradoxically, is the result of a failure in social meanings, values and ideals. . . . If we were sensibly materialist, in that part of our living in which we use things, we should find most advertising to be of an insane irrelevance.[49]

Williams's underlying point is that the measure of the good of a culture should be related to its ability to satisfy 'real needs'. Though this brings its own problems, at least it is clear that the Marxist objection to 'anti-materialist' moralism is that it disguises these real needs in a cloak of 'other-worldly' values. To be a materialist in the Marxist sense is to reject these values on the grounds that they have, historically, been used to legitimate oppression, or at least to recommend toleration of material inequalities in the hope of a heavenly reward, 'Pie-in-the-Sky'. As Marx puts it in *The German Ideology*, social values should spring from the 'real material condition' of human beings, and not 'descend from heaven to earth'.[50]

So the moral critique of consumerism which trades on an 'anti-materialism' is full of ideological pitfalls for Marxists, and we shall see that it is possible to fall into these whilst pursuing quite different lines of critique from the overtly 'moralising'. There is a danger of left critiques of consumerism tugging towards a sort of puritanism almost by default, out of a broad distaste for the irrationality of capitalist waste and consumer excess. This danger was grasped nicely by the Frankfurt School theorist Max Horkheimer: 'Whenever sociologists inveigh against egotism what they actually want is to talk people out of their happiness.'[51] The implication is that a critique of consumerism should focus on human satisfactions, not on ascesis.

Not all moral critiques of consumerism are of this anti-materialist bent; there are, for example, the quite independent moral judgements about the wrongness of waste or of inequality. Marxists and any other rational critics necessarily take a moral position on issues like these. But the distinction between a moral critique and a *moralising* one is that the latter rests on moral assumptions that are ideologically suspect. This suspicion of the ideological function of established moral codes has led some Marxists to dismiss any moral judgement as hopelessly ideological: a position which I think is both mistaken and incoherent.[52] Yet we certainly cannot afford to take any moral position for granted – and this is the real danger of 'moralising' criticism. The need to scrutinise moral premises is even more apparent when we consider our main concern: the objections to consumer culture that might be raised, as it were, on behalf of cultures being led down this road. For objections of the 'anti-materialist' sort will clearly cut little ice here, being premised on moral-religious systems (for example the Judaeo-Christian) which may be quite alien to other cultures. The fine irony would be to commit one form of cultural imperialism in the attempt to avoid another.

Critical Theory and consumerism

The critique of consumerism has been broached from many different neo-Marxist positions: the British 'culturalist' position associated with Raymond Williams; the French 'Arguments' group, most notably the work of Henri Lefebvre; the poststructuralism of Althusser and more recently Baudrillard; by Freudo-Marxists such as Michael Schneider and by many other independent thinkers of the left: Wolfgang Haug, Stuart Ewen, Hans-Magnus Enzenberger and others.[53] It is probably true to say that the ideas of the Frankfurt School Critical Theorists – Theodor Adorno, Max Horkheimer, and particularly Herbert Marcuse – have been the most widely influential. They do, at least, bring us to the hub of the problems of criticising a cultural practice which enjoys at least a superficial popularity, and it is on their approach that I shall focus here.

The Frankfurt School's critique of consumerism is sometimes understood as part of a more general theory of 'incorporation', whereby the working classes are seduced by the superficial attractions of the culture of capitalism into acceptance of the terms of its economic structure: their subordinated and exploited class position. Associated with this view is the belief that their position rests on the problematic notion of the 'false consciousness' of the masses and the manipulative power of the media or, as Horkheimer and Adorno put it in a much-cited article, 'The Culture Industry'.[54] There are places in the output of the Frankfurt School where a false consciousness in consumers seems to be implied, and we shall consider one well-known example of this presently. But it has to be said at the outset that to treat Critical Theory as simply and solely a version of the false consciousness thesis is seriously to misinterpret it. Its political and intellectual project needs to be seen in terms of the use of reason (in its broadest sense) in the emancipation of agents from social domination.[55] 'Emancipation' may involve freeing agents from ideological delusion but this is not all that it implies. To put matters briefly, the mistake often made is to read the Critical Theorists simply as critics of ideology, when their much more subtle approach relates to domination at many levels of social and cultural practice.[56]

The central argument of the Frankfurt theorists vis-à-vis consumerism is therefore not the 'incorporation thesis' (which, incidentally, would not qualify as a cultural theory but as the sort of functionalist, 'culture as tool of capitalism' argument we considered earlier), but the contention that consumerism is part of a broader oppressive 'totality' of capitalism. The idea of a capitalist 'totality', and even of the 'totalitarianism' of capitalism, is most famously described in Herbert Marcuse's book, *One-Dimensional Man*. Marcuse's central argument about consumerism here is contained in his discussion of 'true and false needs'. Because this distinction has been at the centre of so much argument about consumerism, and because it has been taken to imply a widespread false consciousness in people in capitalist cultures, it is worth quoting the relevant passage at some length:

We may distinguish both true and false needs. 'False' are those which are superimposed upon the individual by particular social interests in his repression: the needs which perpetuate toil, aggressiveness, misery and injustice. Their satisfaction might be most gratifying to the individual, but his happiness is not a condition which has to be maintained and protected if it serves to arrest the ability (his own and others) to recognize the disease of the whole and grasp the chances of curing the disease. The result then is euphoria in unhappiness. Most of the prevailing needs to relax, to have fun, to behave and consume in accordance with the advertisements, to love and hate what others love and hate, belong to this category of false needs.

Such needs have a societal content and function which are determined by external powers over which the individual has no control; the development and satisfaction of these needs is heteronomous. No matter how much such needs may have become the individual's own, reproduced and fortified by the conditions of his existence; no matter how much he identifies himself with them and finds himself in their satisfaction, they continue to be what they were from the beginning – products of a society whose dominant interest demands repression.[57]

Whatever its flaws, this is direct criticism of capitalist *culture*, not a displacement of cultural criticism on to the supposed functionality of culture in the class struggle. Marcuse is making claims about the experience of life in capitalist culture and these are not claims based on a moralising criticism but on the *falsity* of the satisfactions offered by consumerism. But it is here that Marcuse's critics accuse him of attributing false consciousness: to speak of true and false needs and to suggest that the broad practices of mass culture belong to the latter category seems to imply this. Alasdair MacIntyre, one of Marcuse's sternest critics, puts the matter bluntly, '. . . how has Marcuse acquired the right to say to others what their true needs are?'[58] Marcuse's claims about the 'one-dimensional' nature of modern capitalism lead inevitably, argues MacIntyre, to an 'elitism' in which the critical theorist exempts his own analysis from the general thesis of social manipulation. Critical Theory thus claims a privileged position in relation to social reality.

MacIntyre does scant justice to the subtlety with which the Critical Theorists approached the problem of a rational grounding of their theory, but he obviously has a point when it comes to the problem of legislating for other people's needs. The 'sovereignty' of individual needs is a very strong card in the liberal pack, since 'needs' are in large part a matter of what an individual experiences, and it is difficult to maintain the claim that someone is mistaken about their own experience, except in quite narrow terms. We can reasonably say someone is mistaken about their needs if they are simply unaware of, say, their body's needs for certain vitamins and minerals and thus maintain an inadequate diet. Similarly, if someone believes that drinking a bottle of gin a day is a healthy practice, we may say they are labouring under a misapprehension about the relationship of this experience to their *interests* in health. Such examples of delusion are really simply cases of lack of appropriate information. However the really contentious issues of false consciousness arise where there is an attempt to speak for either the 'raw experience' or the 'life goals' of others.

In the case of the gin drinker, if he knows the consequences of his actions and still maintains that he 'needs' his daily bottle, it becomes difficult to contradict him. For to do so would involve either denying his experience or enforcing one set of 'life goals' – the maintenance of health and prolonging of life – over another – the immediate, short-term satisfaction of a craving. Short of denying that the drinker is, in the condition of his craving, a rational agent, we have to grant that cirrhosis of the liver may be a valid existential choice. For what, ultimately, is the transcendent value of a long healthy abstemious life over a short one? If this value seems obvious to us it is not because health and long life are universal and unchallengeable goals, but simply because they are *widely shared* goals.[59]

At the centre of the liberal argument about the sovereignty of needs, then, is the insight that needs are always related to certain goals or endstates, and that these endstates ultimately suppose different versions of 'the good life'. In most cases relevant to arguments about consumerism, the ill effects of consumption are far less obvious than in the limited case of a craving for alcohol. To try to suggest that agents are mistaken about either their experienced needs for a range of consumer goods like televisions, microwave ovens, cars, hi-fi sets and fashionable clothes, or about the 'life goals' that these needs represent, is a short route to paternalist social philosophy. The fact that this doctrine of sovereignty is extremely convenient to the proponents of the capitalist market system has caused some critics of capitalism to be suspicious of its ideological content, but it remains, nonetheless, a fairly compelling argument. Marcuse recognised the claims of the sovereignty of needs:

> In the last analysis, the question of what are true and false needs can only be answered by the individuals themselves, but only in the last analysis; that is, if and when they are free to give their own answer. As long as they are kept incapable of being autonomous, as long as they are indoctrinated and manipulated (down to their very instincts), their answer to this question cannot be taken as their own. By the same token, however, no tribunal can arrogate to itself the right to decide which needs should be developed and satisfied.[60]

Marcuse has an answer to some of the liberal charges: he agrees that individual needs cannot be legislated for and that, finally, the individual is the expert on her or his own experience. But he still maintains that people in capitalist culture lack the *autonomy* to make proper judgements about their needs. In arguing that people should be autonomous Marcuse is still well within the bounds of liberal political thought. The problem is that the false consciousness thesis seems to arise again where he claims that people lack autonomy. Clearly Marcuse's claim about lack of autonomy cannot be sustained at the ideological, and even less at the 'depth psychological' level at which he pitches it here. Bryan Turner puts the problem in relation to critiques of consumerism generally:

> Much recent analysis of consumption is in this respect largely negative (Baudrillard,

1975; Lefebvre, 1971; Marcuse, 1964); modern consumption is seen to produce a passive, subordinated population which is no longer able to realize its 'real' needs. . . . The critique of consumerism is thus a version of the dominant ideology thesis . . . in which consumers are uniformly incorporated by all commodities. It is simply not the case that consumers inevitably absorb the meanings and purpose of mass advertisements.[61]

Turner is right to say that the ideological power of consumerism is massively overstated by its critics and Marcuse can certainly be faulted on this point. The danger of this sort of ideological attribution is that it risks misrepresenting human agency, casting people as 'cultural dopes'. Even sympathetic critics of Marcuse, such as Douglas Kellner, recognise these problems. Kellner goes further in arguing that it is precisely the 'totalising' tendency in Marcuse's approach that is at fault:

For global critical theories of the commodity, *all* commodities are *uniformly* seductive instruments of capitalist manipulation. . . . There is both a manichaeism and a puritanism in this perspective. Commodities are pictured as evil tools of class domination and a covert distinction is often made between (bad) exchange value and (good) use value. . . . It assumes that when individuals submit to (bad) consumerism they are weak, malleable and deficient as human beings (or at least Marxists) – precisely the Puritan attitude toward sex and pleasure.[62]

Kellner is well aware that Marcuse's general position is far removed from anything which could be called 'puritanism'. The point he makes is that the failure in Marcuse's 'totalising' critique to discriminate between more or less enjoyable, satisfying and 'autonomous' forms of consumption pushes him in the direction of a sort of 'puritan' condemnation of all modern purchasable pleasures. This tendency is structured into the logic of the 'true/false needs' distinction, for Marcuse is almost obliged to offer examples of 'true needs' and these inevitably turn out to be very basic ones: 'The only needs that have an unqualified claim for satisfaction are the vital ones – nourishment, clothing, lodging at the attainable level of culture.'[63]

Marcuse is frequently misinterpreted as arguing that 'true needs' are only these rather austere basic physiological requirements. This is not what he is saying; he says these are the only needs which have an *unqualified* claim to satisfaction. What he means is that the satisfaction of these basic needs is the only one which we can be reasonably sure doesn't involve some ideological manipulation: in satisfying the basic physiological needs of the body we can be fairly certain we are acting 'autonomously'. So it is the ideological suspicion implicit in his 'totalising' theory of 'one-dimensional' capitalist culture which seems to push Marcuse towards an apparent puritanism in his catalogue of 'true needs'.

The inference Kellner draws is that we need to be more discriminating in our criticism of consumer goods. He wants to retain Marcuse's 'true' and 'false' needs distinction but to introduce more detailed and specific criteria for the 'falsity' involved. Thus he suggests that the critique of consumerism needs to begin with a scrutiny of actual individual commodities:

> If a commodity after critical scrutiny, reveals itself to be life enhancing, truly useful, well constructed, and fairly priced, then a need for it can be said to be a 'true need'. If the commodity fails to offer the satisfactions promised, if it is not beneficial, life-enhancing and useful, but, rather needless, poorly constructed and overpriced, then a need for it can be said to be a 'false need'.[64]

But, as Kellner recognises, things are not quite as simple as this. The value judgements involved in deciding what is 'life enhancing' or 'truly useful' still return us to the problem of the 'sovereign consumer' and her or his degree of critical autonomy: is an electric can-opener 'truly useful'; are personal stereos 'life enhancing'? What is still needed is a way of deciding, or perhaps remembering, what the grounds of cultural satisfaction are within a community. These are major questions which lie far beyond the empirical scrutiny of commodities. But we can scarcely make any useful judgement about the satisfaction of commodities without addressing them. I agree with Kellner that answering these big questions, if it is possible at all (we are, after all, speaking of the meaning of full social happiness), means reaching a form of rational consensus on cultural values. Pursuing this critical project takes us beyond the critique of consumerism and into problems of the rational basis of 'modernity' itself, and this is something which we shall consider in the next chapter.

Kellner's reconstruction of Marcuse's critical theory perhaps raises more questions than it answers. Nonetheless, he is quite right to tackle the problem at this grass-roots level, since, as he says, to speak in the language of 'totalising' theories is simply to preach to the converted. The point of a Critical Theory is to engage with all social agents in a dialogue about their experience, and there is plenty of evidence, not least in the current wide concern with 'green' issues, that people in the West experience the consumer culture as, at least, a mixed blessing.

Kellner ends his paper with a reference to a socialist Third World country, Cuba, which makes the point about the 'tactics' of a Critical Theory in relation to the issue of cultural imperialism. Cubans, he found, were proud of some aspects of their socialist political culture – such as education and health care. But they were unhappy at the 'undeveloped' sphere of consumption – scarcity of consumer goods, long queues in the shops, the general low priority afforded to non-essential consumer goods. In short, the Cubans Kellner spoke to seemed to want a higher level of consumption *within* a socialist economy and culture:

> Although there is certainly no desire in Cuba to model a consumer society on advanced capitalism, there is certainly no hostility toward commodities and consumption. This position tends to be the stance of alienated intellectuals rather than socialist militants. Instead the Cubans, and other socialist societies, see commodities and consumption as integral parts of a socialist society where people's basic needs will actually be fulfilled for the first time in history.[65]

As I write this towards the end of 1989, massive and almost unbelievably rapid political change in the planned socialist economies of Eastern Europe

– the USSR, Poland, Czechoslovakia, East Germany, Romania – lends irresistible weight to the suggestion that people in these societies aspire to a higher level of material consumption. Of course, it is not only the desire for more consumer goods which lies behind these changes and it would be foolish to assume that precisely the same factors were at work in every case. But nor would it be sensible to deny the importance of the desire for the material plenty that is seen as characteristic of life in the West: this is, after all, a good 'materialist' explanation of such historical developments. What is interesting about the changes in the planned socialist societies is that the desire for more consumer goods is linked with the desire for the political freedoms of liberal democracies, but not necessarily with the desire for capitalism. Whether these desires can be achieved without full assimilation into the global capitalist system must remain an open question since in the West, capitalism, liberal democracies and broad relative material affluence have been co-extensive historically. This means we have not experienced one without the others, but it does not at all mean that any one is dependent on the others. Capitalism, certainly, is not the necessary begetter of a liberal political climate, as many examples of repressive capitalist states in the Third World show.[66] Nor does it guarantee a wide and equitable distribution of wealth. It does not follow, then, that any system evolving according to the popular demands for material plenty and political liberty *must* be a capitalist one, even though the pressure from existing global capitalism will clearly push it in this direction. So the mistake of drawing hasty conclusions about events in the Eastern bloc is to see them as necessarily signalling the triumph of capitalism as the 'end of history'.

The obvious rejoinder to any such triumphalism on the part of enthusiasts for capitalism is to point out the many ills that attend the material affluence of developed capitalist societies. We can agree that people desire material goods, and perhaps even that these desires are open-ended, expanding as production expands.[67] But people have other desires: for health, security, freedom from anxiety, and for autonomy (particularly in the way they spend their time). It is by no means clear that capitalist culture delivers these 'goods' with the same efficiency that it delivers consumer goods. The most telling criticisms of capitalist culture are those which reveal the ambiguous context of consumer satisfactions. It is this context that Marcuse points to in his memorable description of the experience of consumerism: 'euphoria in unhappiness'. This phrase, with its echoes of an unresolved Hegelian dialectic, grasps the Critical Theory notion of a social 'totality' in which the available satisfactions always fall short of what agents would choose, in conditions of maximal autonomy. But this cultural context admits of other interpretations than the 'true/false needs' distinction, with all its problems. It can be understood in terms of a broader critique of the *structural* context in which consumer satisfactions are 'bought'. We can conclude this consideration of the critical response to consumer culture by looking briefly at the work of a 'second generation' Critical Theorist, Clauss Offe, who shifts the critique of 'false needs' in just this direction.

Consumption and the structural context of capitalism

Offe's approach to consumer culture stresses the structural differences between this sort of culture and other cultures. The key difference he identifies is that of the *structural differentiation* characteristic of consumer societies. This refers to the processes characteristic of modern societies by which various spheres of life become progressively separated. The most obvious separation is that of domestic life from the sphere of work, a process obviously related to (capitalist) industrialisation and marking one of the most important distinctions of modern industrial societies from 'traditional' societies, in which family life and work form a more integrated cultural pattern. This differentiation extends in modernity to many other spheres: church is separated from state, law from morality, state from civil society, there is a division of labour in the production process and so on. As Offe says, this process has generally been celebrated as the 'opening up' of modern societies to wider possibilities and new liberties: for example the possibility to consume products not produced in the domestic household or the liberty to hold various religious and moral convictions without prejudice from the state. Structural differentiation is often seen, then, as part of the 'rationalising' process of modernity, though there is also a body of thought that maintains this differentiation process has advanced too far in modern societies and has created new problems.

This, Offe maintains, is directly relevant to the analysis of consumption in modern societies, for the concept of 'the consumer' only has meaning within this pattern of differentiation:

> In societies such as our own, the concept of 'consumer' designates an array of actions, interests and situations that are clearly delimited from other interests, situations and actions. In so-called primitive societies, but also in medieval societies divided into estates and, therefore, already affected by the processes of differentiation, the concept of 'consumer' is simply not meaningful. . . . Only modernized social structures, with their differentiated systems of action, make possible relatively clear-cut distinctions between individuals acting 'as' consumers, workers, voters, heads of family and so on.[68]

On this view, the distinctive feature of a consumer culture is not the simple fact of a high level of material consumption, but the fact of the differentiation of the sphere of consumption from other social spheres. This has implications for the critique of consumer culture. In the first place, it turns out that the consumer is in a relatively weak position of power in relation to the other players in the differentiated 'game' of consumption (manufacturers/suppliers and the state) and therefore not generally in a position to command his or her own interests. But it also turns out that the differentiated roles individuals play (as consumer, worker, parent etc.) can determine consumption practices. Offe suggests that structural differentiation can produce 'structurally imposed needs'. What he means is that needs people express on the market (and which are taken, on the liberal reading, as the 'sovereign' felt needs of agents) are not necessarily all expressions of subjectively experienced needs and desires, but may be needs *imposed* on agents by the conditions in which they live. Offe illustrates this with two examples. The first relates to the need for medicaments created by the poor environmental conditions that many people have to endure at work or at home. The need for medicaments expressed in the sphere of consumption can be seen as imposed by conditions related to other spheres over which the individual has little real control – most importantly the sphere of work. The second, and I think more powerful, illustration relates to one of the main emblems of consumer culture, the automobile:

> Consumers often regard automobiles not as a means of satisfying a 'need' (such as the desire for mobility or the pleasure in driving) but, rather, as a response to urban living conditions which often make it 'impossible to live without a car'. In such frequently heard expressions, there is the suggestion that the apparently paradoxical need for an automobile is a need we could, in fact, do without: there is, in other words, a more or less vague awareness of the gap that exists between our needs and the demands forced upon us by the conditions in which we live.[69]

Offe recognises that the concept of structurally imposed needs 'opens up very difficult theoretical terrain', but he insists, rightly, that these structural conditions cannot be ignored. Private cars are certainly the source of pleasure and even objects for the investment of personal identity for some. But they are also undeniably sources of anxiety, frustration and even danger. They are, moreover, clearly an irrational form of transportation when viewed from an environmental perspective or even in terms of simple traffic volume on the roads. The fact that agents can recognise these problems and frustrations while still looking forward to the next model change seems to me to exemplify Marcuse's 'euphoria in unhappiness'. The unhappiness in this instance is a 'background' of routine practices – traffic jams, low-level nervous tension and aggression, polluted city air, noise – against which the 'euphoric' pleasures of driving – the experiences of power, control and liberty – stand out, and are (rationally) embraced as options within the immediate grasp of the individual.

The case of the automobile thus seems to me a clear one of the attendant discontents of consumer culture. In offering our cultural practices to other cultures we simultaneously offer our discontents. And these discontents are, as it were, 'deeply structured' into capitalist modernity. They are a function of the differentiated spheres of action which produce not only 'structurally imposed needs' but also contradictions and tensions between differentiated roles and interests: driver versus pedestrian; producer versus consumer; private interest versus communal interest; capital versus labour. Looked at this way, as a complexly structured 'package', capitalist modernity becomes an offer that other cultures can't refuse. This is because, unlike the offers of discrete consumer goods made by the advertisers, it is not made at the level of the individual at all. The context of consumer culture is the structural context of urban, industrial capitalist modernity and this is not something any individual 'buys'. It is not even something which it is plausible to think of a society fully 'opting for' in the sense of taking considered communal decisions about: short-term economic considerations will generally force the hand of Third World governments towards programmes of 'modernisation'.

The critique of consumer culture, then, has its real force, not when addressed to the supposed 'false satisfactions' of material commodities, but when it exposes the structural determinants and boundaries of individual 'life-worlds' in which consumption is experienced as a central preoccupation. Again the critical key is the notion of autonomy. Offe suggests that the structural context of modernity makes the recognition of autonomous individual needs and desires very difficult:

> The methods of ascertaining one's own needs are quite precarious under modern conditions characterised by a high degree of 'differentiation'. Deluged by 'options', modern consumers find it difficult to choose, recognise and maintain needs as their own. This difficulty becomes greater the less recourse can be had to traditional habits and conventional standards of 'normality'.[70]

This last point raises the question of whether autonomy is increased, as is generally supposed in liberal thought, in the 'pluralist' context of modernity. Offe suggests precisely the opposite: that autonomy may actually diminish with the recognition of vast choice without the 'anchorage' in stable self-perception offered by 'traditional' cultural norms and practices. He shifts his ground somewhat here and introduces new problems. We shall return to the question of autonomy in the following chapter, where we shall reformulate some of the problems raised here in terms of the broader category of social modernity. It is worthwhile drawing together the main strands of quite a lengthy discussion to see where it leaves us in assessing the discourse of cultural imperialism as the critique of capitalist culture.

The culture of capitalism

Many of the problems we have encountered in this chapter stem from the way theorists have conceived of capitalism. The central problem is to do justice to the nature of capitalism as, at once, an economic and a cultural system. Daniel Bell provides a useful simple definition which grasps this dual nature:

> Capitalism is an economic-cultural system, organized economically around the institution of property and the production of commodities and based culturally in the fact that exchange relations, that of buying and selling, have permeated most of the society.[71]

The arguments we considered earlier tended to separate out this complex in a curious way such that the 'cultural' aspects were seen simply as instruments to ensure integration of societies into the global 'economic' system. On this view, cultural imperialism is seen as the 'tool of capitalism'. The motivations for such a view are understandable. Economic domination generally commands a certain priority on the critical agenda and, in the case of the ills facing people in the Third World, economic issues (in their broadest material sense) are rightly prioritised. Marx's claim that 'life involves, before every-thing else, eating and drinking, a habitation, clothing and many more [material] things'[72] is particularly compelling when we consider the drudgery, injury and anxiety that is the daily experience of millions of people pursuing simply these 'basic' goals (see note 15). In so far as the economics of capitalism can be held responsible for this immiseration it is understandable that its critics see this as the main enemy.

We saw that the 'tool of capitalism' approach was mistaken for two reasons. First, because it failed to engage with the problematic of cultural imperialism itself: it reverted quickly to questions of economics rather than engaging with the cultural experience which it assumed to be functional in integrating societies into the capitalist system. Secondly, because in failing to engage with these issues of the 'lived culture' of capitalism it also failed as a theory of the spread of capitalism. This is because it tended, rather naively, to assume both that people are generally (and massively) ideologically manipulable and that capitalism relies on the ideological manipulation of people. In fact, there are senses in which some sort of integration with the world capitalist system is an economic *fait accompli* for all societies in the modern world. The mistake of the 'culture as tool of capitalism' theorists can be seen as that of viewing culture narrowly as a (redundant?) ideological instrument, rather than approaching it in the broader and more complex terms of the 'life-world' that capitalist production brings with it.

Turning to critiques which engaged more with this broader view, we first considered the common notion that there is a homogenising principle built into capitalist modernity. Though it is not clear that global marketing in itself has the power to produce global cultural homogenisation, it is fairly clear that a broad process of convergence seems to be occurring in the cultures of the world. These changes, which include urbanisation, mass communications and so on, are clearly related to the spread of capitalism and may be grasped in the term 'capitalist modernity'. But how is this process to be considered a threat? I suggested that this very much depends on where you stand in the world. The critique of homogenisation may turn out to be a peculiarly Western-centred concern if what is argued is that cultures must retain their separate identities simply to make the world a more diverse and interesting place. The material advantages that come with modernity represent a strong case in favour of homogenisation in some important ways. What has to be shown is that there is a 'downside' to this process – and this involves a quite different order of criticism.

So critique has to show there is something wrong with the cultural experience that capitalism serves up. We saw that attempts like Hamelink's to criticise the impact of Western capitalism on Third World cultures are dogged by the problems of speaking for others. However sincerely meant, they slide both towards paternalism and towards a curious, almost shame-faced critique of Western capitalist culture itself: a critique by proxy. This is not to deny that there are principles of domination at work in the cultural relations between developed and 'developing' worlds. But it does seem necessary to establish the grounds of critique of capitalist culture as it exists in the West first.

We focused on what Bell and many others put at the centre of capitalist culture: the practices of consumption and the 'commodification' of experience. One of the interesting things about consumer culture is its uneasy conscience. Most cultural commentary (from both the left and the right) finds some fault in a culture dedicated to consumption, and we had to distinguish between 'moralising' and 'critical' approaches. Perhaps the reason for this widespread cultural unease is the fact that 'consumerism' has grown around, and to some extent 'colonised', a moral-cultural space left by other developments in modernity. This is something we shall return to. We did establish that approaches to consumer culture which remain too closely tied to notions of the false satisfactions offered by consumer goods fetch up in an impasse in the conflict with the 'sovereign consumer' argument. A better approach is one that reveals the ambiguous *context* of consumer satisfactions. As the work of Claus Offe suggests, consumerism is perhaps best grasped as part of a wider *structural context* of capitalist modernity, and in terms of the 'routine' discontents which this brings.

Where does this leave the discourse of cultural imperialism? It looks as though critics of the spread of capitalism need to engage with issues beyond the most salient cultural feature of capitalism, its preoccupation with consumption. It may be that the significance of consumer culture can only be fully understood in terms of a broad shift in cultural practices from 'tradition' to 'modernity'. Both terms are ambiguous and contentious, particularly for Marxists. But they nonetheless offer a framework in which the political-economic structures of societies – and most significantly the political economy of capitalism – can be related to cultural practices and experiences. So the critique of capitalist culture seems to entail the critique of (capitalist) modernity.. The next chapter will examine one final move in the discursive strategy of cultural imperialism: the sense in which all cultures are, in the words of Octavio Paz, 'condemned to modernity'.[73]

Notes

1. H.I. Schiller (1976) *Communication and Cultural Domination*, New York. M.E. Sharpe, p. 9.
2. K. Marx (1975) 'Economic and Philosphical Manuscripts', in *Karl Marx: Early Writings*, trans. R. Livingstone and G. Benton, London, New Left Review/ Penguin, p. 359.
3. Schiller, op. cit., p. 6.
4. See A. Giddens (1979) *Central Problems in Social Theory: Action, Structure and*

Contradiction in Social Analysis, London, Macmillan, p. 7, on the general mistake of attributing teleology to systems; and J.O. Boyd-Barrett (1982) 'Cultural Dependency and the Mass Media', in M. Gurevitch et al. (eds) Culture, Society and the Media, London, Methuen, p. 278, for a criticism of Schiller along these lines.

5. C. Flora and J. Flora (1978) 'The Fotonovela as a Tool for Class and Cultural Domination', Latin American Perspectives, Vol. 5 (2), pp. 134–50 (p. 135).

6. Ibid., p. 142. The Braverman reference is: Braverman, H. (1974) Labor and Monopoly Capitalism: The Degradation of Work in the Twentieth Century, New York, Monthly Review Press.

7. Ibid., p. 149.

8. R. Salinas and L. Paldán (1979) 'Culture in the Process of Dependent Development: Theoretical Perspectives', in K. Nordenstreng and H.I. Schiller National Soveriegnty and International Communication, New Jersey, Ablex, p. 83.

9. Ibid., p. 84.

10. Ibid., pp. 90–1.

11. See F.H. Cardoso (1982) 'Dependency and Development in Latin America', in H. Alavi and T. Shannin (eds) Introduction to the Sociology of 'Developing Societies', London, Macmillan.

12. Salinas and Paldán, op. cit., p. 91.

13. Ibid.

14. I use this phrase, originally coined by Trotsky, to refer to the general way in which the spread of capitalism involves differential effects on the economies of societies across the globe, thereby producing what we know as 'development' and 'underdevelopment'.

15. See A.G. Frank (1981) Crisis in the Third World, London, Heinemann Educational (especially Chapter 5, 'Superexploitation in the Third World').

16. See Marx, op. cit. Also B. Ollman (1971) Alienation: Marx's Conception of Man in Capitalist Society, Cambridge, Cambridge University Press.

17. Salinas and Paldán, op. cit., p. 92.

18. Ibid.

19. C.J. Hamelink (1983) Cultural Autonomy in Global Communications, New York, Longmans, p. xiv.

20. Ibid., pp. 2–3.

21. Ibid., p. 3.

22. Ibid., p. 4.

23. Ibid.

24. Ibid.

25. Ibid., p. 1.

26. Ibid.

27. Ibid., p. 15.

28. Ibid., p. 5.

29. Marx's distinction, in the third volume of Capital, between the 'realm of necessity' and the 'realm of freedom' is relevant here. See Ollman's discussion, op. cit., pp. 118–19.

30. Hamelink, op. cit., pp. 22–3.

31. J. Sinclair (1987) Images Incorporated: Advertising as Industry and Ideology, London, Croom Helm, p. 166.

32. Ibid., p. 167.

33. Hamelink, op. cit., p. 14.

34. Sinclair, op. cit., p. 161.
35. Hamelink, op. cit., p. 14.
36. Ibid.
37. R. Geuss (1981) *The Idea of a Critical Theory*, Cambridge, Cambridge University Press, p. 49.
38. Ibid., p. 53.
39. Hamelink, op. cit., p. 15.
40. Sinclair, op. cit., p. 158.
41. C. Lévi-Strauss (1973) *Tristes Tropiques*, London, Jonathan Cape, P. 383.
42. Ibid., p. 384.
43. Ibid.
44. Ibid.
45. C. Castoriadis (1985) 'Reflections on "Rationality" and "Development" ', *Thesis Eleven*, No. 10/11, pp. 18–36 (p. 34).
46. W.W. Rostow (1960) *The Stages of Economic Growth*, Cambridge, Cambridge University Press. See the discussion of 'Modernisation Theory' in Chapter 5, pp. 143–44.
47. C. Lasch (1985) *The Minimal Self: Psychic Survival in Troubled Times*, London, Picador, p. 24.
48. C. Turnbull (1973) *The Mountain People*, London, Picador.
49. R. Williams (1980) 'Advertising: The Magic System', in *Problems in Materialism and Culture*, London, Verso, p. 185.
50. K. Marx and F. Engels (1970) *The German Ideology*, London, Lawrence and Wishart, p. 47. See also F. Engels (1978) *Ludwig Feuerbach and the End of Classical German Philosophy*, Moscow, Progress Publishers.
51. M. Horkheimer, quoted in M. Featherstone (1983) 'Consumer Culture: an Introduction', *Theory, Culture and Society*, Vol. 1 (3), pp. 4–9 (p. 8).
52. See, for example, L. Althusser (1969) *For Marx*, London, Allen Lane. For a critique of Althusser's 'anti-humanist' position see Geras, N. (1983), *Karl Marx and Human Nature: Refutation of a Legend*, London, Verso.
53. The literature in this area is extensive, but see particularly: Williams, op. cit.; H. Lefebvre (1971) *Everyday Life in the Modern World*, London, Allen Lane; J. Baudrillard (1981) *For a Critique of the Political Economy of the Sign*, St Louis, Telos Press; E. Fromm (1956) *The Sane Society*, London, Routledge and Kegan Paul; M. Schneider (1975) *Neurosis and Class Struggle*, New York, Seabury; W. Haug (1985) *Critique of Commodity Aesthetics*, Cambridge, Polity Press; S. Ewen (1976) *Captains of Consciousness*, New York, McGraw-Hill; H-M. Enzenberger (1976) *The Consciousness Industry*, New York, Seabury; W. Leiss (1976) *The Limits to Satisfaction*, London, Marion Boyars; C. Myers (1986) *Understains: The Sense and Seduction of Advertising*, London, Comedia; and the collection of articles on 'consumer culture' in *Theory, Culture and Society*, Vol. 1 (3), 1983.
54. T. Adorno and M. Horkheimer (1979) 'The Culture Industry: Enlightenment as Mass Deception', in *Dialectic of Enlightenment*, London, Verso.
55. See Geuss, op. cit., and D. Held (1980) *Introduction to Critical Theory: Horkheimer to Habermas*, London, Hutchinson. See also the discussion in Chapter 5, pp. 144–46.
56. See, in this connection, Lodziak's subtle reading of the Frankfurt School theorists: C. Lodziak (1986) *The Power of Television: A Critical Appraisal*, London, Frances Pinter, Chapter 5.

57. H. Marcuse (1972) *One-Dimensional Man*, London, Abacus, p. 19.
58. A. MacIntyre (1970) *Marcuse*, London, Fontana, P. 64.
59. See Geuss, op. cit., p. 46ff. for a discussion of these points.
60. Marcuse, op. cit., p. 20.
61. B. Turner (1984) *The Body in Society*, Oxford, Basil Blackwell, p. 26. See also N. Abercrombie, S. Hill and B. Turner (1980) *The Dominant Ideology Thesis*, London, Allen and Unwin. Turner's references are: J. Baudrillard (1975) *The Mirror of Production*, St Louis, Telos Press; H. Lefebvre (1971) *Everyday Life in the Modern World*, London, Allen Lane; H. Marcuse (1964) *One-Dimensional Man*, London, Routledge and Kegan Paul.
62. D. Kellner (1983) 'Critical Theory, Commodities and Consumer Society', *Theory, Culture and Society*, Vol. 1 (3), pp. 64–84 (p. 71).
63. Marcuse, op. cit., p. 19.
64. Kellner, op. cit., p. 77.
65. Ibid., p. 80.
66. See, for example, Roxborough's discussion of the political formations of the Third World: I. Roxborough (1979) *Theories of Underdevelopment*, London, Macmillan, Chapter 8.
67. See, for example, Marx's discussion of 'the transformation of what was previously superfluous into what is necessary, as a historically created necessity' under capitalism: K. Marx (1973) *Grundrisse*, London, New Left Review/Allen Lane, p. 528.
68. C. Offe (1984) *Contradictions of the Welfare State*, London, Hutchinson, p. 221.
69. Ibid., p. 225.
70. Ibid., p. 226.
71. D. Bell (1979) *The Cultural Contradictions of Capitalism*, London, Heinemann Educational, p. 14.
72. Marx and Engels, *The German Ideology*, op. cit., p. 48.
73. O. Paz, quoted in M. Berman (1983) *All That is Solid Melts into Air: The Experience of Modernity*, London, Verso, p. 125.

5

Modernity, Development and Cultural Fate

Our final way of speaking of cultural imperialism is via the discourse of cultural modernity. This is a discourse rich in paradox and ambiguity. To begin with, the very term 'modernity' is ambiguous and chronologically elastic. It is commonly used to refer simply to the cultural *present*, but social and cultural theorists have typically attempted to grasp some fundamental change – a shift to modernity – occurring at some point in (European) history. Determinations of this point range from the sixteenth right through to the twentieth century, hence the elasticity of the term. Apart from the difficulties of situating 'modernity' historically, there are problems and ambiguities in relating the idea to other frameworks of social or cultural analysis; how, for example, does modernity relate to class analysis, or, if we take some of the earlier datings of its inception, to theories of 'industrial society'? Despite (or even, perhaps, because of) these ambiguities, the idea of modernity has become the most general way in which we in the West represent our cultural experience to ourselves. What this chapter will ask is how modernity is to be *criticised*. For if all global cultures are 'condemned to modernity', in the words of Octavio Paz, then the critique of cultural imperialism fetches up in the critique of modernity.

Octavio Paz's phrase is peculiarly resonant in the context of twentieth-century Western thought. It echoes, for example, a theme of existential philosophy – one of the major Western responses to the dilemmas of its own cultural modernity. Jean-Paul Sartre's famous claim that human beings are 'condemned to freedom' encapsulates the paradoxical fatalism at the core of his ultra-voluntarist philosophy: we are condemned – fated – to existential *Angst* and insecurity by the very freedom that defines us. Radical freedom, understood in Sartre's existentialism as the awareness of a lack of any determination of human consciousness, issues in a curious but decisive human destiny: 'we are not free to cease being free'.[1] The human agent, for Sartre, is thus caught up in an inescapable, but futile, pursuit of self-definition. Freedom is an ambiguous gift, but one we cannot refuse.

A similar paradox can be read in Paz's formulation. Socioeconomic modernity is the 'fate' of all cultures in that they are integrated at a structural

140

level in the orders of the nation-state system and the global capitalist market; but this integration – which is a structural *fait accompli*, not a cultural 'option' – alters the terms of culture irrevocably, since it entails a one-way journey from 'tradition' to 'modernity'. As this journey is made by human agents and involves the emergence of new senses of possibility – new options, new desires, new freedoms – it too can be understood in 'existential' terms. 'Cultural fate' becomes linked with the realisation of individual human freedom. Cultures are 'condemned to modernity' not simply by the 'structural' process of economic development, but by the human process of *self-development*.

This way of approaching the drift of global cultures – as the outcome of a 'dialectic' between self-development and socioeconomic structures – has one major advantage over most of the discourses of cultural imperialism we have considered. It understands cultural processes as involving the complex cultural choices made by agents, though not, to paraphrase Marx, in conditions of their own choosing. This is, I think, an advantage in that it can avoid many of the problems we have met so far in conceptualising 'cultural domination'. For understanding cultural change in terms of choices made under certain 'determinate' social conditions is to resist seeing cultural agents as 'cultural dopes', and to resist the temptation to despise everything capitalism brings in its cultural wake.

A discourse of cultural modernity which is responsive to the claims about human agency that have been made throughout this book promises well as a context in which to understand the order of cultural domination involved in the spread of capitalist consumerism, of urban industrialism, of the mass media and so on, across the globe. But the ambiguities involved in this discourse are such that it is possible, within it, to lose any sense of cultural domination: to speak of modernity can be to speak of cultural change as 'cultural fate' in the strong sense of historical (albeit 'tragic') inevitability. This would be to abandon any project of rational cultural critique. We shall resist this tendency by maintaining, for example, the close connection suggested in the last chapter between capitalism and modernity. Although capitalism cannot be seen as the single principle behind cultural modernity, it certain *inflects* modernity in a particular way in which what may be called 'structures of domination' are identifiable. Probing such structures may reveal a more deep-seated set of social principles which can explain the 'success' of capitalism as a global economic-cultural system – and questioning these deep-seated principles may be the key to a critique of modernity itself.

Because the scope of the discourse of modernity is so enormous, we must restrict our discussion quite severely. We shall begin by exploring what is at stake in the widespread claim that modernity is an *essentially ambiguous* cultural condition. This insight was shared, in one way or another, by all the great nineteenth-century social theorists, and it has defined the terms of social and cultural critique ever since. The way in which these ambiguities are formulated and addressed has vital implications for the sort of cultural critique which is imagined in the discourse of cultural imperialism. In short, though the ambiguities of the modern cultural condition need to be fully recognised, the danger of a discourse which cannot get beyond them is that it ceases to be a critical discourse. The following discussion of the work of Marshall Berman and Cornelius Castoriadis should be read in terms of this central problem: how to understand modernity, as it spreads around the globe, in a way which does not lose a critical edge – which does not reduce the cultural discontents of modernity to the order of cultural fate.

The ambiguities of modernity

The idea of 'modernity' was a central one for the classical European social theorists of the nineteenth century. Marx, Weber, Durkheim and others, including Simmel and Tönnies, constructed their theories around the idea of a dramatic set of changes in European societies issuing in the 'modern world'. These changes may be seen to pose the problematic of sociology itself. There were crucial differences between the accounts given by these theorists, and even in the categories used to grasp the transition – 'tradition' to 'modernity'; 'mechanical solidarity' to 'organic solidarity', 'pre-capitalist' to 'capitalist'; *Gemeinschaft* to *Gesellschaft* and so on. These differences have fed streams of social thought which, regardless of various points of confluence, still represent antagonistic positions in social theory, the most politically salient being the distinction between Marxist and other perspectives. The crucial point of agreement, however, was that the societies these theorists inhabited were not just 'modern' in the sense of being the social present – the latest point on a continuum of historical change – but that they were of an entirely different order from what had gone before. On this crucial point there was, and still is, agreement across the political spectrum.

Another point on which there was agreement amongst the classical theorists was that the modern world was ambiguous in its capacity to deliver human happiness and fulfilment: its attractions are bound up with its woes. 'Traditional' or 'pre-capitalist' – let us merely say 'pre-modern' – societies were characterised by all manner of social and material ills and unfreedoms: a low level of technical development meant that life was, for most, a continual struggle with nature and material scarcity; the consequence of this struggle for sheer survival was a narrowness, for the majority, in cultural experience and a limitation on the possibilities for self-development; people were held in thrall to a variety of superstitious or dogmatic religious beliefs; civil and political rights were few and authoritarian rule the norm. Modernity, in particular the scientific rationality and the liberal-democratic political projects associated with 'enlightenment', delivered emancipation from many of these forms of domination. But modernity didn't deliver complete emancipation. Marx, Durkheim and Weber each wrote of the *costs* of modernity, using concepts which tried to grasp new forms of cultural pathology: 'alienation', 'anomie', the 'iron cage' of instrumental reason.[2] In each of these views there was a sense that one form of domination had given way to another – where they differed was in the precise analysis of the source of this domination.

Social and cultural theory in the twentieth century has varied in the degree to which it has acknowledged the discontents at the core of modernity. At one end of the scale there have been bodies of thought which fail entirely to grasp the ambiguities of modernity. One of these has a certain bearing on our argument, since it relates specifically to the countries of the Third World.

This is the so-called 'modernisation theory', which was influential in the sociology of development in the 1950s and 1960s and which was mentioned in Chapters 2 and 4. Modernisation theory can be seen as the attempt by the mainstream intellectual apparatuses of the capitalist West, particularly the United States, to provide a theoretical underpinning for their 'development policies' towards the countries emerging from colonialism into nominal political independence. This body of theory has been massively and justly criticised across a broad front – for its clear ideological basis, its theoretical simplicities and incoherences and its huge historical blind spots.[3]

Modernisation theory is ostensibly an attempt to explain the economic 'underdevelopment' of post-colonial countries by focusing on development as a purely *endogenous* process – a process determined solely by features internal to the society itself. This may be seen as the main ideological strategy of the theory, for, of course, this view very conveniently ignores the external determinants of 'underdevelopment': the history of economic exploitation under colonialism and the continuance of this within the market structure of global capitalism. It was possible to ignore these difficult truths by producing a discourse of 'modernisation' which simply borrowed the categories of the classical sociologists (with the obvious exception of Marx!) and pretended that the countries of the Third World were progressing independently from 'traditional' to 'modern' as Europe had in the period between the sixteenth and the twentieth centuries. Underdevelopment was therefore attributable to stubborn 'traditional' attitudes and cultural practices and the answer to the desperate problems of poverty, lack of social provision and political instability was in the 'diffusion' of modern attitudes via educational programmes and so on. Third World countries were to be 'helped' into the modern world by their grown-up cousins in the West. Used in this way, the categories of 'tradition' and 'modernity' become a mere excuse for the historical dirty work of capitalism in the ages of imperialism and neo-imperialism.

Not surprisingly, critical theorists of development have tended to reject modernisation theory bag and baggage, and this has been no loss in one sense, since the violence the modernisation theorists did to the classical theories of modernity crippled them as cultural theories, often by reducing them to simplistic accounts of psychological traits.[4] However, in another way the reception of modernisation theory has meant a loss for radical theories of development, since it has for a long period drawn the battle lines between theories invoking the themes of tradition and modernity and those centred on the history of the relations between countries of the 'developed' and the 'underdeveloped' world. Alavi and Shannin write in the introduction to a reader on the critical sociology of development:

> Sociology of developing societies must begin not with stereotypes of 'traditional' and 'modern' societies but with a historical analysis of the making of the contemporary Third World – the world we live in.[5]

They are quite correct. But to begin in this way should not mean to end without addressing the cultural problematic of modernity. The problem for cultural analysis is that the modernisation theorists have tarred all theories of cultural modernity with their brush and so there has been a reluctance amongst radical theorists, until quite recently, to speak of development and modernity in the same breath. This reluctance has partly been because modernisation theory has substituted its simplicities for a proper account of the cultural implications of modernity as it is imposed by the spread of global capitalism; partly, as I have suggested, because its ideological work was in the disguising of material structures of domination; and partly because the account of the experience of modernity it offered was optimistic to the point of being Panglossian. In imaging, and celebrating, capitalism as the destination of all societies, modernisation theorists ignored all the discontents and ambiguities addressed by the classical theorists. Indeed, by reducing these theories to the level of psychological characteristics of individuals, some even thought it was possible, using psychometric testing, to 'prove' that modernity as it was 'transferred' to developing societies was entirely sweetness and light.[6]

In theorising the cultural relations between First and Third World, it is necessary to distance the concept of 'modernity' from the vacuities of 'modernisation theory'. But at the other end of the spectrum of responses to modernity are those which tend to romanticise tradition and ignore any of the benefits of capitalist modernity. We saw how this is a constant pitfall for critics of cultural imperialism. What is needed is a critical approach that recognises the embeddedness of modernity's discontents in a political-economic system which simultaneously offers attractions over 'traditional' societies.

But this is easily said: in practice it turns out to be exceedingly difficult to produce such a critique. One of the most significant attempts to develop the critique of the nineteenth-century theorists was in the work of the Frankfurt School. Horkheimer and Adorno's *Dialectic of Enlightenment* demonstrates in its title the acute perception of the ambiguities of modern rationality which informed the work of these theorists. What they tried to do was to chart the false turns that Western civilisation had taken in its progress out of the unfreedoms of traditional societies, to discover why 'mankind, instead of entering into a truly human condition, is sinking into a new barbarism'.

'Enlightenment', as it was expressed in the ideas of thinkers from Francis Bacon onwards, aimed at 'liberating men from fear and establishing their sovereignty'. Writing in the 1940s, under the shadow of Nazism, Fascism and Stalinism in Europe and in the light of an emerging consumer capitalism in America, they tried to explain how this project had failed: how 'the fully enlightened earth radiates disaster triumphant'. Their point was that these 'disasters' were not contingent historical accidents, but were tied up with the very project of enlightenment itself. They set themselves the philosophical task of investigating the ambiguities of reason itself:

> We are wholly convinced – and therein lies our *petitio principii* – that social freedom is inseparable from enlightened thought. Nevertheless, we believe that we have just as clearly recognised that the notion of this way of thinking, no less than the actual historic forms – the social institutions – with which it is interwoven, already contains the seed of the reversal universally apparent today . . . In the enigmatic readiness of the technologically educated masses to fall under the sway of any despotism, in its self-destructive affinity to popular paranoia, and in all uncomprehended absurdity, the weakness of the modern theoretical faculty is apparent.[7]

There is no doubt that the early Frankfurt school theorists grasped the central problem of modernity: it is not merely a matter of the injustices of the capitalist system or of various forms of social bigotry or of the ideology of possessive individualism. What is at stake is the ordering of all modern societies according to a particular narrow principle of reason – what Max Weber called *Zweckrationalität* ('instrumental reason') – the sort of reason that lies at the heart of our major social institutions: the 'economy', bureaucratic agencies of social control, science and technology. Horkheimer and Adorno traced the unfreedoms of modernity to the operations of these supposedly rational institutions. The task of reason is to set people free, but the political and historical record, they argued, shows its abject failure. So far their argument is convincing. Few would dissent from the view that modern societies fall far short of the ideals of rationality. However, as is now generally agreed, the early Frankfurt School theorists painted themselves into a theoretical corner in their attempts to explain the failure of enlightenment reason. Their problem centred on the self-imposed strictures on their critical standpoint. To criticise the central tenets of 'reason' itself required the search for a point outside of this reason. This is a fairly tall order – how can we think outside the (admittedly historical) structures of rational thought? Their very concepts, for example the notion of truth, became fugitive in the face of the distorted rationality they claimed was pervasive in the society they inhabited. Jürgen Habermas puts the problem like this:

> The 'dialectic of enlightenment' is an ironic affair: It shows the self-critique of reason the way to truth, and at the same time contests the possibility 'that at this stage of complete alienation the truth is still accessible'.[8]

The philosophical conundrums with which the Frankfurt School grappled were not merely academic: they were attempts, at a high level of abstraction, to make sense of the contradictory experience of modernity. They were forced to reject an institutionalised 'reason' which provided a high material standard of living, 'conspicuous consumption' and waste in close proximity with abject poverty; which could channel the highest levels of technical expertise into technologies of warfare; which could make culture into an industry and 'amusement . . . the prolongation of work'.[9] But the ironies of their critique stem from the attempt to think outside of this 'reason'. It is one thing to say that reason fails, quite another to provide alternatives.

Contemporary Critical Theorists like Habermas have grappled with the same problems as the early Frankfurt School but have taken a rather different, perhaps less uncompromising, approach. Roughly speaking, Habermas feels Horkheimer and Adorno's attack on enlightenment reason itself to be mistaken: the discontents of modernity are not due to *inherent* problems of *Zweckrationalität* but to 'the failure to develop and institution-alize in a balanced way all the different dimensions of reason opened up by the modern world'.[10] Habermas's work is at the centre of a major, and very complex, debate about the nature of modernity.[11] There is not space to do justice to the complexity of these debates here and Habermas has been very cautious about extending his theories from what he admits is a 'euro-centrically limited view' to the Third World context.[12] We will return, briefly, to one aspect of Habermas's work in the final section of this chapter.

The Frankfurt School critique of modernity shows how deep-seated the ambiguities of modernity really are: at the root of these questions of culture lie enormously difficult problems to do with the nature of reason and the possibilities of any rational social critique. Though we need to be aware of these problems, there is a sense in which we can avoid becoming entangled in the 'meta-discourse' of critical theory. This is the sense in which we are interested in culture as the *experience* of modernity. There are ways of thinking about this experience which need not immediately transform themselves into anxieties about the rational foundations of criticism.

Modernity as cultural fate

One of the most interesting attempts to come to terms with the ambiguities of cultural modernity is Marshall Berman's book. *All That is Solid Melts into Air*. The book is subtitled 'The experience of modernity', and this signals the approach he takes. It is a rich and eclectic cultural essay which contains fascinating and original readings of European thinkers and writers – Goethe, Marx, Baudelaire – as well as accounts of the literary and artistic genres of 'modernism'. But all these readings are through the lens of 'modernity', not as style, form or structure, but as a mode of common *cultural experience*. Berman begins the book with a passage that firmly establishes this experiential approach:

There is a mode of vital experience – experience of space and time, of the self and others, of life's possibilities and perils – that is shared by men and women all over the world today. I will call this body of experience 'modernity'. To be modern is to find ourselves in an environment that promises us adventure, power, joy, growth, transformation of ourselves and the world – and at the same time, that threatens to destroy everything we have, everything we know, everything we are. Modern environments and experiences cut across all boundaries of geography and ethnicity, of class and nationality, of religion and ideology: in this sense, modernity can be said to unite all mankind. But it is a paradoxical unity, a unity in disunity: it pours us all into a maelstrom of perpetual disintegration and renewal, of struggle and contradiction, of ambiguity and anguish. To be modern is to be part of a universe in which, as Marx said, 'all that is solid melts into air'.[13]

Berman's description of the lived experience of modernity throws its ambiguities into high relief. This is one of the main aims of his book: he claims that thought about the cultural condition of modernity has 'stagnated and regressed' during the twentieth century and he aims to restore the acute sense of linked possibilities and dangers that he finds in nineteenth-century thinkers, 'simultaneously enthusiasts and enemies of modern life'.[14] By contrast, twentieth-century thought has, he claims, flattened out the ambiguities and contradictions of modernity into simple polarities. On the one hand, modernity is 'embraced with a blind and uncritical enthusiasm'. Here he cites, for example, the crypto-Fascist extravagances of the Futurist movement before World War I, the modernist movement in architecture – Mies van der Rohe, Le Corbusier – 1960s prophets of high-tech utopia – Alvin Toffler, Marshall McLuhan – and, interestingly, the modernisation theorists in development studies. On the other hand, critics of modernity condemn it with 'a neo-Olympian remoteness and contempt'. Berman sees these critics as developing Max Weber's famous description of the 'iron cage' of modernity in a way that loses crucial aspects of his critical insights and that issues in a contempt for 'the masses'. Here he mentions right-wing cultural critics of 'mass-society' – Ortega, T.S. Eliot – and also figures of the New Left in the 1960s, particularly Marcuse for his pessimism in *One-Dimensional Man*.[15] Both positions are indications, for Berman, that we in the twentieth century 'don't know how to use our modernism; we have missed or broken the connection between our culture and our lives'.[16]

The way we should understand this connection is in terms of a 'dialectic' in which the experience of modernity is the central mediating term. Berman thus speaks of *modernisation* as the set of 'world historical processes' which generate the experience of modernity. He describes these processes with all the vivid intensity with which he describes the experience of modernity: the dramatic discoveries of the physical sciences, the industrialisation of production that radically transforms human environments, demographic changes, 'severing millions of people from their ancestral habitats, hurtling them halfway across the world into new lives', 'rapid and often cataclysmic urban growth', mass communications 'enveloping and binding together the most diverse people and societies', powerful nation-states and their associated bureaucracies, and so on. Behind all this, driving all along he sees the 'ever-expanding, drastically fluctuating capitalist market'.[17] Berman isn't interested in giving a detailed account of the relationships between these factors. He doesn't want to enter the social-theoretical debates about, for example, the distinction between capitalist and industrial society. What is important for him is simply to capture a set of objective conditions – largely, but not entirely socioeconomic – within which modern people find themselves. These conditions form the dialectical moment of 'modernisation'.

It is the human responses to modernisation that form the other moment in Berman's dialectic: these responses, which he says aim to 'make men and women the subjects as well as the objects of modernisation, to give them the power to change the world that is changing them', he calls *modernism*. Berman uses this term in a much expanded sense from that normally found in, say, literary or visual-art theories. 'Modernism' for him, though it includes aspects of, for example, literary and architectural modernism,[18] is perhaps more importantly a matter of mundane cultural practice – what he elsewhere calls 'the signs in the streets'.[19] Thus he writes:

> To be a modernist is to make oneself somehow at home in the maelstrom, to make its rhythms one's own, to move within its currents in search of the forms of reality, of beauty, of freedom, of justice that its fervid and perilous flow allows.[20]

This dialectical formulation: modernisation → modernity ← modernism allows Berman to stress the active involvement of ordinary people in the production of modern culture – something he rightly suggests has been undervalued in the more pessimistic critiques of modernity. So, to compress a long and subtle argument into one broad central theme, Berman wants to slip between the horns of the dilemma constructed by the polarities of twentieth-century cultural analysis, and to understand modernity as the cultural environment in which objective socioeconomic structures and 'subjective' constructions of reality interact. Seen in this way, modernity is admittedly an anxious, uncertain and even dangerous place to live: but it is ultimately 'our world' and we can, somehow, be the cultural masters of it. To despise modern culture is, moreover, to despise the attempts of people to make themselves at home in the context of modernisation: out and out rejection of modernity, whether from the right or the left; is, for Berman, a reactionary position. Berman's book is written from the perspective of the broad left, but there is no doubt that it is a celebration of modernity, if only in the way that it reacts against the weight of negative left criticism of modernity seen (narrowly) as the imposed culture of capitalism. This is, then, a bold and provocative account, and it poses some interesting questions to the formulation of the problem of cultural imperialism as an imposition of modernity.

Berman begins his whole argument with an appeal to experience; modernity is 'a mode of vital experience . . .'. The obvious challenge to this is the question, whose experience? Berman places a certain faith in his reader's intuitive recognition of this mode of experience. He is a New York intellectual, reading the 'signs in the streets', and the images of vibrancy, energy and danger that he invokes reflect his own cultural milieu. To extend this claim to global proportions – 'shared by men and women all over the world today' – clearly risks a certain ethnocentrism. Yet I think the risk is worth taking, for it allows the cultural aspects of modernity to be posed at the level of experience. We can treat the description of the experience of modernity which he gives as a set of *deductions* from the conditions of modernisation he describes. Here he is on much firmer ground, for there is clear evidence that these conditions are becoming, increasingly, the context of all global cultures. *Modernisation*, as a set of objective political-economic structures, certainly seems to be a global fate. The question is whether the dialectic he supposes is in operation in all cultures. At certain stages in his argument Berman makes particular reference to countries in the Third World and here it is clear that he thinks it is. For example he discusses attempts by some Third World governments (he does not specify which) to 'protect their people from modernism for their own good':

> If this culture were really exclusively Western, and hence irrelevant to the Third World as most of its governments say, would these governments need to expend as much energy repressing it as they do? What they are projecting onto aliens, and prohibiting as 'Western Decadence', is in fact their own people's energies, desires and critical spirit. When government spokesmen and propagandists proclaim their various countries to be free of this alien influence, what they really mean is merely that they have managed to keep a political and spiritual lid on their people so far. When the lid comes off, or is blown off, the modernist spirit is one of the first things to come out: it is the return of the repressed.[21]

Here we have almost a reversal of the standard cultural imperialism argument. Berman seems to be saying that cultural domination occurs where Third World governments fight a futile battle to preserve 'tradition' in the face of popular wellsprings of modernist energy. Modernity is thus not a cultural imposition but rather a liberation of the human spirit. He cites the famous 'boom' in Latin American literature, dissident wall-posters in China and so on.[22] These instances show, he claims, that modernist culture 'keeps critical thought and free imagination alive in much of the Non-Western world today'.

We must understand that Berman is no naive enthusiast for the processes of economic *modernisation*. His argument about the futility of the repression of modernism is predicated on the objective structures of modern society being in place. He says that Third World governments find themselves in this reactionary position as a result of being 'forced to sink or swim in the maelstrom of the world market, forced to strive desperately to accumulate capital, forced to develop or disintegrate' or, as he goes on to say, often to do both.[23] Elsewhere he accuses some Third World governments of pursuing ill-conceived development projects in a spirit of neo-Faustian grandiosity and megalomania, with no thought for their people's real needs.[24] His major point seems to be that the centres of power in Third World societies have to accept the cultural consequences of economic development – whether or not such development is tied up with their own personal ambitions and conceits. Modernisation begets modernism as popular response, and it is this which cannot be suppressed.

This way of approaching cultural modernity has the advantage referred to at the start of this chapter, of understanding it in terms of choices made under determinate conditions – and of respecting these choices. Berman's 'populism' is a serious attempt to build cultural criticism on non-paternalist foundations. But it does make certain assumptions, which issue in a curious cultural fatalism and a sort of critical impasse. To understand this, we can turn to a most perceptive critique of Berman's book by the Marxist critic, Perry Anderson.

Anderson's key insight is to see the central concept of *All That is Solid Melts into Air* as development. Modernisation clearly involves the processes of economic and scientific-technical development that have been associated with the capitalist market, but no less important to Berman's dialectic is the notion of *self-development*. This, Anderson claims, is what is at stake in Berman's notion of the experience of modernity:

> What is this experience? For Berman it is essentially a process of unlimited self-development, as traditional barriers of custom or role disintegrate – an experience necessarily lived at once as emancipation and ordeal, elation and despair, frightening and exhilarating. It is the momentum of this ceaselessly ongoing rush towards the uncharted waters of the psyche that assures the world-historical continuity of modernism . . .[25]

Limitless self-development is the assumption which gives Berman's view of modernity its 'existential fatalism'. This is how the story goes. The emancipation provided by technical and economic development entails an abrupt and irreversible break with the past. Thus traditional worldviews, values and beliefs can no longer have any claim on individuals, but neither can they provide the resources of moral and existential meaning and certainty that have hitherto supported stable cultures. So far the story is a familiar one: it has, since Max Weber, provided the context for the Western debate over cultural values. The slant Berman puts on matters is at once heroic and fatalist. He suggests that modern men and women simply have to adapt to a world in which nothing can be taken for granted, a life lived, as Sartre might have put it, 'without guarantees'. Self-development means *essential* lack of stability, constant changes and continuous undermining of values. The reason why this cultural fate is inescapable is precisely because it is *chosen* by individuals: it is impossible to will the sort of domination that is a feature of traditional beliefs. It is impossible, for example, to see human potential limited simply by the dead weight of unchanging cultural practice – 'the way things have always been' – once one has experienced cultural plurality – the way things are for other cultures. And exposure to the media is just one aspect of modernity to deliver such experience. Modernisation is a one-way journey in that it alters the terms of human self-understanding.

A good illustration of this sort of irreversible change is provided by another theorist of modernity, Peter Berger. Berger tells the story of a visitor to a collective agricultural settlement in Tanzania. The inhabitants of this village were from different tribes now coexisting co-operatively. This was a community in transition from tradition to modernity. The visitor enquires whether the various tribal dances are still performed and is told by a village elder that, yes, this is done on special occasions once or twice a year. The elder adds that this is good for the community since it helps the different tribal members to understand one another better. Berger takes this instance as illustrative of his claim that modernisation involves 'a shift from givenness to choice on the level of meaning'. He comments:

> While tribal dances were previously performed at times designated by tradition, they were now staged for occasions chosen by the village council. Previously the performances was given as inevitable, now it was decided upon in an act of choice – and, by definition, the choice could be *not* to hold the event on a particular date . . . Finally, a rationale was now attached to the enterprise: Previously the people danced because it was necessary to do so – they probably reflected on it as little as they did about eating and breathing. Now they danced because, supposedly, this was a good thing for the morale of the village . . . Barring catastrophic events which would literally make people forget what has happened, the modernizing shift from givenness to choice appears irreversible. Once an individual is conscious of a choice, it is difficult for him to pretend that his options are a matter of necessity.[26]

The comparison of Berman and Berger is quite instructive, for though they write from quite different cultural-political perspectives, Berger being politically far to the right of Berman, they agree on seeing something like an existential condition – self-awareness, consciousness of choice – as at the core of the cultural condition of modernity. Social structures can be changed, but individual self-development is a one-way journey. This is where the paradoxical cultural fatalism arises.

For Berman, self-development, once unbounded by the conditions of modernisation, throws all cultures into constant flux and instability. His most powerful invocation of this restlessness is in the central 'melting' image which gives the book its title. This is inspired by a forceful passage in Marx's *Communist Manifesto* in which he describes the cultural consequences of the 'bourgeois epoch':

> Constant revolutionizing of production, uninterrupted disturbance of all social relations, everlasting uncertainty and agitation, distinguish the bourgeoise epoch from all earlier times. All fixed, fast frozen relationships, with their train of venerable ideas and opinions are swept away, all new-formed ones become obsolete before they can ossify. All that is solid melts into air, all that is holy is profaned, and men at last are forced to face with sober senses the real conditions of their lives and their relations with their fellow men.[27]

One way – perhaps the 'standard' way – of reading this has been to put the emphasis on the first and last part of the quotation. This is to see Marx describing a clarification of the 'real foundations' of society that emerges with the era of bourgeois capitalism: as the 'two great contending classes' of capitalist and proletariat arise, so people will come to see 'the real conditions of their lives' in these economic relations of 'forced dependency'. This is Marx the critic of ideology and the political economist. Berman, however, stresses the cultural experience in the middle of the quotation and produces a reading of Marx as 'modernist'. Marx's very prose here becomes 'luminous, incandescent' and of a 'breathless intensity', sweeping his readers along with descriptions of the melting away of all solid foundations of practice and belief. In this sense, Berman argues, the *Communist Manifesto* can be seen as a manifesto for cultural modernism.

Berman finds plenty of textual support for this reading of Marx. But he cannot avoid a crucial implication: if *everything* is melting down in the heat of capitalist modernity, where does this leave the foundations of communism? It is, he says, as though Marx has been carried by his perceptions of the iconoclastic dynamics of capitalism, 'far beyond the range of this intended plot, to a point where his revolutionary script will have to be radically reworked'. This is where Berman parts company with most orthodox Marxists. According to the story he tells, 'revolution' becomes a *permanent* state of cultural being and the Marxist notion of a punctual revolution issuing in the communist society as a form of stable rational modernity becomes hard to sustain:

> What is to prevent the social forces that melt capitalism from melting communism as well? If all new relationships become obsolete before they can ossify, how can solidarity, fraternity and mutual aid be kept alive? . . . Ironically, then, we can see Marx's dialectic of modernity re-enacting the fate of the society it describes, generating energies and ideas that melt down into its own air.[28]

It is not surprising that such a view should be resisted by Marxists, for it strikes at the heart not only of the theory of historical materialism but also of the assumptions of minimal cultural stability – that is, 'solid' socialist values – that support it. Perry Anderson sees Berman as presenting an over-individualist version of Marx – a Marx nearer to Rousseau. All the cultural instability that Berman stresses derives from his notion of the unlimited dynamic of self-development unleashed by modernisation. But the very idea of such a lack of limits assumes an individualist view of human nature that, Anderson says, is not Marx's:

> For Marx, the self is not *prior to*, but is *constituted by* its relations with others, from the outset; women and men are *social* individuals, whose sociality is not subsequent to but contemporaneous with their individuality . . . If the development of the self is inherently imbricated in relations with others, its development could never be an *unlimited* dynamic in the monadological sense conjured up by Berman: for the coexistence of others would always *be such a limit*, without which *development itself could not occur*.[29]

Anderson's defence of the Marxist project comes down, here, to the assertion of a different view of human nature: against the restless individualism of Berman's account he offers the image of an inherently social, 'co-operative' human being – the limits to self-development are in our necessary interdependence. On this account, the prognosis for rational cultural stability looks much improved. Who is right? As interpretations of Marx, it has to be said, *both*: as with many other issues, one can find passages which will support either view in the corpus of Marx's work.[30] Beyond this purely exegetical argument, it is difficult to say, since views of human nature are always, in one sense, simply speculations about dispositions towards (cultural, political) behaviour. It is probably more useful to discuss the social and cultural factors that might bear on such behaviour.

The political-economic processes of modernisation are, in Berman's account, the major factors involved. But there are others. There are the great cultural narratives of modernity: the collective stories we tell ourselves about our experience, the possibilities of fulfilment we see for ourselves, our common conceptions of human goals, and so on. These cultural 'imaginings' do not spring from some 'inner dynamic' of human self-development; they are, rather, *stories* about development itself – attempts at social self-understanding valorised and preserved within the interpretive texts of a culture. Berman recognises this: in his discussion of Marx he notes the obsession, expressed throughout his work, with the concept of development, embracing and linking both individual-psychological and socioeconomic senses. One way of understanding Marx's influence in this respect is to see him adding to a great modern narrative in which the ideal of development in central. All the modernist thinkers Berman discusses – and, indeed, his own book – add to this narrative. So, when Berman sees Third World cultures as 'condemned to modernity' it is not just in terms of the 'objective structures' of the capitalist market, urbanism and so on, it is in terms of being caught up in the cultural narrative of development – a narrative with clear beginnings in the culture of the West.

There is at least one way out of the critical impasse that Berman creates for himself. This lies in the critique of the cultural narrative of modernity as 'development'. To be open to the possible hubris of this cultural imagining is to escape from Berman's heroic but nevertheless determinist view that people in all cultures must 'learn not to long nostalgically for the "fixed, fast-frozen relationships" of the real or fantasized past, but to delight in mobility, to thrive on renewal, to look forward to future developments in their conditions of life . . .'.[31]

Let us now have a closer look at this cultural narrative of 'development', to see whether it allows us to understand modernity as cultural imposition rather than as global cultural fate.

The discontents of modernity: development as 'social imaginary'

In Berman's story of modernity, modernisation as a set of social-institutional processes produces the experience of modernity in dialectic interaction with the self-formative cultural actions of individuals. Now what sets this dialectic in motion is modernisation itself. The 'lived culture' of capitalist modernity is transmitted by the major social-economic institutions of the West – the capitalist market, bureaucracy, science and technology, mass communications and so on – what Peter Berger calls the 'carriers of modernity'.[32] There is a clear 'political-economic' sense in which these processes can be seen as imposed on non-Western cultures since they are bound up with the history of political-economic imperialism and colonialism, a history in which the West has been and still is in a position of dominance. The sense in which they are a *cultural* imposition is not so clear. This is because the material and sociopolitical benefits of modernity represent their own emancipation from the domination of 'traditional' economies, polities and worldviews. It is also because the rationality at the core of modernity enables a set of choices which expand individual human possibilities and, decisively, represent a point of no return in the self-understanding of a cultural community. These benefits of modernity are generally collected under the concept of 'development' – a concept which, as we have seen, enlists in its affirmative stance even critics of capitalism such as Marx.

Berman's critical impasse arises out of a perception that certain key aspects of development escape any rational critique – development as continual cultural, normative *undermining* defeats any established critical position, any 'fixed, fast-frozen' rules. We will now examine a critique of development which avoids this impasse.

Cornelius Castoriadis presents this critique in his paper, 'Reflections on "Rationality" and "Development"'. 'Development'. he argues, has become the dominant theme of institutional relations between the First and the Third World ('development policy'; 'development studies'; institutions of economic development, the very term 'developing societies') by virtue of its defining role in the culture of the West. It is important to realise that the entire institutional apparatus of Western development agencies and so on demonstrates development's Western provenance. The notions of progress, expansion and growth, Castoriadis says, are clearly not 'virtualities' – that is, inherent potentialities – of all human societies, but, rather, specific properties and values of the West – properties the West feels it needs to 'teach' other societies. Although this instruction takes place predominantly at the level of the economic, it represents a much broader attempt to transfer some of the fundamental ideas and concepts that have formed the societies of the West and 'by means of which the West has conquered the world and would conquer it still even if it was to be materially destroyed'.[33]

The economic dominance of the West is therefore tied in, for Castoriadis, with the need to assert its discovery of '*the* way of life appropriate to all human societies'. This is as much a question of the stabilisation of Western societies themselves as a project of global domination: nonetheless, the relations it establishes between 'developed' and 'developing' worlds may be described as a form of cultural domination.

Castoriadis goes on to unpack the idea of development which is at the core of the West's assumed 'one true story' of human history, beginning with its place in Greek philosophy:

> What is development? An organism develops when it progresses towards it biological maturity. We develop an idea when we explicate as far as possible what we think it implicitly 'contains'. In short, development is a process of realisation of the virtual, of the movement from *dunamis* to *energeia*, from *potentia* to *actus*. Obviously this implies that there *is* an *energia* or *actus* which we can determine, define, assess, that there *is* a norm pertaining to the essence of what is developing; or, as Aristotle would say, that this essence is the becoming-adequate to a norm defined by a 'final' form: the *entelecheia*.[34]

We can clarify Castoriadis's use of Aristotelian terms by saying that the sense he describes is one in which 'development' as a process has *natural limits*. Development was, for Aristotle, a process of the realisation of inherent potentials, most simply of 'natural' objects – the potential flower in the seed; the physical adult in the child. The limits of development are clear in these cases – we do not think of growth in plants or animals as being 'open ended', but as having an obvious 'goal' or *telos* in the mature form. If we take our models of development from nature as the Greeks did, then development is a limited, finite process. The important point about this early view is that the natural 'goal' of development provided an intrinsic social *norm*: 'proper' development is simply the 'becoming' of the pre-given mature state. The Greek philosophers extended this model from the consideration of organisms to the areas of education, socialisation and political thought; a norm of political socialisation for the young was seen in the idea of the fully developed citizen. But here, as Castoriadis says, the problematisation of such norms – their perception as 'culturally relative' (what sort of 'city', politically speaking, defines the universal norm of the 'good citizen'?) – would have posed insuperable problems to the Greek thinkers, it was 'an obscure point at the frontier of their thinking'.[35]

The Western notion of development has its roots in a system of thought and a related system of values which was quite different from that of Western modernity. The key difference lay in conceptions and valuations of the 'infinite', the 'without end'. For Greek thought, this did not have the positive value of 'infinite possibilities' given in modernity, it had the sense, rather, of the unfinished or the incomplete. In short 'open-ended development' was unthinkable.

A transformation both in cosmology and in values occurs, Castoriadis argues, first with the spread of Judaeo-Christian theology: in the understanding of God as infinite. But this understanding was for a long period limited in its implications, since it is God who is considered infinite, and God is elsewhere – out of this world. So in the value system of Christianity

God ultimately provides the limits and intrinsic norms of a finite human nature. Judaeo-Christianity simply introduced the (absent) *principle* of the infinite; 'the transformation occurs when infinity invades *this* world'.[36] Castoriadis does not attempt a detailed historical analysis here, but he does sketch out 'the "coincidence" and convergence' between patterns of events from roughly the fourteenth century onwards: the rise of the bourgeoisie as a class, the mathematisation of the sciences, the demise of the medieval system of representation, the Reformation, the idea, in Enlightenment philosophy (Descartes, Leibniz), that Reason is the key to the human mastery of Nature. These events – it is difficult to avoid the term 'developments' – mark out for him a significant, if historically extended, conjunction. He argues that 'there is a layer of historical truth which can only be represented by the bizarre cross-section attempted here, traversing Leibniz, Henry Ford, IBM and the activities of some unknown "planner" in Uganda or Kazakhstan who has never heard of Leibniz'.[37]

What Castoriadis is trying to describe is the entry into Western culture of a major organising principle, the idea of infinite development as possibility, value and cultural goal. He calls such an idea an 'imaginary social significa-tion'. This is an important concept in Castoriadis's work and it is worthwhile exploring, briefly, what he means by it.

To do this we must turn to Castoriadis's major work, *The Imaginary Institution of Society*. This is a complex and difficult work which ranges widely over contemporary social-theoretical, historical and cultural debates. Like Marshall Berman (and in this respect, like a therorist we shall consider in the next section, Jürgen Habermas) Castoriadis is a thinker of the left, originally of the Marxist left, who now situates his critique of capitalism within a broader critique of modernity – a modernity in which Marxism itself is implicated. His concept of the 'social imaginary signification' is at the centre of this broad critical reappraisal of social theory, and Castoriadis presents it in the context of lengthy critiques of the major perspectives in social theory – in particular Marxism, structuralism and functionalism. We shall have to recover from this the basic meaning of the concept. Perhaps the best way is to consider an example Castoriadis gives, that of the place of God in a religious culture:

> Whatever points of support his representation may take in perceived reality, whatever his rational effectiveness may be as an organizing principle of the environing world for certain cultures, God is neither a signification of something real, nor a signification of something rational. . . . God is neither the name of God nor the images a people may give him, nor anything of the sort. Carried by, pointed at by all these symbols, he is, in every religion, that which makes these symbols religious symbols – a central *signification*, the organisation of signifiers and signifieds into a system. . . . And this signification, which is neither something perceived (real) nor something thought (rational), is an imaginary signification.[38]

So, an imaginary signification is a representation which is neither 'real' in the sense of being available to perception and empirical scrutiny nor 'rational' in the sense of being deducible via the rules of thought of a culture. But this does not mean it is either *unreal* or *irrational* in the pejorative sense these terms possess in modern Western culture. For Castoriadis the imaginary is *prior* to the real and the rational: it is the product of an act of cultural creation which is fundamental to any subsequent system of cultural representation. This is a difficult idea to grasp because it requires us to think beyond the terms of our cultural discourse and to recognise its origins. But the example of God is a helpful one, for we can easily accept the idea that God is a principle which is neither an object of perception nor an entity whose existence must be logically presumed, but which, nonetheless, is extraordinarily powerful in its cultural effects. Thus God as an imaginary signification is an 'a-reality', something which 'offers itself only on the basis of its consequences, its results, its derivations' – the entire system of religious thought and practice.

Another way of approaching the idea is via the language of semiotics that Castoriadis uses. On the plane of the imaginary, unlike that of the real or the rational, the signified to which the signifier refers 'is almost impossible to grasp as such, its "mode of being" is a mode of non-being'. Thus God has no (worldly!) existence in the way that 'trees' or 'democracy' have: the signified of the word or the image 'God' has no 'independent' existence except as an originating condition of the discourse of religion. Imaginary social significations thus, '*denote* nothing at all, and they *connote* just about everything'.[39]

Now that we have some idea of this rather tricky concept we can consider the role Castoriadis says it plays in social formations. This is a major one – that of providing the *orientation* of a society:

> Every society up to now has attempted to give an answer to a few fundamental questions: who are we as a collectivity? What are we for one another? Where and in what are we? What do we want; what do we desire; what are we lacking? Society must define its 'identity', its articulation, the world, its relation to the world and to the objects it contains, its needs and its desires. Without the 'answer' to these 'questions', without these 'definitions', there can be no human world, no society, no culture – for everything would be an undifferentiated chaos. The role of imaginary significations is to provide an answer to these questions, an answer that, obviously, neither 'reality' nor 'rationality' can provide. . . .[40]

Castoriadis goes on to say that the terms 'questions' and 'answers' are only used metaphorically: it is really in social practices that 'answers' are given and 'this social doing allows itself to be understood only as a reply to the questions that [a collectivity] implicitly poses itself'. This is quite an important qualification since Castoriadis wants to avoid the 'idealism' involved in the notion that social collectivities reproduce themselves simply in terms of a set of disembodied 'ideas'. He agrees with the 'materialist' drift of Marxism to the extent of seeing social meaning as tied to social action, to 'praxis'. As such he is sensitive to the common Marxist charge that religious and philosophical notions fulfil a certain ideological function in class societies. But where he thinks Marxism goes wrong is in seeing the meaning of social practices as simple and 'self-evident' – for example in the quasi-functionalist terms of 'satisfying material needs'. Collectivities engage in practices which can be understood as satisfying needs, but which are simultaneously acts of *definition* of needs in terms of a cultural self-understanding which is given in the social imaginary. Castoriadis thus thinks Marxism yields to a form of functionalism where it resists the sense in which human beings posit and 'answer' large 'existential' questions in their material practices: this he says, turning a famous Marxist metaphor, is what distinguishes human praxis from the activity of bees.[41]

Social imaginary significations are therefore major organisers of cultural practices. Their imaginary nature is relatively clear to us when we consider 'traditional' cultures, for example in religious or magical systems, but it is a feature of our modernity that we tend to ignore or deny the imaginary core of our own culture. Modernity pretends to a total rationality and thus, 'allows itself to despise – or to consider with respectful curiosity – the bizarre customs, inventions and imaginary representations of previous societies'. The thrust of Castoriadis's argument is to show that 'the life of the modern world is just as dependent on the imaginary as any archaic or historical culture'.[42]

For example, he speaks of the domination of the concept of the 'economy' by the social imaginary. The economy appears as the central figure of 'rationality' in modern societies: as the reference point for nearly all rational decision-making. But this rationality is only a 'functional' one, since the actual *point* of economic activity in capitalism cannot be described in rational terms. In a system which has long since passed the simple satisfaction of 'basic needs' the reasons for the continued growth of production and consumption cannot be found in rationality but in an imaginary signification which makes simple quantitative growth the orientation of the society. There is an arbitrariness, a lack of any clear qualitative direction in the economic activity of modernity. This is a point Castoriadis returns to in his discussion of development.

One of the most telling aspects of his discussion here concerns the place of individuals within the economy. The functional rationality of economic thinking issues in a view of people not as agents but as 'functionaries' within a quasi-mechanical system: the worker as 'a cog in a machine', the manager as 'executive'. This sort of description – what Marx called 'reification' – is only possible, says Castoriadis, by the operation of an imaginary signification which allows people to be assimilated to the category of things: this is neither real nor rational, it is the same order of representation as that found in 'primitive' cultures where people are sometimes described as animals or birds:

> To treat a person as a thing or a purely mechanical system is not less but *more* imaginary than claiming to see him as an owl; it represents an even greater plunge into the imaginary. For not only is the *real* kinship between a man and an owl incomparably greater than it is with a machine, but also no primitive society ever applied the consequences of its assimilations of people with things as radically as modern industry does with its metaphor of the human automaton. Archaic

societies always seem to preserve a certain duplicity in their assimilations, but modern society takes them, in its practice, strictly literally in the most naive fashion.[43]

Castoriadis does not merely want to demonstrate the relativism of cultural systems, he wants to show the common appeal to the level of the imaginary at the core of cultures and, perhaps most importantly, how this imaginary in modern societies is far more problematic than in 'traditional' ones. The reason for this is that, as he puts it, 'the modern social imaginary *has no flesh of its own* . . . it borrows its substance from the rational, from one moment of the rational which it thus transforms into a pseudo-rational. . . .'[44] What he means is that the 'orientation' of modern societies does not derive from any convincing independent narrative of cultural purpose – as might be provided by theology or animistic beliefs. The rationalising processes of modernity have made these notions untenable. But neither does 'reason' alone answer any of the major existential-cultural 'questions' of a society. What happens, then, is that the social imaginary of modern society simply 'borrows' its contents from fragments of rationality. The result is an imaginary which is empty of any existential purpose or comfort – which can no longer play its cultural role. It is here that Castoriadis locates the central cultural discontent of modernity.

To return now to Castoriadis's discussion of development as a social imaginary signification, we can see that it displays in its modern 'open-ended' version precisely the 'pseudo-rationality' of its borrowings from the functional rationality of economics, science and technology. The idea that modern societies are about growth and progress is one of their central imaginary significations – but what the imaginary can no longer provide are *qualitative goals and visions*, any sense of a completion to progress, any sense of where communities are going. So the idea of 'development' is realised simply in terms of constant movement along an undefined axis; growth becomes simply the provision of 'more' – 'more commodities, more years to live, more decimal points in the numerical values of universal constants, more scientific publications, more people with Ph.Ds . . .'[45] 'Development' is just as powerful as 'God' in terms of the organisation of cultural practices and representations but it fails, crucially, in its role of providing qualitative cultural orientation. There are two aspects to this failure: first in the pseudo-rationality of the actual practices the social imaginary of development sets in train, and secondly in the crisis of values which results from the vacuity of the concept of development as 'nothing except the capacity to attain new states'.

Castoriadis illustrates the first failure with a critique of a number of postulates which he says arise directly from the imaginary signification of development. Just one example will illustrate the drift of his argument. This has to do with the place of technology in modernity, a central preoccupation in Castoriadis's work.[46] Technology, he says, is imagined as having a 'virtual omnipotence', that is, the potential power to control and order all of the natural world. Stated in these bald terms this idea of total mastery appears, as

he says, absurd: no one believes in it as a formal proposition. Nonetheless
the myth of technological omnipotence is constantly reinforced by, and
sustains, technological practices. Technology works *as though* everything
will some day yield to its control: in this it is abetted by another derivative
postulate of development, what Castoriadis calls the idea of an 'asymptotic
progression'. An 'asymptote' in mathematics is a line which continually
approaches a curve without ever meeting it within a finite distance: an
asymptotic progression is thus the idea that the capacity for expanding
human power, though not absolute, is *almost* infinite: we can simply keep
extending control to more and more aspects of the natural world. The deep
error of this idea is becoming clear in the enormous ecological problems now
being recognised by the green movement and Castoriadis refers to some of
these to illustrate the argument that the exercise of power at one point
creates disturbance – 'increased powerlessness or even "anti-power"' – at
another. Problems like the depletion of the ozone layer, acid rain, the
'greenhouse effect' and the pollution of the seas are not simply technical
problems of modernity – problems which can be solved with more
technology. They are problems of the imaginary institution of modern
societies. There is, for example, the problem that the conceptualisation of
technological control operates within a radically truncated perception of
significant time. Castoriadis comments here on the contraceptive pill: the
social discourse in relation to this reproductive technology is limited to the
possible side-effects on the women who use it and technical developments
are concentrated on these problems. But no one asks about the long-term
effects on the human species at the genetic-biological level, of interference
with fundamental regulatory processes of the human organism. These
questions have relevance on a time scale of maybe 1000 generations (25,000
years) which is, in effect, meaningless to us. So, 'given linear time and an
infinite time horizon, we act as if the only significant interval of time was the
very near future'.[47] Part of the pseudo-rationality – and the hubris – of
modernity is its impoverished grasp of relevant time. In comparison
Castoriadis speaks of the Greece of his grandparents' generation:

> even into their old age they continued to plant olive trees and cypresses,without
> considering costs and returns. They knew that they would die and that they
> should leave the earth in good order for those who would come after them,
> perhaps simply for the earth itself. . . . They did not think of the infinite, perhaps
> they would not have understood the meaning of the word; but they acted, lived
> and died in a time which was truly *without end*. Obviously the country was not
> yet developed.[48]

At the quite simple level of the capacity to manage the physical resources of
the global environment, then, there must be major doubt that modern
'developed' societies have a monopoly of wisdom. This does not mean that
we have to yield to a romanticised view of the 'natural wisdom' of traditional
practices. The point, rather, is to recognise that the problems and discontents
of modernity are bound up, not with an inescapable rationality, but with a

social imaginary which is at the centre of the self-understanding of a culture. Thus, the processes of *modernisation* which Berman and, indeed, Marx ('the expansion of the forces of production') take as virtual 'givens' of history are seen by Castoriadis as cultural projects tied to imaginary significations.

This opens up modernity to a level of criticism which escapes Berman, for Castoriadis maintains that we must 'view reason and rationality in an appropriate perspective . . . as historical creations of humanity'.[49] This connects with Castoriadis's perception of the other failure of the modern social imaginary of development: its failure to provide a narrative of cultural orientation. He can agree with Berman that emancipation from the determinism of traditional worldviews (what Castoriadis refers to as the destruction of the idea of *physis* by reason) is irreversible and that this produces a crisis in social values – the instability of all social norms. But, whereas Berman tends to see this in the 'fatalistic' light of a consequence of the inevitable progress of the human spirit, Castoriadis approaches it as a failure of the cultural imagination. The birth of development does not have to mean the death of stable cultural norms since development itself is posited in terms of the creative project of the imaginary. The maelstrom of modernity is thus not 'cultural fate' for Castoriadis. This is because the idea of the social imaginary allows him to see the norms posited in traditional society by 'nature' (e.g. development in the 'closed' sense of the metaphor of natural organic growth) and the demands of 'reason' and 'progress' in modernity as existing in the same *mode*. They are both essentially human creations which humans can change. By putting the notion of development back in its historical-imaginary place, Castoriadis is able to reintroduce human agency into the debate.

This is a crucial move for although Berman respects human choices, his dilemma is traceable to an attenuated view of human agency in cultural production. Berman's account of modernity is full of forces: the 'dynamic and developmental forces' in the individual psyche appearing almost as 'drives' in the psychoanalytic sense, the 'maelstrom of perpetual disintegration and renewal', 'striving', 'melting', 'volatility' and so on. This is a splendid evocation of the taut skin of modern culture (particularly as it stretches over Berman's New York), but it does tend to diminish the sense of human control over culture, except in the 're-active' sense of modernist response. Castoriadis, by contrast, can accept all the institutional forces operative in modernity, and hence the relative powerlessness of the individual, but still – and this is the crucial point – maintain humanity in the driving seat of culture. The kinds of institutions we develop (and which may then come to have power over us) are not determined by something external to humanity, but created via the social imaginary. Culture is never 'fate' but always, ultimately, decision.

To realise this is to see that the existential discontents of modern society are not things which have to be endured for the sake of its material benefits. This is important in political terms for modern societies themselves, for it suggests that the creation of stable norms is not an entirely blocked project.

Castoriadis maintains that the creation of new forms of meaningful social life must remain at least a possibility, even though nothing short of collective will guarantees it.[50]

But the implications of viewing modernity in this way are even more important for 'developing' societies. The major objection to seeing modernity as a cultural imposition by the West is the problem of romanticising the unfreedoms of traditional societies. In so far as modernity increases individual autonomy it is difficult to deny it, with consistency, to other cultures. The result is that modernity appears as the 'choice' of individuals in developing societies under the determinant conditions of socioeconomic modernisation. But viewing this socioeconomic modernisation itself in relation to the social imaginary allows it to be grasped as a form of cultural imposition. For now we can see that the export of technology and capitalist enterprise (economic imperialism) is simultaneously the export of the Western social imaginary signification of development. 'Cultural imperialism' can therefore be said to appear *on the plane of the imaginary*. So, though cultural contact with Western modernity may inevitably result in the decay of traditional worldviews and practices, this does not necessarily mean that these have to be replaced with the (impoverished) cultural narratives of the West. Projects of 'development' by Western nations can be seen as instances of the colonisation of the social imaginaries of Third World societies.

This sense of cultural domination requires careful formulation. To suggest a colonisation of the social imaginary is not, for example, to suggest a manipulation of individual consciousness. It is not as though individuals are seduced by the glitter of Western progress which they fail to see as meretricious, as in the 'standard' account of cultural imperialism. What is at stake is the effects of the imposition of the social institutions of modernity. If we recall that, for Castoriadis, the existence of social imaginary significations is not within some disembodied world of 'ideas' but in the institutionalised practices of a collectivity, we can see that the imposition of the structures of such institutions – capitalism, bureaucracy, urban-industrialism – carries with it a determinant of the scope of the social imaginary. True, social imaginary significations are always acts of human creation. But in the case of the institutionally subordinate societies of the Third World, it can be claimed that this act of creation has been usurped by the neo-colonial activities of the West. In so far as non-Western societies have been institutionally subordinate to Western ones, so have their culturally self-formative capacities. This is not a subordination of human imagination as such, but of the institutions that contextualise and constrain it – the accumulated 'dead weight' of previous praxis.[51] And the praxis which brought about the institutions of modernity was, of course, a Western praxis.

So there is a sense in which Third World societies have not been allowed 'autonomy' at the level of the social imaginary. Given this level of autonomy, they may arrive at quite different solutions to their collective problems of self-definition, their establishment of social norms and so on, from those of the capitalist-consumerist West. But here again we need to be careful with the formulation, for to speak of 'autonomy' at the level of the social imaginary might seem to tug back to the idea of a 'cultural autonomy' in the 'holistic' sense we rejected in Chapter 3. The problem with this formulation was that it seemed to dodge the issue of a culture being inseparable from the acts of its members: the need to refer 'autonomy' to the agents who make up a culture. What must be addressed is how the idea of a colonisation of the social imaginary copes with the instances of popularity of capitalist consumerism in the membership of Third World cultures. I believe it copes rather well. For what is being claimed is precisely that *individual autonomy* is inhibited by the imposition of alien institutions. When individuals express a 'choice' for what Castoriadis calls the 'growth and gadgets' of capitalist modernity this choice must be understood as limited by what the institutions of the society put on offer. Individual choices, then, only reflect autonomy within the range of what is 'imaginable' as the attainable 'good life' within a culture. The colonisation of the social imaginary restricts individual autonomy by imposing a set of ultimately vacuous imaginary significations – significations which Castoriadis claims (with some justification) are already in crisis in the West.

Castoriadis's work provides a useful way of thinking about the cultural domination involved in the processes of modernisation as they spread around the globe. It is a way which both avoids many of the pitfalls of the critique of cultural imperialism that we have considered and resists seeing modernity as 'cultural fate'. What it does not do is to provide easy political solutions to the discontents of modernity. 'Dissatisfactions', he insists, 'can lead anywhere'. There are no historical guarantees of the eventual emergence of the good and meaningful society either in the First or the Third World. A theoretical discourse can reveal some of the 'myths' of modernity, but only the will of agents can actually change the orientation of a society. Castoriadis has to remain agnostic as to the possibilities for such a change:

> How many of the 55 million Englishmen, 55 million Frenchmen, 230 million Americans and so on and so forth, are really willing to act responsibly in order to take on their own fate? That's the problem. Do they have this desire or do they prefer to go on opening their fridge and looking at their T.V.?[52]

It would be to yield to romanticism to deny that this is also the problem for social agents (of course this must refer to those not entirely excluded from modernity by absolute poverty) in the Third World.

What is to blame for modernity?

Castoriadis's critique of the failure of the modern social imaginary suggests the inadequacy of the cultural resources of modern capitalist societies to their task of providing meaning and orientation to social collectivities. What Max Weber first called the 'disenchantment of the world' – the breaking of the spell of traditional beliefs and practices – leaves a hole at the centre of culture, which Castoriadis believes cannot be adequately filled with stories of growth or development.

The implications of this view for the idea of cultural imperialism are that the process of the spread of capitalist modernity involves not an invasion of 'weak' cultures by a 'stronger' one, but almost the opposite – the spread of a sort of cultural decay from the West to the rest of the world. Peter Berger suggests that, from the perspective of traditional societies, modernity may appear as 'a sort of disease, a deeply abnormal and destructive deviation from the way men are intended (by nature, by the gods) to live'.[53] This way of thinking about the spread of modernity is useful because it helps us to see that the interactions between a 'strong' society and 'weaker' ones in terms of their material resources – that is political and economic domination – do not necessarily have precisely the same cultural dimensions. The cultural impact of capitalist modernity can be seen in terms of *loss* rather than of *imposition*. On the surface there may be a lot of activity and intervention on the cultural plane, and it is on this – particularly where it is most evident, in the mass media – that critics of cultural imperialism have typically focused. But the more significant, and probably more sustainable, point of critique may lie in the debilitation of culture that modernity brings in its wake.

Is this the way we should think about the cultural implications of the spread of capitalist modernity? Should we see it as producing a general weakening in the cultural (symbolic, normative, orienting, imaginative) resources of societies? Is this the real issue of cultural imperialism? I believe the answer to these questions is a qualified yes, but the qualifications are most important.

First, it is important not to overstate matters and to end up in a simple cultural pessimism. The complexity of the culture of capitalist modernity is such that it can be represented in quite different ways by the inflecting metaphors used to grasp it. Say modernity is a 'whirlwind' and you have established a discourse of danger but also of energy and dynamism; say it is a 'disease' and change and decay can be seen all around.[54] Ultimately the critique of cultural modernity cannot rely simply on these tempting metaphors. We have to recognise that the complexity of the processes we are dealing with will always escape the attempt to grasp it in single encompassing concepts. To this extent we have to accept the inherent ambiguities of the modern cultural condition. Criticism of modernity can accept ambiguities but still expose those points at which the culture of modernity can be said to be 'failing'.

But, secondly, this failing needs careful formulation. We must avoid the idea that a culture has an existence or a 'function' *independent* of the practices of cultural agents. To speak of a culture as being weakened or as failing might suggest this sort of ontological separateness. And the danger in this is the political one of disregarding the cultural choices that agents make. We saw this danger in Hamelink's claim about cultural imperialism as a threat to the survival of a culture (pp. 111–13). I argued that this sort of formulation oversimplifies matters in that it makes it appear that the integrity, and 'autonomy', of a culture is something quite separate from the choices of the cultural community. But the survival of a culture is a matter of the survival of cultural practices – the work of cultural agents in determinate conditions. So if agents give up certain practices – religious ceremonies, folk dancing – and engage in others – watching TV, playing football – the culture has not 'survived' in its original form, but this is not a matter for criticism unless we want to say these choices are mistaken or misguided.

We must apply the same sort of strictures to the formulation of the notion of a culture failing to provide orientation and meaning. If we see the 'function' of culture as the provision of these resources, in the shape of 'imaginary significations', we must be clear about where the choices of cultural agents figure in this process. We saw in the discussion of Castoriadis that he (rightly) thinks of the social imaginary as the creative act of cultural praxis. But I argued that the institutions of capitalist modernity colonise the cultural space of 'less developed' societies and thereby prevent these 'creative' processes of cultural praxis generating satisfying cultural-existential narratives to replace those lost with the disenchantment of tradition. There is a sense of cultural domination here at the level of institutions. But we must also remember Castoriadis's insistence that people have to *want to* 'act responsibly in order to take on their own fate'. Ultimately people must have both the desire and the institutional space to create narratives of cultural meaning. The upshot of this is that when we speak of the 'weakening' of cultures in modernity we should think of this as *the failure of the processes of collective will-formation*. As global cultures fall into the conditions of modernity through the spread of the institutions of modernity, they all face the same problem of the failure of a collective will to generate shared narratives of meaning and orientation.

The question that arises from this reformulation of the notion of the cultural weakness of modernity is, what prevents the development of this collective will? The answer to this question should also clarify the answer to another which has lurked behind our whole discussion of modernity: what, if anything, is *to blame* for its discontents? The latter is a question we can hardly avoid if we want to retain a strong connection between the spread of modernity and the discourse of cultural imperialism.

Castoriadis's work suggests the general way, at least, that we should set about answering these questions. As we have seen, the institutions of modernity are not the ones which Third World cultures actually 'choose': they are imposed as part of the process of political-economic imperialism. But we can say that these same institutions no longer represent the 'choices' of social agents in the West either: social institutions can become 'alienated' from the will of social collectivities. This process – what Castoriadis calls the 'autonomization' of an institution – means that 'it possesses its own inertia and its own logic, that, in its continuance and in its effects, it outstrips its function, its "ends", and its "reasons for existing"'.[55] The connection between the collective social actions of individual agents and the functioning of institutions becomes broken.

One way of looking at the ambiguous condition of modernity is as a situation in which this 'autonomization' of institutions has become the rule at precisely the same time that individual agents have been released from the unfreedoms of traditional worldviews. To illustrate this I shall return, briefly, to the ideas of Jürgen Habermas. Habermas attributes the cultural discontents of modernity to a phenomenon which he calls the 'colonization of the lifeworld'. By the term 'lifeworld' Habermas means, roughly, the realm of 'taken-for-granted' meanings within which individuals experience the world: the cultural resources on which agents draw in their interactions. He describes it as that which 'stands behind the back of each participant in communication and which provides resources for the resolution of problems of understanding'.[56] The key point here is the tacit, 'background' nature of the lifeworld. Habermas argues that once these background assumptions become explicit (and therefore subject to reflection and criticism) they lose their power to provide existential 'certainty' and an unquestioned horizon of shared meaning.

It is a *positive* feature of modernisation, for Habermas, that the lifeworld loses some of its tacit unquestioned nature – for this is what it means to be emancipated from the pre-rational forces of tradition. So Habermas sees the positive side of modernity as a certain 'rationalisation of the lifeworld'. What this should allow, all other things being equal, is the generation of rational worldviews and cultural norms via social communication. We ought, then, to be able to construct our shared narratives of what it is to be a human being, what our collective goals are, what should govern our interactions with our fellow citizens and with the natural world, according to reason rather than blind belief. In other words, modernity should allow an 'enlightened' process of rational, collective will-formation.

But this is not the case. Habermas argues that what happens is that the space for communicative action made available by the rationalisation of the lifeworld becomes 'colonised' by 'system imperatives' belonging to the major institutions of capitalist modernity: those of the economy and of bureaucratic administration. Like Castoriadis, Habermas sees these institutions as being 'autonomized' or, as he puts it, 'decoupled from the lifeworld'. This means that all questions of social-existential meaning become subordinate to – or, rather, reformulated in terms of – the demands of the 'decoupled' institutional forces which keep the whole system of social organisation going. Habermas speaks of the demands of these institutional forces in terms of two primary 'steering media': money and administrative power. By this he means, roughly, that social actions are steered by the anonymous demands of a system – for example the capitalist market – rather than being decided by communicative interaction. There is a certain form of 'rationality' involved in this, an 'instrumental rationality' related to material-technological provision. But this rationality cannot cope with the major questions of social-existential meaning which have been the province of the lifeworld. In perhaps his most straightforward formulation of the problem, Habermas puts it like this:

> Today economic and administrative imperatives are encroaching upon territory that the lifeworld can no longer relinquish. To grossly oversimplify the case, until now the processes of destruction that have paved the way to capitalist moderniz-ation have occurred in such a way as to give rise to new institutions. These new institutions transferred social material from the realm of sovereignty of the lifeworld into realms of action steered by media and organised by formal law. This went well as long as it only touched on functions of material reproduction that need not necessarily be organised communicatively. In the meantime, however, it seems that system imperatives are encroaching on areas which are demonstrably unable to perform their tasks if they are removed from communicatively structured domains of action. This is true of tasks such as cultural reproduction, social integration and socialization.[57]

The 'colonisation of the lifeworld', then, is the situation in which the space for collective will-formation is colonised by the intrusive logic of economic and administrative systems. Habermas attributes many of the discontents of modernity to this situation: for example the increasing 'monetarization' of everyday life can account for the phenomena of consumerism and possessive individualism since life-goals are not the common subject of collective discussion. There is simply no real place in the secular routine existence of most people for the examination of the economically determined routines into which they are locked. The 'meaning' of everyday life comes to be shaped by a compelling but unexamined logic of earning and spending. This sort of action belongs to the realm of the economic, which has taken on a generalised function of regulating the totality of human social existence.[58] To revert to Castoriadis's language, the *telos* of consumption activities is unexplored in the conditions of a colonised lifeworld, and this may explain the frustrating chase after more and more goods. The cultural space for alternative conceptualisations of 'the good life' has become marginalised. Those challenges to the status quo that do arise in modern capitalist societies, the 'new social movements' such as the peace movement, environ-mental movements, the women's movement, various minority liberation and welfare movements, movements for regional autonomy and even fundamentalist religious movements, are seen by Habermas as precisely 'resistances to tendencies towards the colonization of the lifeworld'. Such 'new politics' express concern not over the distribution of material resources, but concern for 'defending and restoring endangered ways of life': they are expressions of discontent 'having to do with the grammar of forms of life'.[59]

There is not space here to pursue Habermas's analysis of the costs of modernity, but enough has been said to show that he grounds his critique in an analysis of the 'unbalanced' way in which the economic and administrative institutions of modernity dominate social existence. It is this imbalance that can account for the failure of the cultural processes of meaning generation, for as Habermas puts it, the 'false consciousness' of rigid and narrow traditional beliefs gives way, in modernity, to a 'fragmented consciousness' which is not able to construct satisfying rational narratives of social meaning.

Clearly this situation does not have to appear as cultural fate. As Richard Bernstein says, Habermas's insistence that rationality in modern society is unbalanced and 'selective' helps us to 'see through . . . claims that there is an *inevitable* logic of modernization'.[60] So we can say that the sort of modernity that the West has developed and passed on to the 'developing world' is not the only possible historical route out of the chains of tradition. This in itself may suggest that some sort of cultural domination is involved in the spread of modernity. But the nagging question remains – what is to blame for this? This is a peculiarly difficult question, and I do not believe it is possible to give a full and convincing answer to it. But we can, in concluding, try to spell out where the difficulties lie.

To talk about 'the West' being to blame makes only partial sense. It can reasonably be argued that the processes of modernity originated in the West and that the imperialist adventures of Western nations have been central in establishing a context of domination in which 'Western-modern' institutions have been transferred more or less intact. But to blame 'the West' cannot mean to blame a coherent collective project belonging to agents in the West. For we have seen that agents in the West have been as little able to control the direction of their route out of tradition as are agents in the Third World.

It seems to make more sense to speak, in Castoriadis's terms, of the 'autonomized institutions' of modernity being to blame. But, if we take the most significant of these institutions – that of capitalism – we can see that there are more and less appropriate ways of speaking of 'blame' here. If we think in terms of the *practices* of multinational corporations (*à la* Schiller) then we get a picture of something fairly conventionally 'blameworthy': here is a set of institutionalised practices aimed at the generation of profit for one dominant group and entailing the exploitation of another. As we have seen, this holds for a view of economic domination, but not for one of cultural domination. To grasp the order of 'blame' in cultural domination we have to think of capitalism as something wider than the practices of individual capitalist organisations, however large and powerful. This wider view of capitalism as one of the key autonomized institutions of modernity represents it as something within which the routine practices both of ordinary people and of individual capitalist organisations are locked. It is in this wide sense that we can speak of a 'culture' of capitalism. But here the notion of 'blame' is more problematic: it is not individual practices we are blaming, but a contextualising structure: capitalism not just as economic practices but as the *central (dominant) positioning of economic practices* within the social ordering of collective existence.

This rather attenuated sense of blame marks a key difference between the critical discourse of modernity and the other discourses of cultural imperialism we have considered. In the latter, some clear, *present*, agent of domination was identified: the mass media, America, multinational capitalists. There was the idea that this agent was responsible – that criticism meant laying the blame at its door. But here we have to think of a *situation* being to blame and this is less satisfying to the critical spirit. Thinking in terms of modernity seems to mean thinking in a rather different critical mode from that employed in the discourse of cultural imperialism. It seems to mean, for example, accepting that our cultural discontents have complex multiple determinations that have arisen over time and thus that no *present* agent is 'responsible' in any full sense.

But if the discourse of modernity is always to some degree a discourse of ambiguity and of causal complexity it does not follow that it is a discourse of cultural fate. To say that no easy single target of criticism is identifiable is by no means to say that things have to be this way. Thinkers like Habermas identify the various social movements of modernity as precisely resistances to the cultural impoverishment of modernity. This is very different from, say, Berman's story of a modern world in which we simply have to come to terms with the forces that drive us aimlessly forward.

Perhaps one way of understanding the various discourses of cultural imperialism from the perspective of modernity is as articulations of a general refusal to accept the terms of the modern cultural condition. These discourses are full of incoherences and conceptual conundrums. But if one central theme runs through them all it is the claim that people need something modernity has not properly provided. This is a need not for material well-being, or political emancipation, but a specifically cultural need: to be able to decide how we will live collectively in the widest possible sense – what we will value, what we will believe in, what sense we will make of our everyday lives. The failure of modernity which the discourses of cultural imperialism register is the failure of the autonomised institutions of modernity to meet this cultural need. But the very existence of discourses of cultural imperialism, together with all the other critical discourses of modernity – feminism, green politics and the rest – suggests that the cultural terms of modernity are not fixed, but open to challenge and, however difficult it may prove, to change.

Notes

1. J.P. Sartre (1956) *Being and Nothingness*, New York, Pocket Books, p. 576.
2. K. Marx (1975) 'Economic and Philosophical Manuscripts', in *Karl Marx: Early Writings*, Trans. R. Livingstone and G. Benton, London, New Left Review/ Penguin. E. Durkheim (1984) *The Division of Labour in Society*, London, Macmillan. M. Weber (1971) *The Protestant Ethic and the Spirit of Capitalism*, London, Unwin.
3. See, for example, A.G. Frank (1969) *Latin America: Underdevelopment or Revolution*, New York, Monthly Review Press; I. Roxborough (1979) *Theories of Underdevelopment*, London, Macmillan.
4. As, for example, in the work of David McClelland, who claimed to have found lower levels of entrepreneurial drive or 'Achievement need' in the populations of

underdeveloped countries: D. McClelland (1961), *The Achieving Society*, Princeton, New Jersey, Van Nostrand. See the withering critique of this and similar theories in Frank, op. cit., p. 53ff.

5. H. Alavi and T. Shannin (eds) (1982) *Introduction to the Sociology of 'Developing Societies'*, London, Macmillan, p. 4. See also Andrew Webster's discussion of 'modernisation theory': A. Webster (1984) *Introduction to the Sociology of Development*, London, Macmillan.

6. Thus Inkeles and Smith dispute the entire cultural problematics of 'alienation' or 'anomie' by reducing these to matters of 'psychological adjustment' – 'the more modern the individual, the better his psychic adjustment': A. Inkeles and D. Smith (1975) *Becoming Modern: Individual Change in Six Developing Countries*, London, Heinemann Educational, p. 264.

7. T. Adorno and M. Horkheimer (1979) *Dialectic of Enlightenment*, London, Verso, pp. xi–xii.

8. J. Habermas (1984) *The Theory of Communicative Action Vol 1: Reason and the Rationalization of Society*, London, Heinemann, p. 383.

9. 'The Culture Industry: Enlightenment as Mass Deception', in Adorno and Horkheimer, op. cit., p. 137.

10. T. McCarthy (1985) 'Reflections on Rationalization in *The Theory of Communicative Action*', in R.J. Bernstein (ed.) *Habermas and Modernity*, Cambridge, Polity Press, P. 176.

11. See Bernstein (ibid.) and also S.K. White (1988) *The Recent Work of Jürgen Habermas*, Cambridge, Cambridge University Press; J. Habermas (1987) *The Philosophical Discourse of Modernity*, Cambridge, Polity Press.

12. P. Dews (ed.) (1986) *Autonomy and Solidarity: Interviews with Jürgen Habermas*, London, Verso, p. 187.

13. M. Berman (1983) *All That is Solid Melts into Air: The Experience of Modernity*, London, Verso, p. 15.

14. Ibid., p. 24.

15. Ibid., p. 28. Berman, like many recent critics, misses some of the subtlety of Marcuse's argument here.

16. Ibid., p. 24.

17. Ibid., p. 16.

18. Berman recognises that some of the cultural production of the 1970s he discusses has been seen by others as aspects of 'post-modernism'; see ibid., p. 345–8. I agree with him in viewing theories of cultural post-modernism with some caution. Modernity (or, as I suggest in the Conclusion, 'late modernity') still seems to me the more useful critical category here.

19. M. Berman (1984) 'The Signs in the Street: a Response to Perry Anderson', *New Left Review*, No. 144, pp. 114–23. See, particularly, Berman's stress on the need to understand 'ordinary people and everyday life in the streets' (p. 123).

20. Berman (1983), op. cit., p. 346.

21. Ibid., pp. 124–5.

22. The tragic events in China in 1989 may be seen as supporting Berman's position, though it would be unwise to draw hasty cultural conclusions from this.

23. Berman (1983), op. cit., p. 125.

24. Ibid., p. 77.

25. P. Anderson (1984) 'Modernity and Revolution', *New Left Review*, No. 144, pp. 96–113 (p. 109).

26. P. Berger (1974) *Pyramids of Sacrifice*, Harmondsworth, Allen Lane, pp. 197–8.

27. K. Marx and F. Engels 'Manifesto of the Communist Party', quoted in Berman (1983), op. cit., p. 95.
28. Berman (1983), op. cit., pp. 104–5.
29. Anderson, op. cit., pp. 110–11.
30. See, for example, K. Soper (1981) *On Human Needs: Open and Closed Theories in a Marxist Perspective*, Brighton, Harvester Press, and N. Geras (1983) *Karl Marx and Human Nature: Refutation of a Legend*, London, Verso.
31. Berman (1983), op. cit., p. 96.
32. Berger, op. cit., p. 200.
33. C. Castoriadis (1985) 'Reflections on "Rationality" and "Development"', *Thesis Eleven*, No. 10/11, pp. 18–36 (p. 21).
34. Ibid., p. 23
35. Ibid.
36. Ibid., P. 24.
37. Ibid., p. 25.
38. C. Castoriadis (1987) *The Imaginary Institution of Society*, Cambridge, Polity Press, pp. 140–1.
39. Ibid., p. 143.
40. Ibid., pp. 146–7.
41. The allusion is to a passage in *Capital* where Marx writes: ' – a bee puts to shame many an architect in the construction of her cells. But what distinguishes the worst architect from the best of bees is this, that the architect raises his structure in the *imagination* of the labourer at its commencement.' – K. Marx (1961) *Capital, Vol. 1*, London, Lawrence and Wishart, p. 178 (my emphasis). The point is to draw attention to the *cultural* underpinnings of Marx's thought: human beings are seen as creatures of 'praxis', whose productive labour is always informed by (social imaginary) *purposes*. For a comprehensive and lucid discussion of these points see B. Ollman (1971) *Alienation: Marx's Conception of Man in Capitalist Society*, Cambridge, Cambridge University Press.
42. Castoriadis (1987), op. cit., p. 156.
43. Ibid., pp. 157–8.
44. Ibid., p. 160.
45. Castoriadis (1985), op. cit., p. 25.
46. See C. Castoriadis (1984) *Crossroads in the Labyrinth*, Brighton, Harvester Press.
47. Castoriadis (1985), op. cit., p. 33.
48. Ibid.
49. Ibid., p. 35.
50. See ibid., and Castoriadis (1987), op. cit., p. 373.
51. This idea of a determination by previous praxis is not far removed from Sartre's concept of the 'practico-inert': see J.P. Sartre (1982) *Critique of Dialectical Reason*, London, Verso. We return to this problem in the following section where we consider Castoriadis's notion of 'autonomized institutions'.
52. Castoriadis, in B. Bourne, U. Eichler and D. Herman (eds) (1987) *Voices: Modernity and its Discontents*, Nottingham, Spokesman, p. 50.
53. Berger, op. cit., p. 199.
54. Berman takes the image of modernity as a 'whirlwind' from Rousseau, who described European life in his time as *le tourbillon social*. See Berman (1983), op. cit., p. 17.
55. Castoriadis (1987), op. cit., p. 110.

56. Dews, op. cit., p. 109.
57. Ibid, p. 112. See also J. Habermas (1987) *The Theory of Communicative Action Vol 2: The Critique of Functionalist Reason*, Cambridge, Polity Press, p. 384ff.
58. Habermas (1984), op. cit., p. xxxii.
59. Habermas (1987), op. cit., pp. 392–4.
60. Bernstein, op. cit. (note 10), p. 23.

CONCLUSION
From Imperialism to Globalisation

In chapter one I suggested that the idea of cultural imperialism was one that needed to be assembled out of its discourse. Each of the four ways of talking about cultural imperialism we have discussed has its own set of cultural perceptions and political concerns; each stands as a critical discourse in its own right. And yet, as I have tried to show, there is also a certain expansion of the terms of reference as we move from one discourse to another. The first three in fact come together in the critical discourse of modernity. For capitalism, the nation-state and mass communications are all distinctive features of modern societies and determinants of the cultural condition of modernity. In the last chapter I argued that the various critiques of cultural imperialism could be thought of as (in some cases inchoate) protests against the spread of (capitalist) modernity.

However, these protests are often formulated in an inappropriate language of domination, a language of cultural imposition which draws its imagery from the age of high imperialism and colonialism. Such images (one thinks of nineteenth-century European missionaries washing out the mouths of children for speaking their tribal language) invoke an idea of cultural imposition by *coercion*. Now, though these practices need to be remembered as part of the process by which the West placed itself in a position of global dominance, they are clearly not the most useful way of thinking about present-day cultural imperialism. What dogs the critique of cultural imperialism is the problem of explaining how a cultural practice can be imposed in a context which is no longer actually coercive.

By thinking of cultural imperialism as the spread of modernity, these problems are avoided. For what is involved in this spread is a process, not of cultural imposition, but of cultural loss. If culture is taken to be simply a set of cultural goods circulating on the global market then the critique of cultural imperialism seems to be locked into the problems set by the discourse of liberal individualism. It becomes difficult to establish a critique here without falling towards the ideas of false cultural consciousness. But if culture is seen as the resources through which people generate narratives of individual and social meaning and purpose, the terms of the argument shift radically. The complaint about cultural imperialism is now the more defensible one of a complaint about the general, global, failure of these resources in the condition of modernity.

Capitalist modernity, I argued, is technologically and economically powerful but culturally 'weak'. This weakness can be seen in a general failure to direct its enormously powerful forces of production: the results of which are evident in the rapidly developing global environmental crisis. The fact that national governments and multinational capitalism seem impotent in the face of this suggests the problem is not merely one of technological failure but of a failure of *cultural will*. In Castoriadis's terms, the problem lies in the vacuous social imaginary of capitalist modernity. There is plenty of piecemeal 'manipulation and control' of the environment going on, but no real sense of long-term direction. And this is because there is no longer a sense of qualitative, rather than quantitative, social goals. There is a connection, then, between these enormous material problems facing humanity and the problems people now face in understanding why they do what they do. Anthony Giddens describes these latter problems as a crisis of moral legitimacy:

> I think there is a lot of truth in the idea that modern society undercuts the basis of its own moral legitimation. That is to say, for example, we don't really have morally viable ways of handling sickness, death, existential crises of life, because they're undercut by the very nature of the world we live in, which is based on the idea of technology and control. . . . we live day-to-day lives in which for most of what we do we can't give any reason. We dress as we do, we walk around as we do, we appear on T.V. programmes, these things are part of a tissue of day-to-day social activity which really isn't explained. It's hard to say why we do these things except that they're there and we do them.[1]

I think it is vital to grasp this crisis of moral legitimacy in the West in order to understand why we should think of present-day cultural imperialism as a process of loss. This crisis is arguably a feature of the very recent history of modernity – say the last twenty years. The current preoccupation with the idea of the 'postmodern' in Western cultural analysis testifies to this. For example, David Harvey begins an analysis of 'the condition of postmodernity' with a very precise dating: '[t]here has been a sea-change in cultural as well as political-economic practices since around 1972'.[2] The thrust of postmodern cultural theory is to register a very recent crisis in the self-understanding of affluent Western capitalist societies. The idea of 'postmodernity' is notoriously ambiguous and, as we saw in Chapter 2, theorists of 'postmodern culture' are often given to hyperbole. But without being drawn into the morass of problems surrounding the prefix 'post', we can see that there is a widespread general perception that the 'modernity' of the present can be distinguished from that of earlier modern periods.[3] This perception can shed some light on the issue of cultural imperialism, for it implies that the dominant culture of the present is very different from that of the age of 'high imperialism' of the late nineteenth century, from which intuitive notions of cultural imposition are still drawn.

The prevalent mood of 'postmodernity' (or perhaps 'late modernity' is better) is one of uncertainty, of paradox, of lack of moral legitimacy and of cultural indirection. This is clearly very different from the mood of relative cultural confidence which informed the European projects of colonialism of the nineteenth century. It is different, even, from the self-satisfaction of an affluent 1950s America which produced the global developmental agenda of 'modernisation theory'. To quote the title of a recent collection that tries to grasp this transition, we now live in 'New Times'.[4]

In concluding this study, I want to suggest that all the discourses of cultural imperialism we have encountered can be interpreted in terms of a different configuration of global power that is a feature of these 'new times'. This configuration replaces the distribution of global power that we know as 'imperialism', which characterised the modern period up to, say, the 1960s. What replaces 'imperialism' is 'globalisation'.

Globalisation may be distinguished from imperialism in that it is a far less coherent or culturally directed process. For all that it is ambiguous between economic and political senses, the idea of imperialism contains, at least, the notion of a purposeful project: the *intended* spread of a social system from one centre of power across the globe. The idea of 'globalisation' suggests interconnection and interdependency of all global areas which happens in a far less purposeful way. It happens as the result of economic and cultural practices which do not, of themselves, aim at global integration, but which nonetheless produce it. More importantly, the effects of globalisation are to weaken the cultural coherence of *all* individual nation-states, including the economically powerful ones – the 'imperialist powers' of a previous era. John Urry regards this process of globalisation as a symptom of the 'end of organised capitalism':

> There has been a 'globalisation' of economic, social and political relationships which have undermined the coherence, wholeness and unity of individual societies. Such developments include the growth of multinational corporations whose annual turnover dwarfs the national income of many individual nation states . . . the growth of means of mass communication which can simultaneously link 20–30 per cent of the world's population in a shared cultural experience; the possibility of technological disasters that know no national boundaries . . .[5]

To take up Urry's last point, the sense of globalisation as a *disorganised* process is seen most clearly in the unintended consequences for a shared environment of 'late modern' production and consumption practices. It is becoming increasingly obvious that the Western political-economic principles of unfettered economic growth, the free market, and the sovereignty of the consumer are producing awesome problems for the global environment. As Fred Steward says:

> Human capacity to affect the planetary environment appears to have reached a new level . . . Consequences are expressed beyond both the workers in the industry and the direct consumers of its products. A local event like a nuclear

plant melt-down has an impact across the world through the radiation released. Individual consumption decisions on the use of aerosols containing CFCs can affect planet-wide systems such as the ozone layer. Environmental impacts become increasingly cumulative and indirect. They are expressed over new and unpredictable time spans.[6]

As Steward goes on to recognise, the political regulation of the environmental hazards attending capitalist mass production and consumption is now much more problematic. For these effects can no longer be contained within national boundaries, and yet no effective global, supranational political bodies exist with powers to control production and consumption. Environmental globalisation occurs, as it were, beyond the political imagination of 'sovereign' nation-states.

The example of environmental globalisation is just one, albeit the most dramatic, of a number of ways in which the old global order is breaking down. The incapacity of sovereign nation-states to deal with the material side-effects of their own and others' industrial and technological practices has its parallel in the complex and anarchic interdependence of the world money markets. Rumours about the United States economy can produce activity on the Tokyo market which may have the effect of increasing interest rates, and thus mortgages, in the United Kingdom. The cultural experience of people caught up in these processes is likely to be one of confusion, uncertainty and the perception of powerlessness. For who is to blame? All that can be answered here is 'global market forces'. And this is not a satisfying answer, since it does not connect with any of the ways in which people understand their existence as members of a political community. There is simply no way in which the legitimacy of these immensely powerful global economic forces can be established within the existing political framework of nation-states. We cannot vote in or out multinational corporations or the international market system, and yet these seem to have more influence on our lives than the national governments we do elect.

All this can be viewed in terms of a *cultural experience* of globalisation which extends to all countries of the world. In the 'age of imperialism', the cultural experience of those in the 'core' countries was stabilised by the 'imagined community' of the nation-state. This represented, in David Held's words, 'a "national community of fate" – a community which rightly governs itself and determines its own future'.[7] The idea of cultural imperialism in this period drew on the image of relatively secure cultural communities exercising influence over other 'weaker' cultures. As national governments in late modernity are less and less able to act autonomously in the political-economic sphere, all this changes. When people find their lives more and more controlled by forces beyond the influence of those national institutions which form a perception of their specific 'polity', their accompanying sense of belonging to a secure culture is eroded. The average European or North American probably no longer experiences the cultural security their national identity used to afford. So the implicit terms of reference of cultural imperialism seem to be altered in a world where the dominant areas of cultural production do not have a matching sense of cultural confidence.

The general cultural insecurity of globalisation has been described in some of the more considered accounts of 'postmodernity'. Fredric Jameson, for example, speaks of 'the incapacity of our minds, at least at present, to map the great global multinational and decentred communicational network in which we find ourselves caught as individual subjects'.[8] What Jameson is trying to describe is what he calls a new 'cultural space': the 'as yet untheorized original space of some new "world system" of multinational or late capitalism'. This, he argues, is the space created by a third great expansion of capitalism, after the earlier expansions of, first, national markets and then the 'older imperialist system'.[9] The latest expansion of capitalism produces a truly 'global' system, which can be seen not only in the complex networks of international finance and multinational capitalist production, but also in the spatial context of cultural experience that it produces. What Jameson suggests is that people's experiences are shaped by processes which operate on a global level – and this level is beyond our present powers of imagination. Attempts to articulate this experience can be seen in certain elements of contemporary popular culture. For example he points to the vogue in popular fiction for narratives of 'high-tech paranoia':

> – in which the circuits and networks of some putative global computer hook-up are narratively mobilized by labyrinthine conspiracies of autonomous but deadly interlocking and competing information agencies in a complexity often beyond the capacity of the normal reading mind. Yet conspiracy theory (and its garish narrative manifestations) must be seen as a degraded attempt – through the figuration of advanced technology – to think the impossible totality of the contemporary world system.[10]

The *reality* of the networks of global technology which influence our lives (computers shifting capital around the globe in seconds) can be only dimly grasped in cultural terms. This is because we none of us actually 'live' in the global space where these processes occur: an information technology network is not really a *human* space. Our everyday experience is necessarily 'local' – and yet this experience is increasingly shaped by global processes. As we saw in Chapter 3 it is possible for people to 'imagine the community' of the nation-state, even though this community is spatially extended. But this is not possible on the level of the global since there are neither effective global institutions regulating practices at this level, nor any cultural representations of 'global identity'. The cultural space of the global is one to which we are constantly *referred*, particularly by the mass media, but one in which it is extremely difficult to locate our own personal experience. To use Jameson's term, we need somehow to be able to 'map' the new cultural space of the global.

Now, these problems of relating to the globalised context of late modernity seem to me important in understanding the contemporary relevance of critical discourses of cultural imperialism. For, though the world has changed from one in which it was possible to think of a simple division between 'imperialist' and 'subordinate' cultures, there remains a sense of legitimate protest in these critical discourses. We may think of protests against cultural imperialism as claims for a human level of cultural experience in a globalised system. It is interesting to note here the way in which many critics link the processes of globalisation with cultural demands for *localisation*. For instance, Martin Jaques:

> As power moves upwards from the nation-state towards larger international units . . . so there is a countervailing pressure, whose roots are various, for it to move downwards. . . . There is a new search for identity and difference in the face of impersonal global forces, which is leading to the emergence of new national and ethnic demands.[11]

These demands seem to be occurring everywhere: in the First, Second and Third Worlds. Though expressed in the language of nationalism and ethnicity, these may be seen as simply the available categories in which people articulate a more general need. This is the need for viable communities of cultural judgement: for communities on a scale to which individuals can relate, and which can provide satisfying accounts of how and why we live as we live. Most importantly, the need is for communities which can formulate the sort of qualitative cultural goals that Castoriadis describes in terms of the 'social imaginary'. The condition of late-modern globalisation seems incapable of satisfying such needs. It seems likely that some forms of the discourse of cultural imperialism, particularly those articulated in terms of national or ethnic identity, will increase in the future. But the underlying problems they register are unlikely to be solved by any political projects of national or regional autonomy. For the problem goes much deeper. What is required is a radical structural reorganisation of the way in which human cultural goals become defined and enacted. This implies a deconstruction of the 'autonomized' global institutions of late modernity.

This is such an awesome project to contemplate that the temptation to accept the condition of late modernity as cultural fate is strong. However, as Castoriadis observes, 'as far as our eyes can see, nothing allows us to affirm that a self-transformation of history such as this is impossible'.[12] What he means is that the province of the historical is *always* finally the province of human actions. However 'autonomized' and abstractly powerful our institutions seem to be, we cannot allow ourselves to think of them as unchangeable. Ultimately, the shape of the human world has to be conceived as a function of cultural will. Indeed if we don't believe this, the very idea of 'culture' becomes redundant. The sense of cultural agency and assertiveness implicit in critical discourses of cultural imperialism – the demands of people for a voice in the world – should perhaps be seen as the space where wedges can be inserted, from where we might begin to imagine, theorise and work towards different cultural spaces. In which the original, aboriginal TV screen would be neither blank nor peopled with fascinatingly alien images, but with alternatives of their viewers' deriving, alternatives which we can't – shouldn't – begin to imagine here.

Notes

1. Anthony Giddens, in B. Bourne, U. Eichler and D. Herman (eds) (1987) *Voices: Modernity and its Discontents*, Nottingham, Spokesman, pp. 113–15.
2. D. Harvey (1989) *The Condition of Postmodernity*, Oxford, Basil Blackwell, p. vii. Most other writers on 'postmodernity' date the transition from around this time, though few risk an actual year.
3. See, for example, the various discussions in Bourne et al., op. cit.
4. S. Hall and M. Jacques (1989) *New Times: the Changing Face of Politics in the 1990s*, London, Lawrence and Wishart.
5. J. Urry, 'The End of Organised Capitalism', in Hall and Jacques, op. cit., p. 97. See also J. Urry and S. Lasch (1987) *The End of Organised Capitalism*, Cambridge, Polity Press.
6. F. Steward, 'Green Times', in Hall and Jacques, op. cit., p. 67.
7. D. Held, 'The Decline of the Nation State', in Hall and Jacques, op. cit., p. 202.
8. F. Jameson (1984) 'Postmodernism, or The Cultural Logic of Late Capitalism', *New Left Review*, No. 146, pp. 53–92 (p. 84).
9. Ibid., p. 88. Jameson draws on the Marxist economist Ernest Mandel's periodisation here: see E. Mandel (1975) *Late Capitalism*, London, Verso.
10. Ibid., p. 80. See also the connection Jameson draws between this and the spatial disorientation experienced in the built environment of 'postmodernity': 'The Bonaventura Hotel', ibid., pp. 80–4.
11. M. Jacques, 'Britain and Europe', in Hall and Jacques, op. cit., p. 237. See also Hall, ibid., p. 133.
12. C. Castoriadis (1987) *The Imaginary Institution of Society*, Cambridge, Polity Press, p. 373.

Index